LANDMARK VISITORS GUIDE

Devon

Brian Le Messurier

Brian Le Messurier has lived in Devon for 61 years, and
has written eight books about the West Country, and collaborated
with other writers on several more.

He is a qualified Blue Badge Tourist Guide,
and before retirement worked for the National Trust as a
Countryside Interpretation Officer.

D0263737

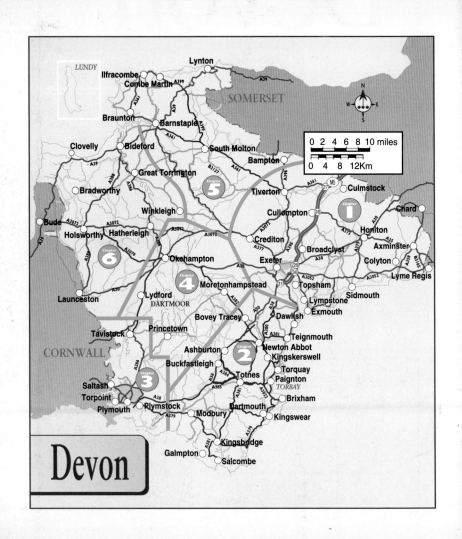

LUNDY

Lynton

Ilfracombe
Combe Martin

SOMERSET

Braunton
Barnstaple

Clovelly
Bideford
South Molton
Bampton

Great Torrington

Chapter 5

Bradworthy
Tiverton

Culmstock

Winkleigh
Cullompton

Chapter 1

Chard

Bude
Crediton
Honiton

Holsworthy
Hatherleigh
Broadclyst
Axminster

Okehampton
Exeter
Colyton
Lyme Regis

Chapter 6

Chapter 4
Moretonhampstead
Topsham
Sidmouth

Launceston
Lydford
DARTMOOR
Lympstone
Exmouth

Bovey Tracey
Dawlish

Tavistock
Princetown
Teignmouth

CORNWALL
Ashburton

Chapter 2
Newton Abbot
Kingskerswell

Buckfastleigh
Torquay
Paignton

Chapter 3
Totnes
TORBAY

Saltash
Brixham

Torpoint
Plymstock
Dartmouth
Kingswear

Plymouth
Modbury

Galmpton
Kingsbridge

Salcombe

Devon

Devon

Brian Le Messurier

• CONTENTS

INTRODUCTION

A Short History
Early Man
The Romans
to the Norman Conquest
1066 to the Civil War
Monmouth to the
    Present Day   16

1 EXETER AND EAST DEVON   18

Exeter   19
Town Centre Tour   20
The Cathedral   24
Topsham   25
Exmouth   28
The Budleigh Salterton –
    Bicton Cross Area   29
Sidmouth   30
Branscombe   32
Beer and Seaton   32
West from Axminster   33
The Cullompton Area   36
Tiverton   36
Bickleigh and Crediton   37
South-West of Exeter   38

2 SOUTH DEVON AND TORBAY   46

Ugbrooke House   48
Chudleigh   48
Newton Abbot and District   49
Dawlish   51
Teignmouth and Shaldon   51
Torquay   52
Paignton   54
Brixham   57
Dartmouth   60

3 PLYMOUTH AND DISTRICT   78

A walk around Plymouth   81
Touring Plymouth by car   88
Around Plymouth   89
The Tamar and the Tavy   95
Buckland Abbey   95
Tavistock   96
Morwellham   97

4 DARTMOOR   102

Flora and Fauna   104
Ancient tracks   104
Archaeology   105
Folklore   106
National Park status   108
Ancient history   108
Bovey Tracey   110
Hay Tor   112
Widecombe-in-the-Moor   113
The Central Area   115
The Western Side, Lydford   117
Okehampton   120
The North-East   120
Castle Drogo   123
Moretonhampstead   125
Princetown   128
The Southern Fringe   129
Buckfastleigh & Ashburton   132
North of Ashburton   133

5 NORTH DEVON 138

North-West of Barnstaple 140
Ilfracombe 142
Combe Martin 144
Lynton and Lynmouth 148
Along the County
   Boundary 150
South Molton 150
Barnstaple 152
Around Barnstaple 153

6 NORTH-WEST DEVON 158

Instow 159
Bideford 160
Appledore and
   Westward Ho! 160
Great Torrington 161
North of Dartmoor 164
Clovelly and Hartland 165
Lundy 169

FACTFILE

How to get to Devon 173
Accommodation 173
Bird Watching Sites 175
Boat Trips 175
Cycling 175
Facilities for the disabled 176
Ferries 176
Fishing 177
Golf 177
Guided City Tours 177
Guided Walks 178
Local events and festivals 178
Maps 179
Public Transport 180
Swimming Pools (Indoor) 181
Tourist Information Centres 181
Walking 182
Watersports 183
Weather 183

• MAPS •

Chapter 1 — Exeter and East Devon 22/23
Chapter 1 — Exeter town plan 26
Chapter 2 — South Devon and Torbay 47
Chapter 3 — Plymouth and District 79
Chapter 3 — Plymouth town plan 82
Chapter 4 — Dartmoor 107
Chapter 5 — North Devon 143
Chapter 6 — North West Devon 162

*I*ntroduction

A SHORT HISTORY

Devon is a large county, with two coastlines, two cities, one complete National Park and part of another.

Cliffs, dunes, estuaries, moorland, heathland, rivers, farmland, woods, plantations, parks and quarries – all provide different habitats for an astonishing range of plants, trees, insects, birds, animals and fish. There can be no other British county with such a diversity of natural species. Perhaps only in stretches of standing water is it deficient; Slapton Ley is its largest freshwater lake. However, a number of newly-excavated trout fisheries have produced more large ponds, and the large reservoir at **Roadford**, west of **Okehampton**, designed to solve Devon's water shortages, will also help.

EARLY MAN

Human beings seem first to have colonized southern England about 200,000BC, probably using the then still-existing continental land bridge, though the evidence for their arrival so long ago is sketchy. The discovery of some primitive stone tools in river gravel on the borders of Devon and Dorset in the nineteenth century points to this era, but unfortunately, the finds were unearthed before modern archaeological techniques were sufficiently advanced to note them in their context. This era was an interglacial period. The land that is now England was subjected to further glacial advances (Ice Ages) in more recent millennia.

The next evidence of man's presence is through numerous finds in **Kent's Cavern** in **Torquay**, which probably date from between 20,000 and 30,000BC. Flint spear heads and scrapers, a bone pin and bone harpoon heads point to hunting activities, but it is not known if Kent's Cavern was a permanent refuge or a seasonal bolt hole. Clearly the people were hunters and gatherers, but little else is known about them. This was the **Palaeolithic era**, the **Early Stone Age**.

As the ice melted for the last time, forests began to take over from the tundra-type landscape, and man – now called Mesolithic, or Middle Stone Age man – had to adapt to hunting the different kinds of animals which had themselves become forest species – deer, pigs and oxen. Flint scatters from this time have been found near the North Devon coast and on Dartmoor.

The **Neolithic people** seem to have come from what is now northern France, and their settlement sites so far uncovered are in south and east Devon at Hazard Hill (Totnes), Haldon, High Peak (Sidmouth) and Hembury (Honiton). All are in elevated positions.

Burial sites are further clues to Neolithic man's culture. A site was excavated at Broad Sands (Paignton) which had a passage leading to a central chamber, all this beneath a circular mound. The best known Neolithic monument in Devon is the so-called **Spinster's Rock** on north-eastern Dartmoor between Chagford and Drewsteignton. It stands in a field, but may be visited from the lane at Shilstone Farm. It consists of three orthostats, or stone uprights, supporting a massive capstone, and the whole structure is large enough to give present-day bad weather protection to some of the cattle who graze the field. When originally erected the four stones were at the middle of an earth mound which has now entirely disappeared.

The beginnings of a lifestyle not dissimilar to our own can be recognized in the Neolithic culture. The cultivation of cereals and the possession of flocks and herds mark an enormous change from the predatory wanderings of small bands of hunters and gatherers in earlier times.

The Neolithic people were now submerged by the arrival of a people who, although the first representatives of the **Bronze Age** culture (they used bronze, an alloy of tin [10 per cent] and copper [90 per cent], in their weapons and ornaments) are often referred to as the **Beaker Folk**. Their beakers were distinctively waisted, decorated pots, possibly used more for ritual or social purposes than for purely utilitarian functions. Although they had

mastered the technique of smelting ore to produce metal, the use of stone in tools and weapons continued.

While the monuments connected with death and funeral ritual are interesting and tend to be more obvious, it is the ruined stone foundations of **Bronze Age dwellings** on Dartmoor which are of the greatest interest to the visitor, and which are most abundant.

There are about 2,000 of these hut remains – 'hut circles' on the Ordnance Survey maps – on Dartmoor. Some are found singly, others in groups, enclosed, or scattered on the open moor. As it is not known how many were occupied at once, any population figure must be guesswork. Dartmoor, however, is the finest repository of Bronze Age remains in Europe; they have survived as they were made of granite, and there has been comparatively little subsequent disturbance.

In the past 40 years or so, aerial photography has revealed a network of parallel field systems with house sites on the lower slopes of high Dartmoor. Archaeological investigation has thrown a great deal of light on this hitherto unsuspected culture, which dates about 1500-1000BC. Separate territorial areas divided by rivers and watershed reaves (boundary banks) have been discovered, but little is known of the system of land tenure or agricultural economy of the people who laid out these wide-ranging occupation patterns.

The Bronze Age gave way to the **Iron Age** (indicating the development of ferrous smelting techniques) during the last thousand years BC, probably about 750BC. As in all these eras, dates are approximate, and in any case the changeover was gradual. The Iron Age is typified by

Stone Monuments

B arrows, cairns and cists (small stone-lined chambers set in the ground) have all yielded objects, and are some of the more easily recognised features of the Bronze Age in the present-day landscape. Barrows tend to be found in lowland parts of Devon, around North Molton, Upton Pyne and Farway, while cairns and cists appear on the more stony areas, such as Dartmoor and, to a lesser extent, Exmoor.

On Dartmoor, cairns and cists are often found in association with the curious and inexplicable linear monuments called stone rows or stone alignments. These are single or multiple lines of upright stones extending across the moor for distances as short as a cricket pitch or as long as 2.25 miles (3.5km), the longest in the world. Carnac in Brittany has similar monuments. Although their purpose remains obscure, a funeral ritual connection seems likely, and a link with astronomical observations is possible.

Other monuments to be seen are stone circles – rings of upright stones, like a kind of mini-Stonehenge – and standing stones or menhirs. They may be found with stone rows or on their own, and can be over 14ft (4m) high (above ground level). Such a prodigious monument can be found at Drizzlecombe in the Upper Plym Valley, in a fascinating group of Bronze Age remains.

the **hillforts** that still corrugate many Devon summits and cliff tops. The building of these enormous earthworks must have occupied hundreds of people for many years, in view of the primitive tools and equipment they possessed; the cult of the tribe seems to have been well developed; and the construction of such gigantic defensive positions suggests that the people were war-like.

The hillforts are often called 'castles'; this may well confuse anyone looking for medieval masonry, and finding nothing more dramatic than concentric banks and ditches. They often contain the place-name element 'bury' – Cadbury Castle overlooking the Exe Valley north of Exeter, and no fewer than three Hemburys (near Honiton, Buckfastleigh and Bideford). In all, there were about fifty or sixty hillforts in Devon, but as there is no way of knowing if they were all occupied simultaneously, no prehistoric population can be postulated.

THE ROMANS TO THE NORMAN CONQUEST

The **Romans** arrived in Devon in AD49 as a conquering force, and the Second Augustan Legion was stationed at Seaton in that year. No doubt the fleet kept pace down Channel with the advancing army (which was commanded by Vespasian, a future emperor), until the site of Exeter was reached. There may have been a local settlement at Exeter before the arrival of the

Above: Dartmouth Castle

Right: Dartmoor

Below: Dart Estuary

Opposite page: Kingswear station

Romans, but this has yet to be proved. The local people were the Dumnonii.

Here the invaders set up a base for their operations in the far west, and the situation was probably rather like a cavalry fort on the North American plains in the early nineteenth century, the Dumnonii playing the part of the Red Indians. The settlement was defended by an earth bank initially, and strengthened later by the construction of a stone wall. Supplies came from the east along what was now the A30 (still a road of Roman straightness east of Exeter Airport) and by ships up the Exe Estuary to what is now Topsham. Again, the road joining Exeter with Topsham is unmistakably Roman.

The Romans had at least two fortlets on the county's north coast: some remains are still visible at **Old Burrow** (near the Somerset border) and at **Martinhoe**.

Evidence of Roman Occupation

For many years it was thought that the Romans did not venture westwards, but archaeological work has proved the existence of interior roads pushing north and south of Dartmoor, the northerly one probably venturing down into Cornwall. Marching camps and forts west of Exeter are also known, but little remains to be seen above ground, apart from a number of Roman milestones in Cornwall.

The most spectacular discovery during the many post-war digs in Exeter was of a **legionary bathhouse** in what is now the Cathedral Close. Unfortunately, as the vast cost of roofing it was prohibitive, the exposed remains were covered with polythene and sand and the whole excavated complex back-filled.

The principal trade of early Exeter was agricultural produce; a possible stockyard was discovered. Evidence of metal working and pottery production attests the self-sufficiency of this focus of Roman culture in a part of the country still largely uncivilized. No temples are known, but a fourth-century pottery sherd bearing the early Christian device, the chi-rho symbol, is proof of a non-pagan influence.

Towards the end of the fourth century most of the Roman garrisons had been withdrawn from Britain to defend Gaul and Italy against the attacks of barbarians. The decline of Exeter is not fully understood, but it shared the loss of the stabilizing Roman influence with the rest of the country. With the departure of the Romans, the public buildings first ceased to be maintained and then collapsed, the structure of the ordered Roman society collapsing with them. A curious effect was a reversion to pre-Roman customs by the indigenous people. Some of the Iron Age earthworks were (perhaps briefly) re-occupied, and old tribal values resurrected. Perhaps they had never been totally suppressed.

With the departure of the Romans, we enter the **Dark Ages**, those secret centuries whose enigmatic annals seem lost for ever. To fill the vacuum, and on the slenderest evidence, commentators have created the Arthurian legends, but they apply to Cornwall and Somerset rather than to Devon.

The **Saxon** invasions of south-east England did not affect the south-west for some time, but gradually the Saxons pushed westwards. Exeter became part of the Kingdom of Wessex in 680, and the Tamar was reached by 780. Devon was now a shire county, like its neighbours to the east.

Here and there a trace of these years survives – a carved stone here, an inscribed monolith there; an example is the splendid cross shaft at **Copplestone**, north-west of Crediton, its interlaced ornamental patterns as fresh now as if it had been carved fifty years ago. But although large monasteries were established at Exeter and Crediton and smaller ones elsewhere, few worthwhile traces of pre-Norman architecture have survived. The Crediton monastic foundation was responsible for the religious development of Winfrith, better known as St Boniface, who was born there about 680 and later established Christianity in central Germany; he is often regarded as the greatest Englishman.

Alfred became king in 871 and began to put the Wessex fortifications in order. The Danes carried out probing raids and occupied Exeter in 876, but Alfred put them to flight in the following summer. The burghs established by Alfred were Exeter, Pilton (now part of Barnstaple), Lydford and Halwell, although the last was later moved to Totnes.

Towards the end of the tenth century, a further flush of Danish attacks up the estuaries of the Tamar, the Teign and the Exe led to much slaughter and plunder, culminating in the sacking of Exeter in 1003. In the meantime Crediton had become the diocesan headquarters, part of the former vast Sherborne diocese. In 1050 it was decided to transfer it to Exeter, as this could be defended, its walls now erect again; and here it has remained ever since.

These were years when the natural forests of Devon were gradually cleared. Most of the villages and settlements we take for granted in the countryside were established in those far-off misty days under the Saxon kings.

1066 TO THE CIVIL WAR

The **Norman** invasion meant little to the people of Devon for over a year. Life went on and, after all, Devon was a long way from Hastings and its aftermath. However, the mother of the defeated King Harold, Gytha, fled to Exeter with her daughter, and this probably strengthened the resolve of Devonians to resist the invaders. Exeter's walls were repaired, the whole area rallied round to defend the city, and William realized that he himself would have to persuade the West Country to tow the line. So he arrived outside Exeter at the head of an army, and after lengthy negotiations peace with honour was agreed.

One of his first actions was to build a castle on the highest part of Exeter's walls, as much to subdue the local population as to defend the city, thus establishing the rule of law from this elevated site. It is an interesting fact that today, after over 900 years, the tradition of law and order is still upheld from the castle. Exeter Crown Court meets in eighteenth-century buildings within its precincts, and indeed the ordinary

people of Exeter regard the castle with something akin to awe and only venture within its walls, whether as witnesses or jurors, with reluctance. A long-standing folk memory perhaps?

Other castles were built at Totnes, Okehampton, Barnstaple and Plympton. The descendants of the first Norman Sheriff of Devon, Baldwin de Brionne, are the Courtenays, the Earls of Devon, who now own Powderham Castle. Their family home was Courtenay, near Paris.

Nearly 20 years after he had become king of England, in late 1085, William decreed that what is now called a national survey or census, should be carried out. The result became known as the Domesday Book. (Exeter is fortunate in possessing the original returns for south-west England in the Cathedral Library.) For the first time we know the structure of society in Britain; details of ownership, land, population, taxes and livestock were all written down. 1,170 places in Devon were listed, the total population being about 60,000, fewer than live in Exeter today; probably one fifth were slaves.

The history of medieval Devon could be told on two planes; the common people left no records but their conditions can be deduced from retrospective observation; or on a wider view, national events have influenced or been affected by incidents in the county. In this introductory chapter, where the national scene is set, the wider view is taken. The later pages of this book, where more local areas of Devon are discussed, are the place for more detailed information.

Another explanation is necessary.

This kind of superficial treatment is bound to be episodic; a series of major events which made their mark on the public consciousness, but which have only this in common – that they relate to Devon, and have influenced it to the extent that they have made it what it is today. We have already seen that much of its early history is bound up with that of Exeter, and so the trend continued into modern times. Plymouth, by far the largest place in present day Devon, is not mentioned in records until 1211.

The third of Exeter's sieges occurred in the middle of the twelfth century, during the civil wars which dogged the reign of Stephen; the first occasion when William's castle was put to the test.

There was considerable movement through the county a few years later as the Second and Third Crusades left England from Dartmouth in 1147 and 1190. Dartmouth was really only a convenient collecting point. At that time it was little more than a splendid natural port, an advantage it still possesses. The South Devon ports came into their own at this time because of the marriage in 1152 of Henry II to Eleanor of Aquitaine, a province in south-west France. Trade was boosted, and Dartmouth and Plymouth (as well as ports in Cornwall) grew in importance as a result.

The middle of the fourteenth century was marked by the arrival of the Black Death, that rat-flea scourge of the **Middle Ages**. It came into England at Melcombe Regis (what we now call Weymouth) in 1348 and soon reached Devon. Perhaps a quarter to a third of the population died. Recent discoveries suggest that whole settlements in the more marginal areas (on the edge of Dartmoor, for example), were wiped out.

The main industry in all these years was cloth (though tin developed later on Dartmoor) and every valley had its fulling or tucking mill. The trade was stimulated by continental links, but suffered in later years when England was at war with the Netherlands, Spain and France.

Cloth and tin supplied the necessary stability to the county when it seemed that all around was changing with the suppression of the monasteries in the years following 1536. They had been vast landowners, but everything was taken over in the name of the king, and allotted to selected gentry. The main houses affected were Plympton, Tavistock, Buckfast, Torre, Forde, Hartland, Dunkeswell and Buckland.

Perkin Warbeck

The West Country has seen the passing of a number of lost causes; the first was that of Perkin Warbeck, who claimed to be one of the princes murdered in the tower. He landed in Cornwall in 1497, but Exeter stood firm for the king. A grateful monarch presented the city with a sword of state and a cap of maintenance, which are still carried before the mayor on all ceremonial occasions. Warbeck was later hanged.

Fifty years after the Warbeck uprising, the **Prayer Book Rebellion** (or the Western Rebellion) occurred. It originated in Sampford Courtenay, near Okehampton, in 1549, an unlikely place for a violent anti-establishment movement to start; large numbers of Cornish people lent weight to the rebellion against the new English Protestant Prayer Book. After much loss of life, the rebels were put down in a battle near Clyst St Mary, after another battle just west of Honiton.

The scene now shifts to Plymouth and the sea. Plymouth was obviously the best base port for the war against Spain. Dartmouth had a haven better protected from south-west gales, but the steep hills prevented easy land access and, what is more, **Sir Francis Drake** and **Sir John Hawkins** lived locally. But practically every port played its part in the sea war, by building the ships that defeated the Armada in 1588. It is said that the Spanish fleet was first sighted in Devon from the cliffs near Hope Cove, although it was first spotted off the Lizard in Cornwall. A system of fire beacons alerted the country to the danger. The development of the New World encouraged trade from West Country ports and Plymouth, Bideford and Barnstaple soon had strong links across the Atlantic.

In the middle of the seventeenth century there was further unrest. The Civil War ebbed and flowed across the land, and family loyalties were split. Exeter was twice besieged, in 1643 and 1645-6, but there were no major battles such as those at Naseby or Marston Moor.

MONMOUTH TO THE PRESENT DAY

The next uprising passed through the east of the county. The ill-starred Duke of Monmouth, who proposed to depose James II, landed at Lyme Regis, just in Dorset, in 1685. He advanced through Axminster (Devon) to Taunton (Somerset), but was defeated at Sedgemoor and executed a month after he landed. **The Devonshire Regiment** (now the Devon and Dorset Regiment) originated as a unit raised to oppose the insurrection.

Only three years later, however, William of Orange landed at Brixham on Guy Fawkes Day 1688 with a vast army, many of them Dutch and German mercenaries; what became known as the **Glorious Rebellion** was successful. James II was ousted, and William and Mary took the throne.

For half of the following 127 years, until Waterloo, England was at war with France. Plymouth developed as a naval base, but trade was thwarted and foreign travel inhibited. Road transport was encouraged by the first of the Devon Turnpike Acts in 1753. Roads were improved, and stagecoaches began to make road travel easier and more reliable.

The British fleet, finding that it could very easily be bottled up in the Hamoaze at Plymouth, began to use the sheltered waters of Tor Bay as an anchorage; until Plymouth Breakwater was built, well into the nineteenth century, Plymouth Sound was a useless refuge for sailing vessels which needed to depart quickly. It was the fleet medical officers, understanding the climatic benefits of the site, who began to recommend Torquay to their consumptive patients; thus it was as a haven for invalids that the village of Torquay became a town and, later, a holiday resort. In the 1840s the railway reached Devon, and the chosen routes soon established the holiday resorts, which have continued, although widespread car ownership has made many people independent of railways.

World War I had little direct effect on Devon, except to cream off the pride of its men-folk, as a glance at any war memorial will show. For this was the end of an era, and things were never the same again.

In World War II the battle came to Devon. Exeter and Plymouth were blitzed out of all recognition by German bombers, and Teignmouth and Exmouth were also badly damaged. Slapton Sands was used by the US forces for invasion exercises in 1943, and 3,000 people from seven parishes in the hinterland covering 30,000 acres (12,000 hectares) were evacuated as live ammunition was used. Dartmouth became an important base for the invasion of northern France.

In the years since the war the railways have contracted, the dual carriageways and M5 motorway have arrived, caravan and camping sites have multiplied, and sailing and self-catering holidays are in vogue. Devon is now in competition with cheap overseas package tours, but, because of its heritage of history and beauty, its accessibility and hospitality, there is an enormous amount to see and do in the county.

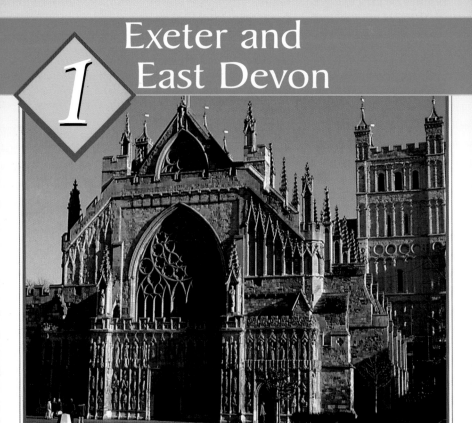

Most people arriving in Devon do so through East Devon. A few come by the northern routes, over Exmoor or through South Molton, and a handful come across from Roscoff, land at Plymouth Airport or enter from Cornwall. Most visitors come by road, down the M5 or along the A30; some by rail or via Exeter Airport (the regional airport for the south-west). This is the corridor, where the peninsula narrows to about 33 miles (53km), through which nearly everyone passes.

If the visitor misses the sign announcing DEVON beside the M5 there will be little in the landscape to inform him that he has left Somerset. The main physical jolt is likely to be the red soil, which he will first see near Cullompton. This is the New Red Sandstone, and is particularly noticeable where it outcrops in sea cliffs for a few miles on either side of the Exe Estuary.

Those who know East Devon better, realize that there is another kind of scenery – a landscape of flat-topped hills and deep valleys north and south of Honiton. The hills to the north are the Blackdowns, shared with Somerset. The main railway into Devon comes through the Whiteball Tunnel and under the county boundary, beneath a shoulder of these hills. The nearby M5 motorist, just after passing the Wellington Monument (in Somerset) will notice a small dome-like structure on the end of one of the Blackdowns' heath-topped spurs. This is Culmstock Beacon, and the little building may have had a connection with the beacon fire. It stands about a mile (1.6km) inside Devon and gives a stupendous view westwards, for despite its modest altitude at 820ft (287m), the ground falls away and there is no higher land until the Haldon Hills (their summit is 826ft, [289m]) are reached beyond Exeter. Entering Devon from Somerset, unless bound for North Devon or North Cornwall, all routes lead to Exeter, reached within 15 minutes of crossing the boundary.

EXETER

Exeter is the undisputed capital of the county. Communications, culture, administration, commerce, education, medicine and religion all focus here. Plymouth is much larger and with the opening of its Theatre Royal in 1982, is now competing in the field of culture, but in no other sense, except its superb natural position beside the Sound and in its role as a port, naval and commercial, is it more important than the ancient city of Exeter. The two are so dissimilar as to make comparisons impossible.

Much has been written about Exeter's history in the introductory chapter, but its visual attractions have not been mentioned. Taking the broad view, one of the appealing aspects is its size; large enough to attract specialized shops, events and institutions, but small enough to be comfortably cosy. Looking down the main street there are green fields only a couple of miles away, and from the highest part of the city (now known as Pennsylvania, as the 1822 builder of Pennsylvania Park was a Quaker who named his terrace after the American province), and from the Exeter Bypass, the sea and the super-tankers off Torbay can be seen due south; Dartmoor is visible due west.

Exeter's old buildings, the cathedral and the Guildhall apart, do not make a great impact, and many of the more interesting features of its heritage have

Left: Quayside warehouses, Exeter

to be searched for. On a dull or wet day in August, when tourists swarm to the city and the car parks show 'Full' signs, the Cathedral Close and High Street teem with life, but few day visitors penetrate to Rougemont Gardens below the castle, walk the line of the city walls, or visit the underground passages.

The latter are, in fact, misnamed. While appearing to be just that, they were built in the fourteenth and fifteenth centuries to bring water into the city from springs outside the walls. The public are taken along the stone vaulted passage by a guide, for a small charge, entering by descending two flights of steps near Boots.

TOWN CENTRE TOUR

Since so much of old Exeter was destroyed in May 1942, the remaining historic buildings and places of interest are slightly off-centre, and can best be linked by a walk round the walls, with a deflection here and there to see something near at hand. Visitors are always surprised at the variety of interest that lies between the ancient core and the newer Exeter outside the walls. The distance is 2,600yd (2,377m) and the area enclosed is 93 acres (37hectares). Five-sixths of the city wall is still visible and the walk round the complete circuit takes between 1^1/$_2$ and 2 hours.

A good place to start is opposite Boots the Chemists, where a line of paving slabs, laid as broken pieces, marks a length of the **city wall** where it has disappeared. (This is the site of the medieval East Gate.) Although it can be followed in either direction, as one way seems to go through the front door of Boots the Chemists the other may be more fruitful!

At once a corner bastion may be seen; a wall plaque states that the city walls were originally built by the Romans about AD200.

As the wall is followed, at Bedford Street one enters Southernhay East, where, on one of Exeter's elegant Georgian terraces, are some curious Coade stone keystones of moulded faces. Turn behind No 9 to rediscover the wall and follow it to South Street where two more wall plaques, one on either side of the street, explain that the massive **South Gate**, demolished in 1819, was for many years a prison. From here it is worth deviating along Magdalen Street to see **Wynard's Almshouses**, opposite the one-time Eye Infirmary. Round a cobbled courtyard, still with its well-head, is a pleasing group of red sandstone cottages and a chapel. Founded in the fifteenth century and rebuilt several times since, the buildings were converted into offices for various voluntary organizations in the 1970s. Now return to the site of South Gate and cross Western Way at the traffic lights and follow the wall to the back of the **Custom House** (1681), the first building in Exeter to be constructed from brick in modern times, and the **Quay House** Visitor Centre where the history of the city, particularly the river quays, is explored. This part of Exeter is also the heart of Exeter's nightlife, with discos and clubs accommodated in old warehouses.

Now resume the wall circuit. Behind the Custom House and along the rather down-at-heel alley, Cricklepit Street, on the left are the remains of Exeter's last **watermill**, with the skeleton of an undershot waterwheel. This mill was first recorded in 1190. On Western Way, across the road is a ruined church, which stands on a bridge now high and dry. This was Exeter's first bridge (1240) and it crossed a much wider river. The Exe now runs in a narrower and deeper channel beyond. There is another wall plaque on the line of the walls at the site of the West Gate.

Stepcote Hill, the cobbled medieval way into the city, climbs steeply up beside **St Mary Steps church.** Until 1778 this was the main road into Exeter from the west. The church has a famous clock, of which various parts can be seen to move when it strikes the hour. Facing it is a wooden-framed Tudor building that was moved here in 1961 and is now known as 'The House that Moved'. It was in the way of the new road, but by strapping it together and jacking it up on rollers the little building was moved to its present site and saved for posterity.

Walk up West Street to Fore Street, now the main way into Exeter from the west. The route is straight ahead up Bartholomew Street, but turn briefly up Fore Street for 50yd (46m), where on the left will be seen the Victorian façade of a 1471 building, the **Tucker's Hall.** Here the craft gild (*sic*) of the Exeter woollen trade, the weavers, fullers and shearmen met, and, in a somewhat altered form, still meet. The roof timbers are original and the panelling is Jacobean.

Return to the foot of Bartholomew Street and carry on up to a walk-way along the top of the walls beside a restored chapel of 1817 with a Doric porch. This leads to a pleasant backwater known as Ash Grove where the wall turns 90 degrees right and follows along the top of the Long Brook Valley. At the corner there was once a bastion known as the Snail Tower, which was designated one of the three common jakes (lavatories) in 1568. Where the path meets the road by some iron gates on the left, enter the gates and go down some narrow steep steps to a lower level. Here one is standing outside the Exeter catacombs, built against the walls in the Egyptian style of 1811 then in vogue and operated in a desultory fashion until 1883. They never caught on as a way of disposing of the dead, and are now sealed off. The stacks of slate 'pigeon holes', some occupied, may be seen by peering through the grill.

A hundred yards away from the wall, in Mint Lane is **St Nicholas' Priory**, a well-preserved part of a once much larger building with many Norman features. The guest hall on the first floor is a particularly handsome room.

The walk is resumed to the foot of North Street (traffic lights) where there was another gate, **North Gate,** and below one can see the **Iron Bridge,** an early example of cast-iron civil engineering. It was built to ease the approach to this side of Exeter for horse-drawn vehicles. Up Northernhay Street, Queen Street contains some of Exeter's best nineteenth-century architecture. The classical **Higher Market** (1838, now adapted as a shopping precinct) and the **Royal Albert Memorial Museum** (1865-6) in Early English revival are worth seeing. The Thistle Hotel and the Central Station opposite were built on made-up ground in the valley of the Long Brook.

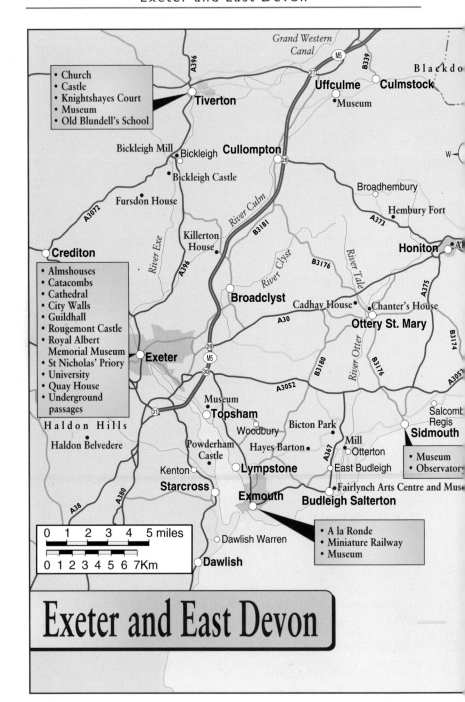

- Church
- Castle
- Knightshayes Court
- Museum
- Old Blundell's School

Tiverton

Grand Western Canal

M5

27

B339

Uffculme **Culmstock**

•Museum

B l a c k d o

A396

Bickleigh Mill •Bickleigh **Cullompton**

28

W•

•Bickleigh Castle

Broadhembury

Fursdon House

A3072

River Exe

River Culm

B3181

A373

Hembury Fort

Killerton House•

Crediton

River Clyst

B3176

River Tale

Honiton A

A375

- Almshouses
- Catacombs
- Cathedral
- City Walls
- Guildhall
- Rougemont Castle
- Royal Albert Memorial Museum
- St Nicholas' Priory
- University
- Quay House
- Underground passages

Broadclyst

A30

Cadhay House• •Chanter's House

Ottery St. Mary

B3174

Exeter

M5

29

30

River Otter

B3180

B3176

A305

A3052

Haldon Hills

•Haldon Belvedere

31

Museum •

Topsham

Woodbury

Bicton Park

Salcomb Regis

Sidmouth

Powderham Castle

Hayes Barton•

Mill •Otterton

A367

- Museum
- Observatory

Kenton○

Lympstone

East Budleigh

Starcross

A380

A38

Exmouth

Budleigh Salterton

•Fairlynch Arts Centre and Mus

| 0 | 1 | 2 | 3 | 4 | 5 miles |

○Dawlish Warren

| 0 | 1 | 2 | 3 | 4 | 5 | 6 | 7Km |

- A la Ronde
- Miniature Railway
- Museum

○**Dawlish**

Exeter and East Devon

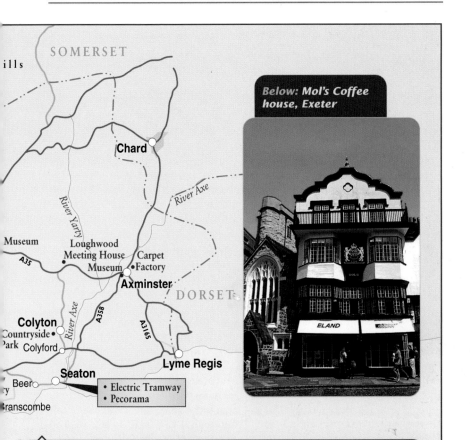

Below: Mol's Coffee house, Exeter

SOMERSET

ills

Chard

River Axe

River Yarty

Museum

Loughwood
Meeting House
Museum

Carpet
Factory

Axminster

DORSET

A35

A358

A3165

River Axe

Colyton
Countryside
Park Colyford

Seaton

Lyme Regis

Beer
ry

• Electric Tramway
• Pecorama

Branscombe

The Guildhall at Exeter

The Guildhall is special, even if the exterior is not particularly attractive. Four great granite columns carry the weight of the Mayor's Parlour above, a room lit by five large original Tudor windows, for this frontage was added in 1592. Passing through an impressive inner door, between small porters' lodge-type rooms, which were once the city police station and the city fire station, one enters the hall itself, with a fifteenth-century arch-braced timber roof. Enormous pictures hang on the walls and the city silver fills a cabinet in the gallery. A feeling of great age pervades the atmosphere, as well it might, for this is the oldest municipal building in the country. Much altered, it's true, it is on the same site as a building mentioned in a deed of 1160.

Across Queen Street are **Northernhay Gardens** with the walls on the right. Head towards the **Exeter War Memorial**. This attractive open area was laid out as a public space as long ago as 1612. A small door in the wall leads into **Rougemont Gardens**. The wide ditch is all that remains of the moat that separated the castle from the city (see Introduction).

At the far end of the gardens from the little door is the Regency building called Rougemont House, now home to the **Connections Discovery Centre**, a hands-on interpretation facility for schoolchildren. Opposite is the gatehouse to **the castle**, now redundant, as the present-day entrance stands alongside. Inside the castle yard are the Palladian (1774) court buildings, but admission is granted only to those on business or jury service as the castle now houses Exeter's Crown Court! On the higher side of the 'moat' one leaves the garden through **Athelstan's Tower**, an attractive viewpoint. Athelstan reigned from 925 to 940, and this tower is part of William's post-conquest fortifications.

On emerging from the tower, **the prison** (1790 and 1853) may be seen across the valley, and beyond, on the lower slopes of Pennsylvania, the twentieth-century West Country equivalent of the 'dreaming spires', the University of Exeter. The campus is beautifully landscaped and well worth a special visit, and includes the Northcott Theatre (plays, films and a licensed buttery) and the Great Hall (concerts). Round the north-east corner of the walls a short walk downhill brings you back to the starting point near Boots.

The city has the narrowest street in the world, **Parliament Street**, at 25in-45in (63-114cm) wide. Its name cannot be explained; find it opposite the Halifax Building Society.

THE CATHEDRAL

Enter the Cathedral Close by Broadgate, where one of several gates into the Close stood in medieval times. Violence to the clergy after dark led to this drastic action; Salisbury's gates are still *in situ*. The simple stone **Devon War Memorial** on the right, designed by Lutyens, stands on the site of the Roman bathhouse excavated in the early 1970s and now covered over. The cobbled approach to the west front is made of granite setts from Portugal. This processional way is designed to improve the rather squat west front.

The cathedral's twin towers are Norman, although perforated by later Gothic windows, and are all that survive of the cathedral built between 1133 and 1160. Bishop Bronescombe became dissatisfied with this building and began rebuilding it in 1270, but his conception was not completed for about a hundred years.

Inside, from beneath the west window is a good view of the 300ft (105m)-long unbroken tierceron vaulting. This weighs about 5,000 tons (5,080tonnes), and stands on columns of Purbeck (Dorset) stone. Much of the cathedral is of stone from Beer in East Devon.

The roof bosses have been restored to their original medieval hues. Churches in the Middle Ages were dazzling, and where possible the brightness has been put back in Exeter Cathedral. Look especially for the complicated boss dating from

1350 in the second bay from the west, which depicts the murder of Archbishop Thomas à Becket in Canterbury Cathedral in 1170. The knights are killing him as he kneels, defended by his cross-bearer. A mirror on wheels enables the bosses to be studied without neck strain.

Other glories to look for are the Minstrel Gallery of about the same date, the Bishop's Throne (1312-17) which is regarded as the finest piece of wood carving of its age in Europe, and the tombs in the attractive Lady Chapel at the east end.

The side chapel behind the throne, St James' Chapel, was destroyed by a bomb in World War II, but fortunately the throne had been taken to pieces and removed to the country for safety; otherwise it would have become so many wood splinters. Shrapnel damage can be seen above the choir. The chapel is now restored.

Of the buildings in **Cathedral Close** the most noteworthy is **Mol's Coffee House**, its bay windows a reminder of Drake and Hawkins when they chatted over their coffee. Though there is nothing else to match Mol's, taken together the Close's buildings comprise a delightful scene. It is here, in St Martin's Lane and along Gandy Street (the other side of High Street) that the essence of Exeter's attraction is most deeply felt.

RECENT DEVELOPMENTS

In recent years, major developments have taken place to expand Exeter's sporting, leisure and artistic life. There are sports centres offering facilities for badminton, basketball, keep fit, gymnastics, swimming, volley ball weight training and more informal activities; while the **Exeter Phoenix** in Bradninch Place is the place to go if you are interested in dance, folk, jazz, rock, film, theatre or cabaret. Classes and courses are always on the go and there is a bar and café.

Exeter has sprawled east and south in living memory, gobbling up the villages of Heavitree, Whipton and Pinhoe, though the residents of Clyst St Mary might object to their village being called a part of Exeter. Here, at Crealy Park, is one of Devon's finest sites for children, with every conceivable ride (on land and water) as well as such favourites as a pets' corner.

TOPSHAM

Exeter has also 'acquired' the desirable estuary port of **Topsham**, 5 miles (8km) away. Topsham is a place of individual character and this has enabled it to retain its independence despite the administrative take-over. Untouched by bombs in World War II, it has a great wealth of buildings of enormous charm. While none of them is of the highest grade in architectural terms, collectively, and as a group, they form a town that is a delight to reside in, as is reflected in house prices. Cheek by jowl the older houses stand, many of them terraced, but deep-set on their narrow sites. Monmouth Street, Higher and Lower Shapter Street, the Strand, Victoria Road and Ferry Road are some of the constricted thoroughfares that reward the explorer.

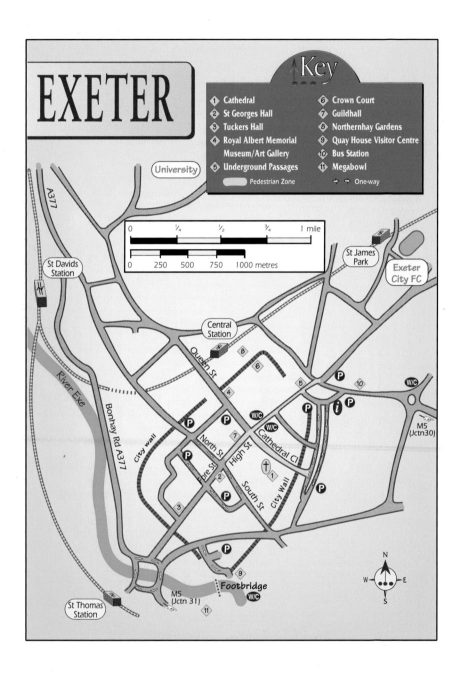

EXETER

The Grand Western Canal

Grand Western was the rather pretentious name for a scheme which went off at half-cock. Originally intended to be part of a through route from Taunton to Topsham, as part of a plan to link the Bristol and English Channels, the Taunton-Topsham canal, with three branches to Cullompton, Tiverton and Wellington, was granted an Act of Parliament (as all canals needed in the 'Great Age' of canal building) in 1796, the projected cost being £166,724. The section of the canal from Tiverton to Lowdwells, on the Somerset border, a distance of 11 miles (17.7km), was started in 1810 and completed in 1814 at a cost of £220,000. Not for another 13 years was any further work carried out. By then the plan to extend the canal to Topsham had been abandoned. Though the section from Lowdwells to Taunton was completed, it was never profitable and was closed in 1869.

Happily, the section from Lowdwells to Tiverton was not allowed to deteriorate too much when it went out of use in 1924, and in recent years the Tiverton end was re-opened as an amenity waterway and Country Park. A horse-drawn passenger barge with bar and refreshments operates from the basin and the whole section can be walked, a beautiful trip through some very pretty country.

Enjoy Topsham on Foot

There is only one way to enjoy Topsham – on foot. Everything is so crowded that cars are a nuisance, and this is Topsham's one drawback. Several car parks exist, but residents prefer to have their vehicles outside their houses, even if it means using the pavements. Do not add to the problem, but park in a car park and explore if possible when the tide is high; as your enjoyment will be enhanced if the slimy, dark silt of the inter-tidal zone is obscured! Not for nothing is the place disparagingly referred to as Topsham-on-mud by those who are jealous of its attractions.

There is a walk of about half a mile to the far end of the Goat Walk, a narrow pedestrian walkway beside the estuary at the southern end of the Strand, thus passing the so-called 'Dutch' houses, attractive bow-windowed residences with flower-bedecked courtyards. A small museum entirely in keeping with the town is reached along the Strand and is well worth a visit.

Topsham developed as a port for Exeter in the Middle Ages, although it had earlier performed this function in Roman times. Small craft could reach the city by coming up the river, but following a dispute, the Countess of Devon built a weir across the river in 1282, thus cutting Exeter off from the sea. From this time, the city's merchandise had to pass through Topsham to the advantage of the treasury of the countess and her successors. A short canal – England's first pound-lock canal – was built to bypass the obstruction in 1564-6, and was later considerably lengthened. The name **Countess Wear** (or Weir) came to be attached to the hamlet (now a suburb) between Topsham and Exeter.

Topsham is no longer a commercial port. However, it still serves as a base for hundreds of recreational sailors. A small salmon fishery exists, and there is no more enjoyable way of passing a fine evening than standing on the cliff at the top of Church Steps with the tide flooding below, the sun setting over Haldon, and the fishermen seine-netting on the far bank of the Exe. Of the numerous public houses here, the Bridge Inn beside the River Clyst on the **Exmouth** road is the most unspoilt.

Perhaps the most satisfying way to experience the appeal of Topsham is to go by bus (they are very frequent) from Exeter and walk back along the canal, after exploring its narrow streets and alleys. The foot ferry across the Exe brings one to the canal, and a level walk of 5 miles (8km) to the city.

Once past Topsham, the Exe Estuary widens to admit the River Clyst (pronounced 'Clist'), and Exmouth is soon reached along a busy switchback road past the Royal Marine camp and the turning to **Lympstone**. This village has charm when the tide is in, but at low tide the expanse of mud is vast and intimidating.

As the main road approaches Exmouth, a sign (left) points to **A la Ronde**, an eccentric building of 1798, owned by the National Trust. The name suggests a circular structure, but it really has sixteen sides. Two 'ladies of quality', the Misses Jane and Mary Parminter, having travelled in Italy, modelled it on the sixth-century basilica of San Vitale at Ravenna. The rooms lead off a central octagon, which is lit by apex roof lights 35ft (12m) above.

The quirky architecture of the house is matched by the interior decoration of shells, feathers and much of the original furniture and *bric-à-brac* collected by the two women. Later additions to the structure, such as the gargantuan Victorian central heating, an early flush lavatory and the gas lighting, have only added to the eclectic atmosphere of this extraordinary dwelling. A little way up the lane a small chapel and almshouses of contemporary date called Point in View are also worth a visit.

EXMOUTH

Exmouth is the fourth largest urban area in Devon after Plymouth, Torbay and Exeter. It is the family holiday resort *par excellence* with a long sandy beach, good parks, undercover entertainments, boat trips, a busy shopping area, and attractive hinterland. At one end of its 2-mile (3.2km) sea front, the longest in Devon and Cornwall, is **Exmouth Dock**, once a busy commercial enterprise used by coasting vessels, but now abandoned. Here the ferry leaves for Starcross, a 1+ mile (2km) trip across the mouth of the estuary.

The broad tidal waters of the Exe are very popular with sailors and water skiers, and naturalists wax lyrical about the birds which choose to winter on the muddy flats, or use it as a migratory stop-over. The Exe has international importance as a habitat for birds.

Excavations carried out in the heart of the town before re-development revealed the foundations of buildings dating from the fourteenth and fifteenth centuries, well before written evidence suggested a settlement here.

On the sea front is the **Great Exmouth 'oo' Model Railway**, the world's largest display at that gauge, set in attractive and realistic landscapes. **Exmouth Museum** is in Sheppards Row, Exeter Road.

The Barn

In 1896-7 the architect Edward Prior built a house in Foxholes Road called **The Barn** (now the Barn Hotel), which has been called 'the most important house of its date in Europe'. It was an expression of the Arts and Crafts Movement, an attempt to return to simplicity and a national style, while being modestly original. As its plan evokes the shape of a butterfly, the quest for simplicity is hardly satisfied, though the desire to achieve originality is eminently successful. The Barn was thatched when newly built, and was burnt down in 1905, being rebuilt the following year. Its main features are two enormous round stone chimneys flanking a central gable which links the two main house components. The structure is of local sandstone intermixed with large sea-scrubbed pebbles.

Just east of Exmouth is **Sandy Bay**, its large caravan site giving wonderful views to Torbay and Berry Head.

At the entrance is the **World of Country Life**, with a comprehensive collection of rural artifacts from simple farm tools to a massive traction engine, together with collections of vintage vehicles and classic motorcycles, farm animals and a pets' corner. There are also exotic animals such as llamas, a host of other country-related items and age-related adventure playgrounds for children. As the display is under cover this makes a fine refuge in bad weather, but a visit is always worthwhile.

THE BUDLEIGH SALTERTON – BICTON CROSS AREA

Budleigh Salterton is the next place along the coast, a genteel watering place with a pebble beach and an attractive, slightly old-fashioned air. Not for Budleigh the lures of amusement arcades and discos. At the Exmouth end of the beach, hand-powered capstans are still used to haul fishing boats up the beach over wooden rollers.

Where the main street meets the promenade, the **Fairlynch Arts Centre and Museum** occupies an attractive *cottage orné* (there are many more to be seen in Sidmouth). Children will love the imaginatively conceived smugglers' cellar.

The East Budleigh road heads north up the Otter Valley and **East Budleigh** is reached after 2 miles (3km). A signposted side road in the village near the church leads in another mile to **Hayes Barton**, Raleigh's birthplace in 1552. A fine example of a Tudor farmhouse, it is not usually open to the public, but it can be seen from the road.

East Budleigh is unspoilt and still

possesses many cob and thatch buildings. Cob is a dry compacted mass of mud and straw, which will last for hundreds of years given a good hat (a roof) and a good pair of shoes (a stone plinth). The Sir Walter Raleigh Inn is a good place for a drink and a meal. The church, on its eminence, contains the Raleigh pew (among many carved bench ends) bearing the date 1537, and some well restored roof bosses.

One of the roads at Bicton Cross leads to **Otterton** and **Otterton Mill**, widely advertised as 'The Museum that Works'. Here, waterpower from the River Otter is used to drive the waterwheel, and food made from flour milled on the premises can be eaten in the restaurant and purchased in the shop. There is often an exhibition in the gallery.

Bicton Park

On the A376 at Bicton Cross a brick direction post (dated 1743) bears a passage of scripture on each face. Bicton Park is a place which can only be described as a total experience; there is so much here to do and see. The owners' claim that it is the 'One Stop Family Day Out' is not made glibly. There are gardens, parkland, a lake, train rides, a wonderful adventure playground, and a couple of hanger-like covered exhibitions, the Hall of Transport and the James Countryside Museum. Not far way is the Bicton Arena, where equestrian and other outdoor events are promoted.

Before leaving the district, the interesting area loosely called **Woodbury Common** should be visited. This is an open unproductive upland, of poor soil, partly used for commercial forestry but largely uncultivated and ungrazed. It extends from the outskirts of Exmouth to beyond the Exeter to Sidmouth road. Much used for walking and riding, it is also ideal for cross country running and orienteering. The Royal Marines train here. A wonderfully scenic road passes along the ridge giving extensive views across to Dartmoor one way and Dorset the other, even though the altitude nowhere reaches 600ft (210m). Many walks can be devised in any direction over such open country.

SIDMOUTH

Sidmouth is the unrivalled aristocrat of the East Devon coast; a town of distinction and character. It occupies the valley of the little River Sid, between the mighty slopes of Salcombe Hill and Peak Hill, and extends back to its satellite Sidford.

Although it was a place of no consequence before the end of the eighteenth century, Sidmouth achieved the respectability of court patronage in 1791 when the king stayed here; in 1819-20 the Duke and Duchess of Kent and their infant daughter Victoria, later Queen Victoria, enjoyed a lengthy winter sojourn in its mild climate. Society soon caught on, and a building boom in the attractive Georgian and Regency style began. Present-day Sidmouth is therefore a product of the first forty years of the nineteenth century, sympathetically brought up to date by sensitive owners.

The best way to discover some of the architectural surprises in Sidmouth is to walk enquiringly around with open eyes. The prominent Regency row known as **Fortfield Terrace** sets the standard for the rest of the town. The Esplanade nearby is similar, for both have elegant first-floor wrought-iron balconies with tent-shaped canopies and trellis supports. The Russian double-headed eagle on No 8 marks the visit there in 1831 of Grand Duchess Helene of Russia, sister-in-law of the Czar.

Rather later is **Coburg Terrace** (1815) and the **Royal Glen Hotel** (1810), each with a castellated parapet and Gothic windows. And peppered around the town, many of them standing in mature gardens, are such stylish residences as Powys, Hunter's Moon and Cedar Shade. Another kind of building represented locally is the *cottage orné*, an attempt to reproduce a rustic building of Romantic design, usually with a thatched roof. Examples can be seen at the foot of Peak Hill – Rock Cottage and Beacon Cottage for instance.

In the town the observant visitor will notice a number of mid- and late nineteenth-century shop fronts, delightfully rare survivals, and protected by the listing process as much as the houses themselves. Amazingly, there are 484 buildings or groups of buildings listed as of special architectural and historic interest in the Sidmouth area. One last house must be mentioned – **Old Chancel**, near the church. This was built by a local antiquary, Peter Orlando Hutchinson, in the 1860s, using the demolished material of the 'restored' parish church, and is partly ecclesiastical in style.

Folk Festival

Sidmouth never developed as a family resort, as it lacked the vital natural element so necessary for the success of a holiday with children – sand. (There is some at low tide at Jacob's Ladder Beach.) However, in recent years it has hosted the annual International Folk Festival, when groups of musicians and dancers from all over the world enliven the town for a week. An after-dark informal procession ends the event, when the lighted torches are dowsed in the sea.

The **Sidmouth Museum** in Church Street is in character with the town. There are displays of Regency prints, Victoriana, lace and the complex geology of East Devon. A curious and little-known Sidmouth connection with the world of commerce, going back a hundred years, began with a Miss Cash, a cripple, who embroidered names and monograms on linen with dyed cotton. This developed into Cash's Name Tapes. She lived at Barton Cottage near Church House.

A very different site is the **Norman Lockyer Observatory**, founded in 1912 by the man now seen as the father of astro-archaeology for his investigations into the astronomical alignments of Stonehenge and other stone circles. The Observatory has a planetarium and several large telescopes.

Continuing eastwards, the A3052 should be taken to the top of Trow Hill, where, round the corner, a sign points to Branscombe. Just off the main road at **Salcombe Regis**, is the **Donkey Sanctuary**, where infirm donkeys are nursed back to health, and elderly animals are given a well-fed comfortable old age. Admission is free, and the visitor can wander around the buildings and paddocks.

BRANSCOMBE

If Sidmouth is unrivalled as a town in East Devon, **Branscombe** is the most delightful village on the East Devon coast, and is perhaps the longest village in Devon. The sea is 1¹/₂ miles (2km) beyond **The Pottery**, at the top of the scattered groups of buildings.

Branscombe church is on the right ³/₄ mile (1km) further on. Its exterior is dominated by the Norman tower, and inside there is an Elizabethan gallery (reached by outside stairs), box pews and a rare three-decker pulpit. A little further on is a thatched blacksmith's forge, and opposite is a thatched cottage set back from the road, the famous **Branscombe Bakery**, where the ovens were heated by ash faggots. This is now a tearoom.

Down at **Branscombe Mouth**, the road ends at the pebble beach, and a car park. It is an interesting place; fishing goes on here, both from the beach and from boats. The Sea Shanty café was once a coalyard (the coal came by sea), there were lime kilns and a gypsum works here, and the coastguard cottages (now the Lookout) hint at the smuggling trade which was rife in East Devon in the eighteenth and early nineteenth centuries.

This is a good place for a walk of 2¹/₂ miles (4km), lasting perhaps 1¹/₂ hours. Walk up the hill to the east, the Beer side, but follow the concrete track into the cliffside caravan site. These caravans occupy the level patches used by generations of Branscombe people to grow early potatoes. The route follows the higher of the tracks between the caravans and soon reaches a good signed path entering the scrub. This is the **Hooken Landslip** which broke away from the cliff in 1790, and the Pinnacles, great turrets of white stone, are the major manifestations of this collapse. The path climbs steeply to the clifftop. Now turn left and follow the path back to Branscombe.

The stone from this area was used for building from Roman times and is known as Beer stone, after the village just beyond. Exeter Cathedral has thousands of tons in its structure, brought by sea and river from Beer. When first taken from the workings, it can be cut with a saw, but it hardens after exposure to air. **Beer Quarry Caves** are open to the public and are enormously exciting to penetrate.

BEER AND SEATON

Beer is now a holiday and fishing village. A stream bustles down the main street. Beer and Seaton are often spoken of together as they almost merge. Seaton presents two faces to the world: a quiet retiring ambience at the Beer end, and a more gregarious outlook near the mouth of the Axe. A holiday camp and limited boat anchorage opportunities no doubt contribute to this ambivalence.

Together the two places have much to offer the holidaymaker. At **Seaton** the disused railway track has been rebuilt into **a tramway**. Open top tramcars (closed trams in bad weather) shuttle along the **Axe Valley** between Seaton, Colyford and Colyton. Children of all ages head for the **Pecorama** where a wide range of attractions including an outdoor model railway and the **Beer Heights Light Railway** will keep everyone happy for hours; lunch can be taken in a Pullman car.

Built-up Devon ends at the east end of Seaton sea front. Beyond is the main landslip area stretching away to Lyme Regis in Dorset, a tortuous tumble of unstable cliff, tangled with wood and scrub, and a haven for wildlife. Naturalists regard it as the last and largest wilderness on the coast of southern England. **The South Devon Coast Path** passes along its length, but there are no escape routes. Either the walker treks all the way from Seaton to Lyme Regis – a distance of 6¹/₂ miles (10km) – or you come back the way you went. At the time of writing the approach from Seaton is over Axe Cliff golf course and through a few fields, and it is well worth attempting a short distance into the landslip to get its atmosphere. But one may have to backtrack. The path goes on, and on... There are buses back from Lyme Regis, but check their times first!

There have been many landslips here over the centuries, but at Christmas 1839 a cataclysmic slip occurred after heavy rain. For naturalists the interest lies in seeing what plants develop from a given point in time, and the area is a National Nature Reserve. The Devon county boundary is crossed just before Lyme Regis is reached. The area was used by John Fowles in his book *The French Lieutenant's Woman*, and subsequently used for the film.

WEST FROM AXMINSTER

Axminster is a name known throughout the world on account of its product – carpets. They are manufactured here in a modern computerised factory, near the station and open to the public. There is a museum in the town. Another old trade can be viewed at the tannery at **Colyton**, a small market town not far away. This particular tannery uses oak bark to produce high quality leather, one of only two tanneries in England to do so.

To the north of Colyton is **Loughwood Meeting House**, built in 1653 and used by dissenters. This tiny chapel lies just below the busy A35, but is seemingly far more remote and well worth a visit for a few peaceful moments.

To the west of Colyton is the **Farway Countryside Park**, which has as its centrepiece a butterfly house, but includes other attractions, such as a putting green, pony rides and a kite flying area.

A few miles to the north is **Honiton,** on the southern route into Devon; here the A30 and A35 roads unite. The town is bypassed, and the wide street with market stalls on Tuesdays and Saturdays is busy all day with unhurried activity. The local museum, called the **Allhallows Museum** after the building in which it is housed, specialises in Honiton lace, a craft still actively pursued.

Broadhembury is the kind of place people think of when Devon is mentioned; a great deal of cob and thatch and a picturesque church. The 'Hembury' of the name refers to the very large earthwork on a spur of the Blackdown Hills, **Hembury Fort**, above the village. When the

Above: Otterton

Opposite The south west coast path is one of the longest routes in Britain and includes both coasts of Devon

Below: Beer

Iron Age people fortified it, the site was already old; it had been a causewayed camp in Neolithic times.

The old road from Honiton to Exeter leaves no-one in doubt as to its origin. The Romans laid it down about 1,800 years ago. Going from Honiton westwards, just before the dual carriageway is reached, on the right is a thatched building of some antiquity. This stands on the site of the St Margaret's leper hospital. In medieval times lepers were not encouraged in towns; this hospice is nearly 1 mile (1.5km) outside Honiton. Latterly it has become an almshouse.

Ottery St Mary is a thriving little town. The church is the showpiece, a miniature Exeter Cathedral, and like its exemplar, a squat structure. Westwards from the church, and past the college, the large building is **Chanter's House**, the house of the Coleridge family, made famous by the poet Samuel Taylor Coleridge, the author of *The Ancient Mariner*. Chanters is unfortunately not open to the public. Two other buildings worth seeing in the college are the Warden's House and the Vicar's House. Notice the flint-stone walling hereabouts.

In **Cornhill**, the pleasant terrace just below the churchyard, are two shops restored by the Devon Historic Buildings Trust from ignominious dereliction. Round the corner in **Paternoster Row** are several good examples of eighteenth-century town houses with dated rainwater heads (1759 and 1779). Lower down the town, in Jesu Street, is a nonconformist church built of brick in 1664, one of the earliest in England.

Historically, much of the countryside east of Exeter and lying now between the A30 and M5 was given over to cider orchards. This area is abutted on the west by the enormous **Killerton** estate of the National Trust, given to the Trust in 1944 by Sir Richard Acland, and centred on the garden and park of Killerton House. Much of Broadclyst is owned by the Trust. Killerton House is not particularly attractive in itself, but the Paulise de Bush costume collection is here, a display which is changed annually. The gardens are a delight: a subtle blend of herbaceous borders, lawns, shrubs and trees, gradually merging into the wooded clump of Dolbury, an Iron Age hillfort on the summit of Killerton's sheltering eminence.

Cadhay, Escot & Whimple

A mile north-west of Ottery is **Cadhay**, a beautiful Tudor manor house built in 1550 by John Haydon, a successful lawyer. The house is approached along an avenue of lime trees, and is open to the public at certain times. Nearby is **Escot Park and Gardens** with an arboretum and rose garden, and collection of wildlife including wild boar, pot-bellied pigs, otters and birds of prey. Also nearby, at **Whimple**, is a fascinating museum of dollshouses and toys, the latter a collection of steam and mechanical toys dating from the mid-nineteenth century.

Easily reached on the other side of the M5 is **Ashclyst Forest** and **Paradise Copse**, also National Trust, an extensive woodland where one can wander all day and not see another human being. Roe deer are there in abundance and may be spotted during the day if all is quiet, but one frequently sees them near the roads through the forest as dusk falls.

THE CULLOMPTON AREA

Cullompton bestrides the B3181 and revels in its freedom from traffic following the construction of the M5. Motorway and railway users should look for its fine church tower (1549), a notable landmark. The interior is completely perpendicular in style. Its two most noticeable features are the bright and beautifully carved roof which extends from end to end, and the rood screen, also coloured, which spans the width.

Beyond Cullompton the highly-regarded **Coldharbour Mill** project at **Uffculme** is worth visiting. Until 1981, it was a working wool mill, and when it closed because of the economic recession, it was converted to a working museum of the woollen trade. An 18ft (6m) waterwheel provides some of the power. These old industrial enterprises are a fascinating feature of the British countryside. Not far from here is the Grand Western Canal.

At **Hemyock**, near Culmstock, to the north-east of Uffculme, **Hemyock Castle** is an interesting medieval building, delightfully set in the Blackdown Hills. The castle, which saw action in the Civil War is rarely open, but worth the effort on those few occasions.

TIVERTON

Tiverton's life has always revolved around its rivers. It stands at the confluence of the Exe and the Lowman (Tiverton means 'two ford town'). For hundreds of years, woollen mills were powered by water from the rivers, but when the woollen industry declined, John Heathcoat set up his lace factory here in 1816, after he had been forced out of Leicestershire by the Luddite machine wreckers. Much of Tiverton's life still focuses on the Heathcoat factory, now diversified and modernised.

Tiverton has some interesting buildings. **Old Blundells School** (National Trust) at the foot of Canal Hill can be viewed from outside. The school, founded in 1599, is one of England's great public schools, and straddles the A373 a mile east of the town, a site to which it moved in 1880. **The Old Police Station** in St Andrew's Street was restored by the Devon Historic Buildings Trust and converted into two modern dwellings. Also in St Andrew's Street is **Tiverton Museum**, a most enterprising collection that has won the Museum of the Year award.

The church should be seen for the Greenway aisle, and Castle Street has the town leat – Tiverton's medieval water supply – running along its length. The **castle,** which is frequently open, is much altered from medieval times, and today serves as a private residence. Originally built in 1106, it last suffered attack in 1645, when Sir Thomas Fairfax, Cromwell's general, captured and slighted its defences.

A grandson of John Heathcoat built **Knightshayes Court** (National Trust), 2 miles (3km) north of

Tiverton. The architect was William Burges, whose wildly fanciful decorative whims set him apart even among the extravagant nineteenth-century practitioners of his profession. His dilatoriness in not completing the interior of the house led to his being superseded by J D Crace. The gardens are splendid, and like those at Killerton, gradually merge into informal woodland. There are some fine topiary animals on the box hedges of the formal garden. The house looks proprietorially down on the town that brought the family so much wealth.

BICKLEIGH AND CREDITON

The Exe Valley is now followed down to **Bickleigh**, where the road crosses the river by a narrow bridge in the midst of the kind of pretty scenery for which Devon is famous. Even if this is quintessential England, there is a successful vineyard here on the western slopes overlooking the bridge. Public houses and thatched dwellings crowd in upon the river, making it the sort of place to linger, and there is plenty of interest for everyone, especially the **Bickleigh Mill Craft Centre and Farm**. Old-time machinery and farming methods, shops, a restaurant and perhaps the most exciting of all, a trout fishery, where even quite small children can catch fish and take them home.

Bickleigh Castle, downriver and detached from the honeypot around the bridge, is a charming relic of stirring times past. Apart from the thatched Norman chapel – probably the oldest complete building in Devon – the chief survival is the three-floors-high gatehouse containing the

most impressive room, the great hall. The castle and the somewhat newer farmhouse alongside are open to the public. Everything is immaculate and in the best taste.

From Bickleigh, the hill road to Crediton is worth taking as a journey into deepest Devon. Up and down and round swoops the A3072 with expansive views north to Exmoor. To the south, the looming tree-topped Raddon (Red Down) Hills block the view to Exeter.

After $2^{1}/_{2}$ miles (4km) take a turning left signposted to **Fursdon House**, which is 1 mile (1.5km) south of the A3072. Here generations of the Fursdon family have lived for over 700 years. The house is small, not particularly attractive, but a warm, lived-in atmosphere pervades the panel-lined rooms. There are walks on the small estate, and delicious teas.

Just before Crediton a visit to **Shobrooke Park** to see the flock of Canada geese on the lake will set them honking excitedly as the visitor approaches along the public footpath.

Crediton, mentioned in the introductory chapter as being the head of the Exeter diocese until 1050 and the birthplace of St Boniface, has not in modern times equalled or surpassed these Dark Age achievements. Some disastrous fires, common in Devon towns in medieval times, have swept away historically important buildings, and their replacements make little impact on the visitor. Only the splendid church, a towering edifice like a small cathedral and unlike any other church in the county, is worthy of Crediton's lustrous past; but one wishes it were set on a more prominent site, a hilltop perhaps, or at least above the

Knightshayes
Court

main road, where it would be better appreciated.

SOUTH-WEST OF EXETER

As one travels south-west from Exeter the view is blocked by the **Haldon Hills**, a flint-topped plateau of greensand and sandstone, similar in many ways to the Devon hills inland from Sidmouth. Being flat-topped and not dipping below 600ft (210m) except in the saddle between Great and Little Haldon and with a modest maximum altitude of 826ft (289m), this range cries out for an artificial eye-catcher. One was provided in the late eighteenth century when Sir Robert Palk built the

three-sided **Lawrence Castle** (often called Haldon Belvedere) on Penn Hill as a memorial to his great friend Major-General Stringer Lawrence. We should now call it a folly. A little way north, on the B3212, is Bowhill House, a fine sixteenth-century mansion whose Great Hall has been carefully restored using original materials and techniques.

Away to the south stretch the coniferous plantations of the Forestry Commission and a number of walks of different lengths have been laid out through the forest, starting from the Commission's information point on **Buller's Hill**. There are directions from the ridge road, and indeed it is signposted from the A38 dual carriageway. Fallow deer can often be seen, and forty-nine resident bird species are known, as well as thirty-six species of butterfly.

Where the A38 passes over the ridge is **Haldon Racecourse**, home of the Devon and Exeter Races since 1769, and the similar hilltop, 1 mile (1.5km) away on the A380, carried an Admiralty telegraph station during the Napoleonic Wars. The name **Telegraph Hill** has been applied to the road ascent on the Exeter side.

The best route to Kenton is the Starcross road going south then east and dropping steeply off the plateau to the rich red Devon soil. A lane leads down to the magnificent red sandstone church of **Kenton**. Inside is the well-restored rood screen (with coloured figure paintings), rood loft and pulpit. It is said that the grooves rubbed in the Beer stone dressings of the porch were caused by the village archers sharpening their arrow points.

Starcross is a short distance away along the west bank of the Exe Estuary. Here the railway travels along the 'sea' wall, blocking off the fine views of the tide-riding boats from the ground floor rooms of the nineteenth-century terrace houses.

The Italianate sandstone tower near the station marks a pumping house of **Brunel's 1846 atmospheric railway**. This well-known engineer decided to power his trains on atmospheric principles. A continuous pipe with a longitudinal slot on top was laid between the rails in which ran a piston fitted to the leading vehicle of a train. Stationary steam engines pumped out air from the pipe in front of the piston, forming a vacuum, while air coming in behind the piston pushed the train along. The system was not successful, as Brunel did not have the materials to match his idea, and after spending £426,368 installing what became known as the 'atmospheric caper', he cut his losses and began running conventional locomotives.

The mouth of the estuary is marked by **Dawlish Warren**, a popular resort which has developed beside the sandspit which protrudes towards Exmouth. The plants and birdlife are of national importance, and there is a visitor facility open in the summer where information on the natural history of the area can be found.

Powderham Castle

The estate should be entered from the south of Kenton on the A379. Powderham Castle, the home of the Courtenay family, the Earls of Devon, since 1390, stands in one of the finest parks in the county; it still has a large herd of fallow deer, and a strange amalgam of architectural styles. Perhaps the most interesting rooms in the house are the marble hall and the staircase hall. The former contains a 13ft (4.5m) longcase clock, by Stumbels of Totnes (1740), which plays a tune at 4, 8 and 12 o'clock. Various events are held at Powderham Castle and in the park throughout the summer and times of opening are widely advertised.

In and around Exeter

The Catacombs

A nineteenth-century attempt to solve the problem of burial space in the city by stacking coffins in a stone mausoleum. Now sealed.

Exeter Cathedral

Gothic nave between massive Norman towers. The Bishop's Throne is notable.
☎ (01392) 255573
Open: 7.30am-6.30pm Monday to Friday; 7.30am-5.30pm Saturday; 8am-7.30pm Suday, all year.

The City Walls

Exeter
Five-sixths of the wall is still visible. Built on a line determined by Roman engineers and rebuilt and restored after every siege.

Exeter Phoenix

Bradninch Place, Exeter
Dance, jazz, rock, films, theatre. Bar and café.
☎ (01392) 667056

The Guildhall

Exeter
The oldest municipal building in the country. The hall itself, with a fifteenth-century arch-braced timber roof, stands behind a Tudor pillared front of 1592.
The Guildhall is still a working building but is open for viewing whenever possible. ☎ (01392) 665500 to arrange a free tour or check opening times.
www.exeter.gov.uk also gives details.

Sports facilities

Exeter
☎ (01392) 265862 for details and opening times

Quay House Visitor Centre

Exeter
An exhibition explaining Exeter's maritime heritage.
☎ (01392) 265213
Open: 10am-5pm daily, Easter to October

Rougemont Castle

Exeter
The shell of William the Conqueror's castle, now housing the Exeter Crown Court buildings.

Royal Albert Memorial Museum

Queen Street
Specialist displays of silver, costume, clocks and watches, paintings, flora and fauna.
☎ (01392) 265135
Open: 10am-5pm Monday to Saturday, all year. Admission free.

Spacex Art Gallery

Preston Street
Contemporary art gallery hosting exhibitions, workshops and special events.
☎ (01392) 431786
Open: 10am-5pm Tuesday to Saturday. Admission free to exhibitions.

St Nicholas' Priory

An impressive part of a once much larger monastic building, containing medieval furniture and fittings.
☎ (01392) 665858
3-4.30pm Monday, Wednesday and Saturday, Easter to October.

Tucker's Hall

Fore Street
A medieval building, the only Exeter trade guild to survive with its headquarters intact.
☎ (01392) 436244
Open: 10.30am-12.30pm Tuesday, Thursday and Friday from June to September; Thursday only from October to May.

Underground Passages (Aqueducts)

Exeter
A medieval civil engineering solution to the lack of water within the old city.
☎ (01392) 265887/665887
Open: 10am-5pm Monday to Saturday, July, August and September and school holidays. 2pm-5pm Tuesday to Friday and 10am-5pm Saturday for the rest of the year.

Wynard's Almshouses

Exeter
Medieval houses for the elderly, now converted into offices for voluntary social services.

Topsham Museum

25 The Strand, Topsham
A small museum largely devoted to the sea and shipping.
☎ (01392) 873244
Open: 2-5pm Easter Sunday to end of October, Monday, Wednesday, Saturday and Sunday.

A la Ronde

Summer Lane, Exmouth (National Trust)
An eccentric sixteen-sided house decorated with shells and feathers, and full of bric-a brac of many kinds.
☎(01395) 265514
Open: 11am-5.30pm Sunday to Thursday, April to October.

The Barn Hotel

Exmouth
The most important house of its date in Europe.

The Great Exmouth '00' Model Railway

Seafront, Exmouth
Fun for both parents and children with model trains.
☎ (01395) 222999
Open: From 10.30am daily from Easter to the end of October.

The World of Country Life

Sandy Bay, Exmouth
A comprehensive display of farm implements and customs.
☎ (01395) 2745433
Open: From 10am daily April to October.

Exmouth Museum

Off Exeter Road
The town's history told in local artifacts.
Open: 10.30am-12.30pm daily, Sunday 2.30-4.30pm.

Fairlynch Arts Centre & Museum

Budleigh Salterton
A decorous museum for the dilettante, housed in a thatched cottage orné.
☎ (01395) 442666
Open: 2-4.30pm daily, mid-April to late October plus 11am-1pm, Monday to Friday, mid-July to mid-August.

Bicton Park Botanical Gardens

East Budleigh
Museums, gardens, train rides and playgrounds in a beautiful parkland setting.
☎ (01395) 568465
Open: 10am-6pm in summer, 10am-5pm in winter, 364 days per year.

Hayes Barton

East Budleigh
Sir Walter Raleigh was born here in 1552. Not open to the public.

Otterton Mill

Otterton, Budleigh Salterton
Restored watermill & craft centre.
☎ (01395) 568521
Open: 10.30am-5pm Easter to October, 10.30-4pm November to Easter.

Sidmouth Museum

Church Street
A repository of Victoriana, East Devon lace and Geographical displays.
Open: 2-4.30pm Monday, 10am-12.30pm and 2-4.30pm Tuesday to Saturday, Easter to October.

Norman Lockyer Observatory

Sidmouth
☎ (01395) 512096 for details of events and public openings.

Donkey Sanctuary

Salcombe Regis
A 'nursing home' for hundreds of donkeys.
☎ (01395) 578222
Open: 9am to dusk daily, all year round.

Branscombe Church

Notable for its Norman tower, three-decker pulpit, box pews and Elizabethan gallery.

In the Honiton area

Beer Quarry Caves

Penetrate the interior of these ancient vaults dating back to Roman times.

Pecorama

Seaton
Railway fun for all the family. Outdoor model railway and Beer Heights Light Railway. Wonderful gardens.
☎ (01297) 21542
Open: April/May to September. Telephone for times or visit www.peco-uk.com

Seaton Electric Tramway

Experience the clanking transportation of the tram as it travels along the Axe marshes.
☎ (01297) 20375
Open: Daily April to October. Weekends only November and December.

The Landslip

between Seaton and Lyme Regis
A 6 mile (10km) long strip of natural landscape on the coast. Geological and floral interest intermixed.

Axminster Museum

Past and present history including the carpet industry.
Open: 11am-1pm and 2-4pm Monday to Wednesday; 11am-4pm Thursday and Friday; 11am-1pm Saturday, June to September

Loughwood Meeting House

Axminster (National Trust)
A tiny, remote, dissenters' meeting house, dating from 1653.
☎ (01392) 881691
Open: all year.

Colyton Tannery

One of the last tanneries in the country to tan leather using oak bark.

Farway Countryside Park

Colyton
Includes a butterfly house, adventure play areas indoors and out, 9-hole pitch and putt, animals and pony rides.
☎ (01404) 871367
Open: 11am-5pm daily, late March to the end of October. Saturday and Sunday and school holidays in the winter.

Allhallows Museum

High Street, Honiton
Specialises in Honiton lace, and is housed in the original Allhallows School building.
☎ (01404) 44966
10am-5pm Monday to Saturday, April to September; 10am-4pm in October.

St Margaret's Leper Hospital

Honiton
One mile (1.5km) west of Honiton. A medieval leper hospice, now adapted as an almshouse.

Ottery St Mary Church

A 'miniature Exeter Cathedral', packed with architectural and historic interest.

Chanter's House

Ottery St Mary
House of the Coleridge family. Not open to the public.

Cadhay House

1 mile (1.6km) NW of Ottery St Mary
A privately-owned Tudor mansion, open to the public at certain times.
☎ (01404) 812432
2-6pm Tuesday, Wednesday and Thursday in July and August plus 2-6pm bank holiday Sundays and Mondays.

Escot Park and Gardens

Ottery St Mary
250 acres of parkland and gardens. Otters, birds of prey and wildfowl.
☎ (01404) 822188
Open: 10am-6pm daily, Easter to September; 10.30am-4pm daily October to Easter.

Whimple Dolls House and Toy Museum

Near Ottery St Mary
☎ (01404) 822607

Hembury Neolithic and Iron Age Hillfort

Blackdown Hills
Probably Devon's largest and finest earthwork, occupied in two prehistoric eras.

North, West and South of Exeter

Killerton

Broadclyst (National Trust)
Georgian house with costume
collection in a series of period
rooms. Extensive gardens and
parkland with spectacular displays
of azaleas and rhododendrons. Iron
Age hillfort on Dolbury.
☎ (01392) 881345
Open: House – 11am-5.30pm daily
except Tuesday; closed Monday in
March and October (except half-
term); seven days a week in August.
Park and garden – 10.30 until dusk
daily, all year.

Cullompton Church

The perpendicular rood screen and
colourful roof are memorable.

Coldharbour Mill

Uffculme
A working museum of the wool
trade, with steam engine and
waterwheel. Giant New World
Tapestry, gardens and walks.
☎ (01884) 840960
Open: 10.30am-5pm daily, Easter to
October. Winter Monday to Friday,
telephone for times.

Grand Western Canal

Tiverton
Built as part of an uncompleted
larger scheme, now a linear
country park with a horse-drawn
boat operating at the Tiverton end.
Day-boat and rowing boat hire.
☎ (01884) 253345
Open: Park all year. Boat trips
April to October. Telephone for
timetable.

Old Blundells School

Tiverton (National Trust)
Serene 1604 buildings where
Blundells School began. Not open to
the public.

Tiverton Castle

Privately-owned, but open to the
public at certain times.
☎ (01884) 253200
Open: Easter to September

Tiverton Church

A splendid town church, richly
endowed in 1517 when the Greenway
aisle and porch were added to the
south side.

Tiverton Museum

An award-winning small town
museum with displays on agriculture, transport, industry and
especially social history.
☎ (01884) 256295
Open: re-opening after refurbish-
ment in summer 2001. Please
telephone for details.

Knightshayes Court

Tiverton (National Trust)
Nineteenth-century house designed
by the eccentric architect William
Burges, standing in beautiful
grounds.
☎ (01884) 254665
Open: 11am-5.30pm Saturday to
Thursday, mid-March to Early
November (opens Good Friday).
Closes 4.30pm and on Thursday and
Friday, after 1 October.

Fursdon House

Cadbury
Tiverton. Walks on estate, teas.
☎ (01392) 860860
Open: 2-5pm bank holiday Mondays;
Wednesday and Thursday in June
July and August.

Bickleigh Castle

The well kept gatehouse of a
medieval castle standing in beautiful
gardens on the bank of the River
Exe.
☎ (01884) 855363
Open: 2-5.30pm Sunday, Wednesday
and Bank holidays from Easter to the
end of May. Daily from June to early
October.

Bickleigh Mill Craft Centre and Farm

Crafts, old farming practices and a
trout fishery all in a small area.
☎ (01884) 855419
Open: all year.

Crediton Church

Stately town church with a fifteenth-
century clerestory and some notable
monuments.

Haldon Hills Forest Walks

Long and short walks through
Forestry Commission plantations.

Lawrence Castle (Haldon Belvedere)

Penn Hill
A folly building erected as a memo-
rial to Major General Stringer
Lawrence.

Kenton Church

Splendid rood screen and restored
pulpit.

Powderham Castle

Starcross
An historic structure incorporating
many different architectural styles
standing in a large deer park.
Children's secret garden and farm
shop.
☎ (01626) 890243
Open: daily all year for shops and
restaurant. Tours of castle every
half-hour 10.30am-5pm April to
October (except Saturday).

Dawlish Warren Visitor Centre

Information on the area's natural
history. Haven for overwintering
birds.
☎ (01392) 265700

Chapter 1 included the top of the Haldon Hills. Once beyond Haldon, the visitor is definitely in South Devon, or on Dartmoor, depending on the direction he takes. South Devon abuts Dartmoor to the north and the hinterland of Plymouth in the west, and includes within its boundaries the South Hams. This sub-region serves to distinguish the fertile countryside between the Rivers Dart and Yealm, and Kingsbridge may justly claim to be the capital of the South Hams. The name 'South Hams' is first found in 1396, but the meaning of 'Hams' is unclear.

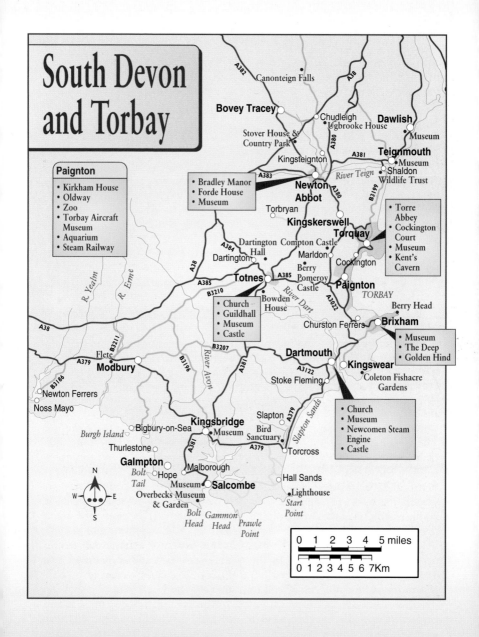

South Devon and Torbay

Paignton
- Kirkham House
- Oldway
- Zoo
- Torbay Aircraft Museum
- Aquarium
- Steam Railway

Canonteign Falls

Bovey Tracey

Chudleigh
Ugbrooke House

Dawlish
Museum

Stover House & Country Park

Kingsteignton

A381 **Teignmouth**
Museum
Shaldon
Wildlife Trust

River Teign

- Bradley Manor
- Forde House
- Museum

Newton Abbot

Torbryan

Kingskerswell

Torquay

- Torre Abbey
- Cockington Court
- Museum
- Kent's Cavern

Dartington Hall
Dartington

Compton Castle
Marldon
Berry Pomeroy Castle

Cockington

Totnes

- Church
- Guildhall
- Museum
- Castle

Bowden House

Paignton

TORBAY

Berry Head

Churston Ferrers

Brixham

- Museum
- The Deep
- Golden Hind

River Dart

Flete
Modbury

River Avon

Dartmouth

Stoke Fleming

Kingswear

Coleton Fishacre Gardens

- Church
- Museum
- Newcomen Steam Engine
- Castle

Newton Ferrers
Noss Mayo

Bigbury-on-Sea
Kingsbridge
Museum

Slapton
Bird Sanctuary

Slapton Sands

Burgh Island

Thurlestone

Torcross

Galmpton
Bolt Tail Hope
Museum **Salcombe**
Overbecks Museum & Garden

Malborough

Hall Sands
Lighthouse
Start Point

Bolt Head *Gammon Head* *Prawle Point*

N
W — E
S

0 1 2 3 4 5 miles

0 1 2 3 4 5 6 7Km

As the county's prime holiday area, South Devon owes its success to three factors: the discovery of its beauty and mild climate at the end of the eighteenth century, when the continent was closed to visitors; the grafting onto these natural characteristics of the social facilities of early watering places such as assembly rooms, accommodation and bathing machines; and the arrival of the Great Western Railway in the late 1840s. The larger resorts, Torquay and Paignton (now, with Brixham, gathered together under the umbrella title Torbay), are still tossing about in the backwash of the developmental surge which came in the second half of the nineteenth century, when they sped headlong into the forefront of British holiday destinations. Most visitors now enter South Devon by road, and the A380 up Telegraph Hill is the main approach.

UGBROOKE HOUSE

A few miles further on the motorist will see a sign reading 'Ugbrooke House', the stately home and estate belonging to Lord Clifford, which sits retiringly in the quiet countryside between the A380 and the A38. The house dates for the most part from about 1750 when Robert Adam rebuilt the earlier Tudor manor house and Capability Brown landscaped the park. He planted trees and formed three lakes by damming the Ug Brook.

However the house's recent history is equally interesting. In the 1930s the 11th Lord Clifford left Ugbrooke as he could not afford to live there, and during the war it became a school for evacuees and a hostel for Poles. In the 1950s several downstairs rooms, now beautifully restored, were used as grain stores. The parents of the present Lord Clifford returned from Australia in 1957, and began the enormous task of bringing life and beauty back into the house and park, and a few years ago it was opened to the public. The interior is noteworthy for the care taken in restoring the fabric, and for the collection of paintings, dolls, furniture and military uniforms.

CHUDLEIGH

A short distance from Ugbrooke is **Chudleigh**, once on the busy A38, but now bypassed by the dual carriageway to Plymouth. Much of medieval Chudleigh was destroyed in the great fire of 1807, when two-thirds of the town was burnt down.

As the town is on a ridge of limestone, there were problems of a reliable water supply in the Middle Ages, but in about 1430 Bishop Lacey provided a town leat (similar to the one at Tiverton), which brought water along a circuitous route 7 miles (11.3km) from a spring on Haldon. Some potwater dipping wells may be seen near the top of New Exeter Street.

At the other end of the town are **Chudleigh Rocks**, a limestone outcrop little visited by strangers. A scramble along its crest is an enjoyable experience, and the view westwards from the top of the cliff is breathtaking. The crags are much used by rock climbers, and, as you would expect on a limestone feature, the rock is penetrated by caves. The Pixies Cave can be entered by visitors – a torch is useful.

About 3 miles (5km) up the B3193, just west of Chudleigh, is **Canonteign Falls and Farm Park**. A natural hillside gorge was landscaped by the first Viscountess Exmouth 160 years ago. Water was fed to a cascade by a leat. After many years of neglect this beautiful corner of the Teign Valley has been restored and the paths cleared. The site now claims the highest waterfall in England.

Westwards from Chudleigh along the A38 for 3 miles (5km) as far as the Drum Bridge intersection, there is a left turn, signposted 'Newton Abbot', and almost immediately a left turn into **Stover Country Park**. A large granite lodge of classical design beside the dual carriageway was built on one of the approaches to Stover House, which dates from 1776; it is not open to the public as it is now a girls' school. The park has become a Country Park managed by Devon County Council. Close to the Park is **Orchid Paradise**, a superb orchid collection housed in a plant nursery. Also near the Park, **Trago Mills** is a shopping complex with a number of play areas for children.

There is a pleasant walk round the lake. A great deal of work was done a few years ago to make the park, which had become derelict, beautiful once again, and available to the public. Birds and dragonflies are present in abundance, and fishing can be tried from special platforms.

In this part of the Bovey Basin, as the low-lying area between the Haldon foothills and Dartmoor is called, are the white workings of the ball clay operations. Ball clay is found at only one other place in Devon, between Okehampton and Great Torrington. (China clay occurs on south-west Dartmoor.) Ball clay differs from china clay in that it is china clay washed down millions of years ago from deposits higher up. China clay is decomposed feldspar, one of the three constituents of granite. Ball clay is used to make pottery and tiles.

NEWTON ABBOT AND DISTRICT

Newton Abbot is at first sight an unprepossessing town. Its attractions have to be searched for, but many decent small buildings are waiting to be discovered. It grew rapidly when the railway arrived, and became a junction for the Torbay and Moretonhampstead branches and a necessary stop for the heavier trains to attach a 'banker' locomotive to assist them over the fierce Dainton and Rattery inclines between Newton Abbot and Plymouth.

As a market town for rural South Devon it retains its usefulness and is highly regarded by country people who find little to attract them to Torquay, where you can buy china animals but not a pair of hard-wearing trousers. For workaday things Newton Abbot is ideal.

The River Lemon passes through the built-up area and is largely culverted, a fact which fails to allow for the occasional flash-flood. The St Leonard's Tower, which stands at the central crossroads, is all that remains of a church built about 1350 and demolished in 1836.

Close to the town centre are the **Hedgehog Hospital** at Prickley Ball Farm on the Denbury road where visitors can learn more about these delightful animals, and **Tucker's Maltings** the only traditional malthouse in the country which is open to the public.

Two outstanding buildings are within easy reach of Newton Abbot, albeit in opposite directions. **Bradley Manor** (National Trust) stands in its own grounds just off the Totnes road, and is frequently open to the public. It is a small fifteenth-century manor house, and its great hall, emblazoned with Queen Elizabeth's royal arms, is a notable feature. In the woods beyond Bradley Manor is Puritan Pit, a deep natural cavity where early nonconformists held their meetings in secret 300 hundred years ago. At the other end of the town **Forde House**, now used by Teignbridge District Council, dates from 1610. King Charles I visited in 1625, and William of Orange read his proclamation here in 1688, on his way to London, after landing at Brixham.

'Racing at Newton Abbot' refers to the national hunt racecourse on the Kingsteignton road. During the rest of the year, it is used for stock car racing, greyhound racing and country shows.

A little way out, and beyond the large village of Ipplepen, is the parish of **Torbryan**, which should be visited for the sake of its church and the Church House Inn. This remote church – it stands at the end of a cul-de-sac – was never restored, and retains to a remarkable degree the fittings of a medieval church. Large clear perpendicular windows admit much light to illuminate the striking hues of the screen, pulpit and altar. A short walk up a nearby public footpath to Tornewton takes one along a delightful valley through

Dawlish Water

limestone country. One of the features of South Devon are these pockets of limestone, and in caves concealed by scrub on either side have been found animal remains from millions of years ago.

DAWLISH

Approaching South Devon down the Exe Estuary, **Dawlish** (not to be confused with Dawlish Warren) is the first of the south coast holiday resorts to be reached. The heart of the town is built on both sides of a pleasant open space called the Lawn through which runs the Dawlish Water, or simply the Brook, much frequented by ducks and black swans, who paddle about above some seemingly unconcerned trout. The railway cuts off the view to the sea and creates its own attractions, overpowering the coastal end of the town.

Dawlish developed early in the nineteenth century as a quiet watering-place, although a small settlement half a mile inland had existed for hundreds of years. The long sandy beach, the coves, and the proximity of the railway assured the town's success, even if the crowded and hilly site prevented expansion.

The town is well worth exploring; here and there one can feel the atmosphere that Jane Austen and Charles Dickens must have encountered when they visited Dawlish. (Dickens contrived to have Nicholas Nickleby 'born' here.) A visit to **Dawlish Museum** will strengthen this feeling, as local history, trades and Victoriana figure largely in the exhibits. Off Exeter Road is a fine recreation ground, including an 18-hole approach golf course and a heated indoor swimming pool.

At the top of the hill heading towards Teignmouth is the award-winning housing development of Oakland Park, a successful attempt to group buildings of intimate scale in a pleasurable composition while echoing Devon's heritage of vernacular buildings.

TEIGNMOUTH AND SHALDON

The road to **Teignmouth** undulates violently, and descends into the town down a long hill from the thatched house called **Minadab**, a well-known landmark of the kind commonly found in Sidmouth. Teignmouth combines a workaday face with a fun-loving holiday image, and it is too facile to say that the former is based on the estuary while the latter faces the sea. To an extent, this is true, as the boat building yards and ball clay exporting quays are on the Teign Estuary; but this makes no allowance for the sailing, wind-surfing or angling holidaymakers for whom the estuary is their playground.

Teignmouth's buildings reflect its ambivalent outlook. Some splendid nineteenth-century houses look across the seafront open space known as the Den, but at the back of the town are the old, narrower, winding streets. There are two parish churches, and that belonging to West Teignmouth, rebuilt about 1820, has cast-iron pillars airily supporting a roof lantern of unusual delicacy.

Teignmouth was largely destroyed by the French in 1690, and was in the front line too in World War II when seventy-nine people were killed in German air raids. Keats stayed at No 20 Northumberland

Place with his mother in 1818 – a plaque marks his sojourn.

Much of Teignmouth's holiday activity takes place near the Den. The pier, theatre, cinema, model railway, tennis and novelty golf are all here. On Dawlish Road is a heated swimming pool. **Teignmouth museum** is in French Street, so-called as it was built with money given in a public appeal after the 1690 raid.

To the north of the town, at Ashcombe, is **Ashcombe Family Activities**, with everything from quad bikes and go karts to paintball and grass sleds. Across the estuary from Teignmouth is **Shaldon**, reached by a long road bridge (only freed from tolls in 1948); its old toll house stands at the north end, and Shaldon's late nineteenth-century church (completed 1902) is at the south end. This building has been likened to a tunnel of stone, and from outside it possesses an air of gloom that a visit inside does little to dispel, even if one knows that connoisseurs of Victorian architecture hold it in high regard.

The village of Shaldon, however, has an air of unspoiled period charm. Lines of simple flower-decked terraced cottages look out on the constantly changing scene of the estuary mouth, at the ferry boats with their lines of imitation gun ports, and perhaps a ball clay ship stuck on one of the ever-shifting sand banks.

At the sea end of the village the great tree-topped headland known as the Ness rears up, and here are found the holiday trappings of the village and the **Shaldon Wildlife Trust**, with a large car park. A tunnel through the cliff to the popular Ness beach is often attributed to

smugglers, but they would hardly have advertised their trade in this way; more likely, it was cut during the Napoleonic Wars.

On the higher slopes of Shaldon is an approach golf course, and just below the Torquay road is a public park.

That part of the **South Devon Coast Path** between Shaldon and Torquay makes a very good day's walk. As it cuts across the grain of the landscape, it is a strenuous expedition, but may be shortened at several places by turning off the coast path to the A379 for a bus back to Shaldon.

The three towns of Torquay, Paignton and Brixham are now gathered together under the title Torbay for administrative and municipal convenience. But in this book, the individuality of the three constituent towns will be retained using the term Tor Bay in its two-word form to describe the natural feature only.

TORQUAY

Torquay has an abundance of interest. The prehistoric and historical scene was set in the introductory chapter with references to Kent's Cavern and the presence of the fleet in Tor Bay during the Napoleonic Wars. The medical officers on duty with the fleet were quick to realise its climatic benefits and recommended a stay in the mild embryo resort to their private consumptive patients. So it was as a haven for invalids that the popularity of Torquay developed, a reputation perpetuated in the present-day Borough motto *Salus et felicitas* – Health and Happiness.

At the same time, of course, when the Continent was out of bounds, a few shrewd entrepreneurs, who owned land or added to their estates, built Mediterranean-type villas with Italian-sounding names like Villa Borghese and Villa Como, and were then in a position to re-sell. Two of these families were the Carys and the Palks, and one is not in Torquay long before these names appear in one form or another. Much of Torquay is therefore nineteenth-century, though the tall apartment blocks and hotels, some with gull-wing fly away roofs, are clearly post-World War II.

An exception is the interesting complex of buildings centred on **Torre Abbey**. Here there flourished, from 1196 until the dissolution of the monasteries, an abbey for Premonstratensian canons. After 1539 the property passed through several owners before being bought by the Carys in 1665, and it was they who built the present mansion early in the eighteenth century. The gatehouse probably dates from 1320, and the so-called '**Spanish barn**', the monastic tithe barn, is another relic from pre-dissolution days. It acquired its name after being used as a temporary prison for 397 Spanish captives from the Armada ship *Nuestra Senora del Rosario* in 1588. The property was bought by Torquay Corporation in 1930 and the house is now used as an art gallery. William Blake's works are well represented and there is a good collection of English drinking glasses. The gardens are immaculately kept, and floral displays of the highest quality draw admiring visitors year after year.

Beaches

Torquay's success as a holiday resort has been achieved despite not having any large beaches. **Torre Abbey Sands** are mostly covered at high tide, and the other opportunities are at **Meadfoot Beach, Anstey's Cove and Oddicombe**, where a cliff railway assists visitors to reach the shore. Petitor is the unofficial naturist beach. It was Paignton which developed as the family resort and remains so to this day, with better sandy beaches, both off the promenade and at Goodrington. Torquay's natural advantage of a Riviera image has channelled its growth along more adult lines, and there is no shortage of entertainment to suit all tastes and pockets.

The **Bygones Museum** in Fore Street, St Marychurch features a life-size Victorian street, together with a World War I trench and model railway. Not far away on Ilsham road is **Kent's Cavern**, awarded Britain's 'Cave of the Year 2000'. Stalagmites and stalactites can be seen, along with finds from the Stone Age, while evening tours are arranged by candlelight for those who enjoy a spooky theatrical experience.

There is one other reminder of olden times within the bounds of Torquay which must be seen – **Cockington**. In the public mind it consists of an ancient forge and Cockington Court, a pleasant but not outstanding mansion in 287 acres (115 hectares) of beautiful grounds. Around this core there are other attractive buildings, notably

Torquay

the Drum Inn (1934) designed by Sir Edwin Lutyens. The survival of Cockington within Torquay is a considerable achievement, even if a price in tourist exploitation has been paid. Horse-drawn carriages are on hand to take visitors to and from this village within a town.

Babbacombe Model Village is far more than its name implies. It is a triumph of landscape miniaturisation, and stays open with illuminations to 10pm until mid-October. Tiny trains move round the site. A very special kind of aquarium is Aqualand, at Beacon Quay, which claims to be the largest display of its kind in the West Country. **Torquay Museum** in Babbacombe Road contains many of the finds from Kent's Cavern and the unique Agatha Christie exhibition, as well as displays of Devon folk life, pottery, archaeology and Victoriana.

Sporting possibilities abound. Several golf courses, pitch and putt, squash, ten-pin bowling and swimming are all there to be tried. Water sports are as varied. Water skiing, windsurfing, sea fishing, sailing or simply taking a boat trip across the bay or round the coast are some of the opportunities available. There

are also two cinemas, three theatres, night clubs, discos and casinos.

Many people enjoy walking along the promenade and the piers. The public gardens entice visitors and a steep climb through the beautiful **Rock End Gardens** behind and above the Imperial Hotel leads to that curiously-named viewpoint, Daddyhole Plain. (A 'daddy' is thought to be a demon in folklore.) The visitor should also walk or motor along the Ilsham Marine Drive, diverting onto the cliffs to get a close look at Thatcher Rock. This is one of the limestone 'horns' of Tor Bay. Berry Head is the other.

PAIGNTON

Paignton developed as the family resort beside Torquay. Children like sand, and there is more of it at Paignton. There are hills in Paignton – very steep ones – but they are further back from the sea than at

Paignton Pier

Above: Berry Pomeroy Castle just off the Totnes to Paignton road
Below: Brixham

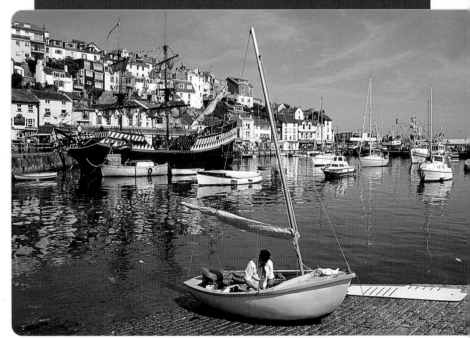

Torquay, and the town was already established before land hunger pushed Paignton to encroach on its hilly hinterland.

Historically, Paignton was some distance inland – the old streets are unmistakable – but when the railway arrived, the settlement grew towards that station, and soon the rapidly expanding town was filling in the land between the railway and the sea. Fortunately, a pleasant open space was allowed to remain between the front row of buildings and the beach.

Architecturally Paignton is not as distinguished as Torquay, although there are two surprises. **Kirkham House** in Kirkham Street may have been a fourteenth-century priest's house; the public are allowed to visit its suite of interesting but unfurnished rooms.

The other surprise, even more unexpected, is an opulent mansion, **Oldway**, built in 1874 for the Singer family (of sewing machine fame) in the French style. Rows of neo-classical pillars around the exterior prepare one for a sumptuous interior of marble staircases and painted ceilings. Incongruity is added by the local authority's interior signing, for this ostentatious building is now owned by the Council and much of it is used as offices. However, it is open to the public as are the equally splendid grounds. This ambitious mansion – ambiguously called the Wigwam by Isaac Singer, its builder – copied many features of Versailles, perhaps because his second wife was of French extraction. The family originally came to Paignton for health reasons, and Oldway was built with the money they made from sewing machines.

Paignton Zoo

Paignton Zoo, on the Totnes road, the largest in Devon, is a constant delight for visitors. A feature of the zoo is the exotic birds which walk and fly around the grounds. On a tree-covered island in the lake, the gibbons woop their eerie cries and swing from branch to branch, bringing up their young in cosy barrels loftily sited in the trees.

Facing Oldway's main entrance is a round building with a pointed roof, looking rather like a miniature Royal Albert Hall. This was originally built as a riding and exercising pavilion, and may well have been based on the Albert Hall which was built 3 years before Oldway, in 1871.

Before leaving Paignton to explore the countryside nearby, there is a final attraction, the **Paignton and Dartmouth Steam Railway** which uses steam engines to haul trains from the GWR station at Paignton to Kingswear. The railway calls first at Goodrington Sands, skirts Tor Bay behind Saltern Cove and Broad Sands, and then calls at Churston before diving into Greenway tunnel. Emerging, the railway follows the River Dart to Kingswear. A ferry links Kingswear with Dartmouth across the water. At Goodrington Sands, **Quaywest** claims to be Britain's biggest water park and includes an awesome waterslide and the highest (and fastest) flume in the country.

'Behind' Paignton, as it were, are two ancient and historic buildings of the highest interest. **Compton Castle** (National Trust) nestles in a valley in a seemingly indefensible site about a mile (1.6km) north of the Torbay ring road at Marldon. The earliest part of the building, dating back to about 1330, is the great hall, with various associated rooms and cellars. The owners were the Gilbert family. Later, in 1450-75, various additions and replacements were effected including a withdrawing room and a chapel.

About 1520 further reconstruction and enlargement took place. The towers and curtain wall with their impressive machicolations (holes through which missiles could be dropped on attackers) were built as well as the portcullis entrances. French raids on Teignmouth, Plymouth and Fowey (in Cornwall) had made the family feel vulnerable, and this protection was adequate against lightly armed raiding parties even in this overlooked site. Civil War activity is unknown, but by 1750 the hall was ruinous. The Gilberts – who had included Sir Humphrey Gilbert (founder of Newfoundland) and his half-brother Sir Walter Raleigh – sold Compton Castle in 1800 and bought it back in 1930. Commander and Mrs Walter Raleigh Gilbert then restored and rebuilt the structure, and gave it to the National Trust in 1951.

The other historic building is **Berry Pomeroy Castle**, not far away, but difficult to find from Compton. It is better to return to the ring road, take the Totnes road at Marldon Five Lanes and look for the sign after a few miles. This is another site where several structures have followed one another, but unlike Compton Castle, the present-day result is a ruin, even if a highly atmospheric one. It stands in dense woods on a spur above a small stream.

Three sides could be easily defended; only the south side needed massive walls, and here is the gatehouse, curtain wall and St Margaret's Tower. This part of the castle, the oldest, was probably built in the fourteenth century, though the records are silent, by the Pomeroy family. Between 1548 and 1613 a large mansion was built inside the castle walls by the Seymours, who acquired it in 1548; the gaping windows of this abandoned house still taunt us with their mystery. Why was it left to fall down? No-one knows. A fire may be the answer. The whole scene is very picturesque, and there are walks in the woods that surround the castle. The castle is privately owned, but open to the public.

The third of the Tor Bay towns is **Brixham**, until not so long ago a quiet fishing backwater, but now caught up in the holiday business, though separated from Paignton's southern satellites of Goodrington and Galmpton by a green belt.

BRIXHAM

Like Torquay, Brixham sits on limestone. Traces of early man have been found here. In medieval times, the town developed as Higher and Lower Brixham, with the fishing industry concentrated round the creek, which is now largely filled in, but which penetrated nearly half a mile beyond where the inner harbour now ends.

The fishing industry was so successful that the ships sought to exploit the fishing grounds of the North Sea, following the migratory shoals, and they were largely responsible for the development of Lowestoft, Grimsby and Fleetwood as fishing ports. Markets for their fish near where they were caught were needed.

On the quay at Brixham is **The Deep**, which explores all aspects of the sea, with animated pirates and other delights for younger visitors. Another nautical connection is the National Coastguard Museum which is incorporated in the **Brixham Museum** at Bolton Cross. This includes fascinating photographs of wrecks and rescues, and of the kind of apparatus used in saving life around the coast.

The quay at Brixham buzzes with industry most of the time. An extensive inshore fishery survives, and there is much coming and going of holidaymakers' pleasure craft, as well as trips to Torquay or round the coast to Dartmouth.

A worthwhile exploration of **Berry Head Country Park** can well take a couple of hours; there is so much here to see, whether one is interested in plants, sea birds, history or technology. Out to sea are the tankers and super-tankers performing their loading or lightening logistics before heading off, shallower in draft, to cope with the Dover Strait, or waiting until the world oil price increases.

The vertical cliffs – do watch children and dogs – provide superb nesting sites for kittiwakes, fulmars, guillemots, gulls of various kinds, kestrels, jackdaws and rock doves; a visit here in the spring is the best time to see hectic avian activity. The limestone rocks carry an unusual flora, which includes autumn squill, fellwort, scabious, rock sea lavender and wall pennywort. As several rarities are known here, visitors are asked not to pick specimens.

Across this elevated promontory in Iron Age times the local tribe built a defensive earthwork. This gave Berry Head its name; Berry is a corruption of Byri or Byrig, the Saxon word for fortification. The huge Napoleonic War fort, now such a landmark and an interesting feature to explore, destroyed most of this. A certain irony must have been felt by the garrison of that fort when *HMS Bellerophon* put in to Tor Bay bearing Bonaparte to St Helena.

The coastguard station monitors maritime comings and goings, and nearby is Berry Head Lighthouse, which is sometimes said to be the highest, the smallest, and the lowest lighthouse in Great Britain. At 191ft (67m) above sea level there is none higher; being only a few feet high it is very small. When originally built it operated by the action of a weight falling down a 150ft (52.5m) shaft; this has been replaced by a motor. Inland is an aircraft navigational device, and by the café is a cloud-determining device; the Royal Observer Corps is also represented. Sometimes on a very clear day Portland is visible 35 miles (56km) away across Lyme Bay.

From Berry Head the **South Devon Coast Path** perambulates St Mary's Bay and Sharkham Point, then runs along National Trust land nearly all the way to Kingswear. Much of this magnificent coast was bought by the Trust in late 1982, and is open for public access. At Inner Froward Point is a World War II gun battery, almost complete except for the guns, and inland a little way, on a high point is the 80ft (24.4m) high, hollow, tapering stone pillar known as the Day Mark, an unlit

Above: Kingswear

Below: Brixham inner-harbour

Dartmouth, looking across the River Dart to Kingswear

navigational beacon dating back to the 1860s. A good walk from Berry Head is to follow the cliff path to Kingswear, returning to Brixham by bus. Four hours are needed for the 10 miles (16km) of strenuous walking.

Tucked in a small valley leading down to the sea near the Day Mark is **Coleton Fishacre Garden** (National Trust), a 15-acre (6 hectares) sub-tropical paradise only begun by the D'Oyly Carte family (of Gilbert and Sullivan fame) in the 1920s. It is open to the public.

DARTMOUTH

Two ways of arriving at **Kingswear** have already been mentioned, by steam train or on foot. **Dartmouth**, the little town across the water, so redolent of our British heritage, must be in the top ten of any Devonian's list of towns. The charm of the place is its cramped site. Steep hills slide straight into high water, or at least they did so before man altered the waterfront. Lacking space on the hillsides, Dartmothians have pushed outwards into the river in the same way as those who live in Brixham.

In about 1600 the muddy creek of Mill Pool was filled in, to become the lowest part of the present town. It met the estuary at the significantly named New Ground and the gardens by the bandstand. The **Market Square** occupies part of this made-up land. Likewise, every building in front of Fairfax Place and Lower Street (in other words, the whole of the South Embankment), is built on land reclaimed from the river. Knowing this, it is easier to understand the pressures for space that must have exercised the local merchants.

They needed flat land near their ships; there was little point in building high up on the hillsides. Dartmouth was the leading trading port of Devon. It possessed a deep-water, sheltered anchorage, easily and well defended by the twin castles of Kingswear and Dartmouth, between which a chain could be strung in times of war. The Second and Third Crusades left from here – what a chaotic turmoil of people, animals and supplies the port must have witnessed – and trade with Spain, Portugal and later Newfoundland burgeoned.

Royal Naval College

Dartmouth, of course, synonymous with the training of naval officers, is so much a part of our naval tradition that one is almost surprised that the **Royal Naval College** was only built in 1905. Before this, the trainee officers lived in superannuated wooden hulks moored in the Dart, but as these began to rot a permanent building became necessary. The college is officially called Britannia after the first of the hulks it succeeded.

Bayard's Cove, just downstream from the Lower Ferry, is a reminder of these rollicking days of sail. Old buildings line the quay in harmonious disarray. Other attractive buildings are the seventeenth-century **Butterwalk**, a Grade I listed building containing the comprehensive **town museum**, and St Saviour's Church, with its splendid gallery dating from 1633.

The castle, already mentioned, should be visited as well as the lesser-known fortifications at Bayard's Cove. Within the precincts of Dartmouth Castle is another church, St Petrock's, rebuilt in the seventeenth century, but containing several memorial brasses.

Much of the coast south-westwards for $1^1/_2$ miles (2km) belongs to the National Trust, and this includes the wooded hill behind Dartmouth Castle called **Gallants Bower**. On its 400ft (140m) summit is a Civil War earthwork, a relic of the Royalists' determination to hold on to Dartmouth in 1645. However, when the Parliamentarians invested the town, the Royalists put up little resistance, and it soon fell to General Fairfax in January 1646.

The cliff walk to **Little Dartmouth** (where there is a National Trust car park) is delightfully varied, with views ahead across Start Bay to Start Point.

The smoke from the steam railway across the Dart prompts one to recall that **Thomas Newcomen** was born in Dartmouth. Newcomen recognised the power of steam, and he produced the first industrial steam engine, although James Watt gained most of the credit when he improved the invention 50 years later. In a building near the Butterwalk can be seen an example of a steam engine based on Newcomen's principle, but in this case built in the early nineteenth century.

Dartmouth's position makes it a good place for boat trips. Pleasure cruises come here from Tor Bay in the summer, and leave Dartmouth for holiday trips along the coast. One of the classic English river journeys is up the Dart to Totnes, a winding, ever-changing voyage of delight. Birdwatchers especially will see much to enchant them. There is one waterside tree where cormorants dry their wings, managing to

Totnes

Totnes is another of Devon's top ten towns. One can go further. In 1965 it was recognised by the Council for British Archaeology as of such quality that it was listed as one of the CBA's forty towns 'so splendid and so precious that the ultimate responsibility for them should be regarded as a national concern'. The reasons for the CBA's assessment can be succinctly listed here:

- Ancient town plan well preserved
- Ancient bridge crossing and approaches
- Georgian bridge
- Waterfront of historical importance
- Town wall, ditch and gates well preserved
- Castle precinct well preserved
- Medieval to seventeenth-century buildings worthy of preservation
- Georgian and Regency buildings worthy of preservation

Above: Alongside the River Dart at Totnes

Right: Totnes

Below: Stoke Fleming with Slapton Sands beyond

look prehistorically sinister in the process. Kingfishers can often be seen where the channel narrows, and occasionally an osprey. The Scottish birds sometimes rest a while on the Dart and feed themselves up before setting off for the tropics.

TOTNES AND DISTRICT

An exploration of **Totnes** is best begun from the top end by visiting the **Norman castle**. As it dominates the town the visitor can quickly get a baron's eye view of Totnes from its walls. The small but perfect keep stands on its motte beside the inner bailey or court. Alongside the castle on the west you will see a housing development, Castle Court, which fits neatly into the town in scale and texture, proving that modern buildings can after all be good to look at. The line of the town walls can be picked out, and are traceable on the ground in several places.

Down **High Street** are the two covered pavement arcades of the **Butterwalk** and the **Poultry Walk**, similar to other pillared ambulatories at Dartmouth, Kingsbridge and Plympton. Clearly this was a fashionable and sensible South Devon convention in the early seventeenth century, as were the slate-hung elevations.

The red sandstone church is worth a visit. The Beer stone rood screen is notable as a superb example of fifteenth-century stone carving. At the 'back' of the churchyard is the Guildhall, built in 1533. The council chamber, court room and mayor's parlour contain a great deal of interest. The Ramparts Walk leads to the East Gate, where High Street gives way to Fore Street.

After passing through East Gate,

Totnes Museum is on the right in the Elizabethan house. An unusual exhibit relates to early computers. Charles Babbage the 'father' of British computer science spent much of his early life in Totnes; he virtually invented the punch-card system and a kind of prototype computer, the analytical engine. He was far ahead of his time and like many such men of genius was not appreciated or understood in his lifetime. The house occupied by the museum is only one of many which preserve their original form, but may have false or later façades, belying their age. A notable feature of many of these early town houses is their decorated plaster ceilings. As these are mainly in private houses they are not often seen, although some owners seem to leave the lights on and the curtains open in the upstairs rooms on summer evenings so that the elaborate plasterwork can be appreciated by passers-by.

Across the road, set in the pavement, is the **Brutus Stone**. A legend links this lump of rock with the Trojan who landed here in 1000 BC. Opposite is Atherton Lane, often festively floral. Indeed, Totnes on summer Tuesdays has local people, mostly shopkeepers, dressed in Elizabethan costume.

Further down still is the distinguished Georgian front of **the Mansion**, now part of the King Edward VI School, and, on the same side, tucked up another lane, is the Gothic House which has a public right of way running through it. **Fore Street** opens out at its foot onto the Plains, where an obelisk stands to local boy William Wills (with Burke, the first person to cross Australia). He died in 1861 on the return journey. The river is crossed by an 1828 bridge designed by Charles Fowler, architect of the old Covent Garden market, and is the lowest bridge on the Dart.

The main street is so crammed with historic buildings that it is worthwhile to walk up and down on opposite pavements. Opposite the Civic Hall is the Devonshire Collection of Period Costume in 43 High Street. It is well worth a visit to see beautiful things delightfully displayed.

At the top of the town, not far from the large car park, are the **Leech Wells** in Leechwell Lane. Water gushes into three stone troughs, and the lepers came here in an attempt to cleanse themselves in what they thought were healing waters. There was a leper hospital nearby through the Middle Ages; the water formed the local supply. Leprosy was rife in this country for thousands of years. Even after the Civil War, in 1646, 257 leprosy burials took place in Totnes.

One mile south of Totnes off the A381 is **Bowden House**, a Tudor dwelling with a Queen Anne façade. The family dress in Georgian costume to guide the visitor, and there is a photographic museum too. Also to the south, near Blackawton, is the **Woodlands Leisure Park** with a huge number of rides and slides (wet and dry) and several play areas.

Continuing up the Dart Valley, the next stop is at **Shinner's Bridge**, where the A384 and A385 meet, our first encounter with 'Dartington'. This many-sided concept began in 1925, when Leonard and Dorothy Elmhirst, both idealists, purchased an 820-acre (328 hectares) estate based on **Dartington Hall**, with the intention of reviving life in the countryside. The estate was run down,

Dorothy Elmhirst had a considerable fortune, and they saw the property as capable of development.

Since then, the activities at Dartington have blossomed and multiplied. The retail trade is carried on at the Cider Press at Shinner's Bridge, where one can buy furniture, good quality gifts, farm foods, clothes and tweed cloth, and eat at an excellent vegetarian restaurant, Cranks. Other activities over the years have been building, forestry, education (adult courses and a boarding school) and the arts in the broadest sense.

Various walks around the estate begin from the Cider Press car park, some short, some long. Dartington Hall itself ought to be visited; but, as it is about 1 mile (1.5km) from Shinner's Bridge, one can turn off the A384 at Dartington church and park in the hall car park. The courtyard is under the arch, and opposite is the Great Hall, a roofless ruin in 1925, but now beautifully restored with timbers drawn from the estate. A chamber music concert here is a sublime experience. Behind the hall in the gardens is the restored tilting yard, with terraced grassy banks and twelve enormous clipped yews looking like giant skittles. Modern tournaments, outdoor plays, masques and *son et lumière* presentations are held here.

FROM DARTINGTON TO KINGSBRIDGE

The rest of this chapter deals with that part of Devon known as the **South Hams**. There is no general agreement about exact boundaries, but the Rivers Yealm (pronounced 'Yam') and Dart on the west and east, Dartmoor to the north and the sea to the south, are usually reckoned to define this fertile rural area of farms and villages. The name South Hams is first noticed in documents in 1396, but scholars have found the meaning obscure. At local government reorganisation in 1974, it was applied to the southernmost district council in the county, with headquarters at Totnes. Kingsbridge, Salcombe, Modbury and Ivybridge are the only other places that could be classed as towns in the area, and for the purposes of this book Ivybridge is included in the Dartmoor chapter.

The A379 coast road from Dartmouth dips, climbs and winds through the villages of Stoke Fleming and Strete, and past **Blackpool Sands**, an attractive cove overhung with Monterey pines, and bearing no resemblance to its north country namesake. The local people repulsed a Breton invasion force here in 1404.

After several switchback miles, the road drops down to sea level at the north end of **Slapton Sands**, a 2¹/₂ mile (4km) bank of shingle and pebbles, thrown up when the glaciers melted after the last Ice Age.

Trapped behind this pebble ridge are the waters of Slapton Ley, the largest natural freshwater lake in Devon, and divided into the Higher and Lower Ley by the road leading to the village of Slapton.

The **Higher Ley**, being smaller and shallower, and receiving the largest stream, the River Gara, has silted up in the thousands of years since it was created, and is now largely reed-grown and bordered with willow. **The Lower Ley**, however, is open water, fringed with reed. The lake is shallow and has an average depth of about 6ft (2m). Eels find the muddy bottom attractive, and four-pounders are regularly taken. The eels, roach and perch fall prey to the pike, as do frogs and ducklings.

As a pike fishery the Ley is highly thought of but it is as a bird sanctuary that the Ley is so important. The scarcity of other freshwater ponds and lakes in the south-west makes Slapton Ley a place of avian concentration, particularly in the spring, and when birds are migrating in the autumn. This diversity of natural interest was the origin of the **Slapton Ley Field Centre**, set up between the sea and the village. The

Slapton Sands

At Slapton Sands, the tall stone memorial obelisk by the roadside – unveiled by the United States General Grunther in 1954 – commemorates the use of the area in late 1943 and early 1944 for beach landing practice prior to the Normandy invasion. Because live ammunition was used, all the inhabitants and their animals from seven parishes in the Slapton hinterland were forced to evacuate. This involved 3,000 people across 30,000 acres (12,000hectares). The difficulties of the operation may be judged when it is realised that transport and motor fuel were scarce, most able-bodied men were in the Services, the days were short and the weather bad. During that time the village (one of several) was deserted; rats roamed the streets unmolested. Leslie Thomas has written about the event in The Magic Army *(1982)*.

Field Studies Council run courses here for many categories of study and student. Investigations do not involve only the immediate locality. Groups range far and wide in South Devon, and the Field Centre minibus may often be seen parked in a Dartmoor layby, while students tramp off through the heather to learn about the Dartmoor tors. Two nature trails have been laid down round the Lower Ley, and leaflets describing the routes are available from the Field Centre. Guided walks are advertised in the summer.

The village of **Slapton** should be visited, too; a pleasing hotch-potch of buildings in the South Hams tradition. The church porch contains a sanctuary ring. In medieval times, it was sufficient to touch it to receive sanctuary, but there then followed a complicated ritual of confession and abjuration, which resulted in the felon having to leave the country. Near the church are the ruins of the chantry, of which the tower is all that now remains.

Along the coast road is **Torcross**, an exposed village partly built on the pebble ridge itself. Torcross is periodically battered by gales, but has not so far suffered the fate of Hallsands 3 miles (5 km) to the south, almost at Start Point. To reach Hallsands, turn left off the A379 in Stokenham and follow the road signs. At Torcross a World War II Sherman tank, recovered from the sea, is on display in the car park.

Hallsands was a row of thirty-seven houses on a rocky ledge beneath the cliff, protected by a shingle foreshore. The men earned a living by fishing, and life was uneventful until the closing years of the nineteenth century, when a contractor engaged in construction work at Devonport

dockyard was given permission to dredge shingle offshore. In a very short time 500,000 tons (508,000 mtn) were taken, and by 1902, when dredging stopped, the beach level had dropped 13 ft (4.5 m). Its natural protection dissipated, the village was exposed to the sea, and in a series of storms all the houses were demolished, the last in 1917. The whole affair was a case of official buck-passing, and little was done for the homeless. The line of ruined buildings can be seen beneath the cliff, and it is surprising that houses were built there in the first place.

Since it is so close, one should visit **Start Point Lighthouse**, which dates from 1836. The light has a range of 20.8 miles (33 km). The name Start comes from the same Anglo-Saxon root *steort* meaning a tail, which is found in the name of the bird, the redstart. From Start Point there is a way through the lanes to **East Prawle**; the route is then signposted to **Prawle Point**, 1 mile (1.5 km) further on. This is the southern extremity of the county. There is a National Trust car park at the road end, a few hundred yards from the Point itself.

Start Point is just out of sight beyond Peartree Point, but the other direction looks across the mouth of Salcombe Harbour to Bolt Head. Near at hand, a mile away by cliff path, is **Gammon Head**, the most photogenic promontory on the South Devon coast. Its massive hump protects a sheltered beach, Maceley Cove, from the south-west gales, and is a lovely spot for a swim, even if the climb down and up is rather a scramble.

To continue the exploration of the South Hams, the A379 leads to

Above: Blackpool Sands between Dartmouth and Slapton

Right: This Sherman Tank stands at Torcross as a memorial to USA servicemen

Below: Hallsands

Kingsbridge, the 'capital' of this part of Devon. All roads lead to **Kingsbridge**, the natural route focus at the head of the Kingsbridge Estuary. This wide expanse of water, with many shallow creeks poking tidal tentacles among fertile fields, is not fed by any large river, and is really what geographers call a ria, or flooded valley. Although the channel to Salcombe is used by pleasure boats and yachts, 80 years ago a weekly 'market packet' steamer ran between Kingsbridge and Plymouth, calling at Salcombe on the way. Where children now feed ducks and swans, ships from far-off places used to tie up to discharge exotic cargoes, and export cider, corn, harness and stone. Ships were built nearby, and the recreation ground is on the site of a tidal millpond. Between Kingsbridge and the sea are the remains of twenty-two limekilns; the limestone came by sea from Plymouth.

Kingsbridge is now a busy, cheerful place with good shops, pubs and restaurants. The appearance of the town is attractive, though there are few outstanding buildings. Perhaps The **Shambles** is the most striking structure. Here the old market building is raised on Elizabethan granite pillars. In **Fore Street** there are quaint passages and alleys on either side. At one time, Fore Street had twenty-six alleys, but some are now closed. Kingsbridge passages have curious names like Squeezebelly Passage, Khartoum Place, Baptist Lane and several named after inns.

At the top of the town, on the east side of the road, is **Knowle House**, one of several fine eighteenth- and nineteenth-century houses. This one was the home of Colonel Montagu, who gave his name to the Montagu's harrier. On the opposite side of the road, and lower down, is the very interesting **Cookworthy Museum** in the Old Grammar School. William Cookworthy (1705-80), the English discoverer of china clay, who made the first English porcelain, was born in Kingsbridge. The exhibition is sponsored by English China Clays Ltd. There are also interesting displays of agriculture and domestic life. To the north of the town, near Loddiswell, is the **Sorley Tunnel Adventure Farm**, where children can feed farm animals or enjoy various play areas. The name is from an old railway tunnel which can be explored. There is also a craft centre.

SALCOMBE

Salcombe is a drive of 7 miles (11km) through West Alvington and Malborough. Look for Malborough's church spire, a prominent landmark for miles around. The problem at Salcombe in high summer may be finding a parking space, but it is worth the effort! Everyone in Salcombe in July and August seems to be in the boat business. Blue jeans, guernseys and yellow boat boots are as common as top hats at Ascot and as de rigueur, for this is a sailing mecca. As a calling place for coastal cruising, it is a convenient one-day's journey from Dartmouth, Plymouth being the next port of call. Salcombe is also a retirement base, the salubrious climate of Devon's southernmost town helping to make it so.

Salcombe's fame in history is concerned with her fleet of yacht-like clipper schooners, which always brought home the first fruits from the pineapple pickings in the West Indies or the orange harvest in the

Azores. Local trades are well portrayed in the Salcombe **Museum of Maritime and Local History** at Custom House Quay, where mementos and maps of the Slapton World War II battle training area – described above – are also found.

Another collection of bygones is at the **Overbecks Museum** at **Overbecks House** (National Trust) at the southern end (Sharpitor) of the built-up area. To reach here one passes the sandy beaches of North Sands (with the remains of one of Henry VIII's castles on one of its promontories; it withstood a siege in the Civil War) and South Sands, and at low tide, other enticing beaches will be seen across the bay.

Overbecks House also accommodates **Salcombe Youth Hostel**, and looks over the dreaded Salcombe Bar, a sea-covered sand spit waiting to snag deep-keeled ships, especially at low tide in a storm. In 1916, thirteen of the crew of fifteen of the Salcombe lifeboat were lost in turbulent seas on Salcombe Bar. This hazard may have inspired Tennyson's famous poem *Crossing the Bar*. The gardens at Overbecks are another attraction. The mild climate allows plants and shrubs to grow that one would not expect to find in England.

From here round the cliffs via **Bolt Head** to **Bolt Tail** and **Hope Cove** is a walk of 6 miles (9.5km), and there is no public transport for the return.

There is one 2-mile (3km) walk, however, which the visitor should on no account omit. Up the steep lane behind Overbecks is a pleasant high-level path leading to a viewpoint indicator on the top of **Sharp Tor**, overlooking Starehole Bay, the last resting place of the four-masted Finnish barque the *Herzogin Cecilie*, which was wrecked in 1936. Along this high path, a steep path leads down to the back of the bay. The return to Overbecks can be made along the lower path, the Courtenay Walk, which cuts through the spiky rocks of Sharp Tor.

WESTWARDS FROM SALCOMBE

Beyond Hope Cove, which nestles behind the protecting arm of Bolt Tail, the coastline changes in character. Tall cliffs give way to a mixture of low cliffs, sand dunes and popular beaches. Inner Hope is a

Gateposts

One other aspect of the man-made South Hams landscape which remains to be remarked upon is the massive masonry gateposts, or abutments. Instead of using a wooden post, farmers in times past – the date unknown – built up buttresses of stone on which to hang their gates, and went to some trouble to make a feature of them. A National Trust warden, asked if he knew why the practice had developed, replied 'Have you ever tried to drive a post into shallow soil with rock not far below the surface?' This may not be the whole answer as one sees these structures where one expects the soil to be good and deep.

piece of Devon miraculously preserved from a hundred years ago, a square of thatched cottages unspoilt by modern development.

Off **Thurlestone** (the name means 'holed stone') is the famous arched rock that gave the parish its name, and after the small estuary of the Avon, **Bigbury-on-Sea** is reached, with its sands, shops and sea tractor. This strange contraption is employed to maintain the link between **Burgh Island** and the mainland when the tide is in. It can operate in 10ft (3.5m) of water and cope with seas up to a force nine gale. A large hotel dominates the island and the Pilchard Inn provides refreshments.

One further popular beach, **Challaborough,** will be found along this stretch of coast before access becomes difficult (unless the continuous South Devon Coast Path is used). The next estuary belongs to the Erme, rising, like the Avon, many miles away on southern Dartmoor, and lacking any sort of ferry or bridge near its mouth. Fortunately, at low tide it may be waded from slipway to slipway, but care must be taken especially during stormy weather or when there is a good deal of floodwater coming downriver.

The **Erme Estuary** is the quietest, most unspoilt river mouth on the whole of the south coast of England; a fact probably due to the benign ownership of the Mildmay family whose presence at **Flete** (near the A379) and Mothecombe (on the western side of the estuary) has been so protective. Flete is a curious amalgam of mixed architectural antecedents. A house rebuilt in 1620 and a Jacobean wing look one way, while a partial rebuilding by Norman Shaw in 1878 faces another

direction. The house is privately owned, but is open to the public on certain days of the week.

Modbury is the chief settlement in this part of the South Hams. Standing astride the busy A379, it has a Georgian elegance that surprises the first-time visitor. The slate-hung front elevations are very typical of South Hams' buildings.

The last slice of the South Hams before the outskirts of Plymouth are reached lies between the Erme and Yealm Estuaries. (The many estuaries along this seaboard make the walking of the South Devon Coast Path as much a triumph of planning as of execution. As some of the ferries are 'summer only' the walk is tedious if attempted off-season.)

The Yealm reaches the sea via a delightfully circuitous fjord-like channel, dressed with hanging oak woods. Up a wide creek stand the twin villages of **Newton Ferrers** and **Noss Mayo,** the latter a jolly name for a picturesque village. From here the coast path may be traced round the headland for a good distance before cutting back across the peninsula to the starting point at Noss. The path follows a planned route – the **Revelstoke Drive** – cut in the last century by Lord Revelstoke as a horse carriage drive round his property, the Membland estate. Made with horses in mind, it is nowhere steep, and as it constantly changes direction the views are varied. Down the cliff near **Stoke Point**, and somewhat submerged in a permanent caravan site, is the ruined, but partly restored, church of St Peter the Poor Fisherman, or **Revelstoke church.**

Although this part of Devon in the peak season hums with activity, by going only a short distance, perfect peace is attainable.

Above: *Salcombe*

Left: *Overbecks House, Youth Hostel*

Below: *Salcombe*

In and around Newton Abbot

Ugbrooke House

Chudleigh
Clifford family home in a lovely park, rescued from decay and now a splendid stately home.
☎ (01626) 852179
Open: Grounds 1-5.30pm, admission to the house by guided tours only, at 2pm and 3.45pm, Tuesday, Wednesday, Thursday and Sunday from second Sunday in July until first Thursday in September.

Canonteign Falls and Farm Park

West of Chudleigh
A nineteenth-century landscaped gorge and cascade brought dramatically to life.
☎ (01647) 252434
Open: 10am-5pm daily March to mid-November. 11am-4pm Sundays and school holidays in winter.

Chudleigh Rocks

Limestone crag with climbing rocks and caves.

Bradley Manor

Newton Abbot (National Trust)
Small fifteenth-century manor house on the edge of the town.
☎ (01626) 354513
Open: 2-5pm Wednesday, April to September plus some Thursdays in April and September.

Forde House

Newton Abbot
A 1610 house, restored by Teignbridge District Council. Viewing by appointment only:
☎ (01626) 361101

Prickly Ball Farm and Hedgehog Hospital

North of Newton Abbot, off A381
Hands on farm and hedgehog sanctuary
☎ (01626) 362319
Open: 10am-5pm daily, April to September; telephone for times October to March or check on www.hedgehog.org.uk

Stover Country Park

Newton Abbot
A pleasant open space with woods and a lake, conveniently sited beside the A38 and A382.
☎ (01620) 352541

Orchid Paradise

North of Newton Abbot at Forches Cross
Artificial climate housing large variety of orchids.
☎ (01626) 352233
Open: 10am-4pm daily except for winter bank holidays.

Torbryan Church

Colourful medieval church with original fittings.

Dawlish Museum

Local history, trades and Victoriana reflecting the town's interesting past.
☎ 01626 865974 for opening times

Teignmouth Museum

A small collection of artifacts reflecting the history of this port and holiday town.
☎ (01626) 777041 for opening times.

Shaldon Wildlife Trust

A small seaside zoo.
☎ (01626) 872234
Open: 10am-6pm daily, Easter to end of September. 11am-4pm daily October until Easter (not Christmas Day and Boxing Day).

Babbacombe Model Village

Torquay
Internationally-known triumph of landscape miniaturisation.
☎ (01803) 315315
Open: daily except Christmas Day; 9.30am-10pm Good Friday to end of June; 9am-10pm July and August; 9.30am-10pm September; 9.30am-9pm October; 10am to dusk November to Good Friday.

Cockington Country Park and Village

Torquay
A forge, the Drum Inn and Cockington Court, preserved within the town by Torbay Council.
☎ (01803) 690495 for details of special events

Kent's Cavern

Ilsham Road, Torquay
Man's earliest home in the area - 20,000 to 30,000 years BC.
☎ (01803) 215136
Open: from 10am daily, all year. Evening tours during summer months.

Oddicombe Cliff Railway

One of Devon's two cliff railways, drops steeply down to Oddicombe beach.

Torquay Museum

Babbacombe Road
Many artifacts from Kent's Cavern are here as well as folk life displays and Victoriana.
☎ (01803) 293975 for Opening times.

Bygones

Fore Street, Torquay
Look back in time through recreated street scenes, domestic interiors and World War I trench. Model railway and miniature fantasyland.
☎ (01803) 326108
Open: 10am-6pm, daily March to October; 10am-10pm Sunday to Thursday in July and August. 10am-4pm daily, November to February.

Torre Abbey

Kings Drive, Torquay
Interesting complex of buildings including a tithe barn. Torquay's art collections are housed in the eighteenth-century mansion.
☎ (01803) 293593
Open: 9.30am-6pm daily, Easter to November

Kirkham House

Paignton
Fourteenth-century priest's house.
☎ (01803) 522775
Open: on selected days from Easter to end of August, telephone for details.

Oldway

An enormous mansion modelled on Versailles and paid for by the money made by the Singer sewing machine family.
☎ (01803) 201201
Open: 9am-5pm Monday to Friday, all year.

Paignton Zoo

Devon's largest collection of exotic birds and animals.
☎ (01803) 697500
Open: from 10am daily, all year.

Palgnton and Dartmouth Steam Railway

A scenic, privately-operated steam railway run on authentic GWR principles.
☎ (01803) 555872
Open: Steam trains run Easter bank holidays, selected days in April, May and October; daily from June to September.

Quaywest

Goodrington Sands, Paignton
Large outdoor waterpark plus other amusements for all the family.
☎ (01803) 555550
Open: 10am-10pm daily, Easter to October. Shorter hours for the water attractions depending on the season.

Compton Castle

Marldon (National Trust)
Splendidly restored medieval castle with impressive defensive works.
☎ (01803) 872112
Open: 10am-12.15pm and 2-5pm Monday, Wednesday and Thursday, April to late October.

Berry Pomeroy Castle

A slightly spooky ruined mansion within the remains of a medieval castle. Open to the public.
☎ (01803) 866618
Open: 10am-6pm daily, April to September; 10am-5pm in October.

Berry Head Country Park

Brixham
Spectacular limestone cliff scenery and birdlife. Wide ranging views, lighthouse and coastguard station. Interesting remains of huge Napoleonic fort.

The Deep

Brixham
Sited on the quay. Recently-opened attraction which explores all aspects of the sea.
☎ (01803) 858444
Open: from Easter, telephone for times

Below: Gardens at Coleton Fishacre, National Trust

Brixham Museum

Bolton Cross, Brixham
Tells the story of Brixham. Includes the National Coastguard Museum, displaying apparatus, techniques and records relating to the coastguard service.
☎ (01803) 856257
Open: 10am-5pm Monday to Friday, 10am-1pm on Saturday, Easter to October

Golden Hind

Brixham quayside
☎ (01803) 856223
Open: from Easter, telephone for details.

Coleton Fishacre House and Garden

(National Trust)
House designed for the D'Oyly Carte family in the Arts and Crafts tradition and a well wooded coastal garden with a stream.
☎ (01803) 752466
Open: House – 11am-4.30pm Wednesday to Sunday, April to October. Garden – as house but from 10.30am to 5.30pm, and on bank holiday Mondays, plus 11am-5pm on Sundays in March.

Day Mark

Kingswear
Prominent hollow stone navigational aid from 1860s.

Inner Froward Point Gun Battery

Kingswear (National Trust)
Well preserved survivor from World War II in beautiful pine tree and cliff setting.

Dartmouth and Totnes

Dartmouth Museum

A small but fascinating collection of memorabilia connected with the town, in the Butterwalk, a listing building.
☎ (01803) 832923
Open: 11am-5pm Mondays to Saturdays, April to October

Newcomen Engine

Dartmouth
Thomas Newcomen produced the first industrial steam engine, and was born in Dartmouth. A beam engine based on his principles is preserved here.
☎ (01803) 834224
Open: 9am-5pm Monday to Saturday, 10am-4pm Sunday, Easter to October. 10am-4pm Monday to Saturday, November to Easter.

St Saviour's Church

Dartmouth
Notable for its splendid 1633 west gallery.

Dartmouth Castle

A stern estuary-mouth castle containing within its walls a church having several memorial brasses.
☎ (01803) 822588
Open: 10am-6pm daily, April to September; 10am-5pm October; 10am-1pm and 2-4pm Wednesday to Sunday, November to March.

Gallants Bower

(National Trust), Dartmouth
A hilltop earthwork, dating from the Civil War.

Dartmouth Castle

Devonshire Collection of Period Costume

Totnes
A well-displayed collection of clothing through the ages.
☎ (01803) 862423
Open: telephone for details

Leech Wells

Totnes
Cleaning troughs for local lepers in medieval times.

Totnes Castle

A small but perfect Norman keep stands beside the inner bailey.
☎ (01803) 864406
Open: 10am-6pm daily, April to September; 10am-5pm October; 10am-1pm and 2-4pm Wednesday to Sunday, November to March.

Totnes Guildhall

Built 1533. Open to the public.
☎ (01803) 862147
Open: 10am-1pm and 2-5pm Monday to Friday, April to October.

Totnes Museum

Excellent local history museum in a half-timbered building. Special room devoted to Charles Babbage, the father of British computer science, who lived in Totnes.
☎ (01803) 863821
Open: 10.30am-5pm Monday to Friday, 11am-3pm bank holidays, April to October.

Bowden House

One mile S of Totnes. Haunted Tudor dwelling and photographic museum.
☎ (01803) 863664
Open: from 12 noon Monday to Friday, Easter week and late May to end of September.

Woodlands Leisure Park

Indoor and outdoor playzones for all ages. Rides, toboggan run and falconry centre.
☎ (01803) 712598
Open: 9.30am-5pm (later in high summer) daily, mid-March to beginning of November; 9.30am-5pm weekends and Devon school holidays only, November to mid-March.

Dartington Cider Press

The retail side of the Dartington Hall enterprise.
Shinner's Bridge
☎ (01803) 864171
Open: 9.30am-5.30pm Monday to Saturday all year plus 10.30am-5.30pm on Sunday from Easter to Christmas.

Dartington Hall

A medieval estate rescued by two idealists in an attempt to revive the many-sided activities of country life.

Slapton Ley Field Centre

The base for natural science and bird research in South Devon. Two nature trails are marked out nearby. Slapton Sands American Memorial Commemorates the use of the area by Americans in World War II for battle practice.

Hallsands Ruined Village

A row of cottages between the beach and the cliff demolished by a storm in 1917.

Start Point Lighthouse

Significant feature on the South Devon coastline.

Prawle Point (National Trust)

Devon's most southerly point.

Cookworthy Museum

Kingsbridge
Largely celebrates the work of William Cookworthy, the English discoverer of china clay, who was born in Kingsbridge. Also good displays of agricultural and domestic items.
☎ (01548) 853235
Open: 10am-5pm Monday to Saturday, late March to September; 10.30am-4pm in October

Sorley Tunnel Farm and Craft Centre

North of Kingsbridge
☎ (01548) 857711
Open: telephone for details

Overbecks Museum & Gardens

Salcombe (National Trust)
Maritime miscellany and beautiful gardens in memorable surroundings.
☎ (01548) 842893
Open: Museum – 11am-5.30pm, April to July and September, Sunday to Friday. August daily. October Sunday to Thursday. Garden – 10am-8pm (dusk if earlier) daily all year.

Salcombe Museum of Maritime and Local History

A local history museum with details of the World War II training area at Slapton.
☎ (01548) 843927 (Tourist Information Centre)
Open: 10.30am-12.30pm and 2.30-4.30pm Easter to October.

Flete

Modbury
Owned by the Mildmay family, the house is open at certain times.
☎ (01752) 830308 for opening times.

Revelstoke Church

A cliffside church left to decay in the 1860s and now partially restored.

3

Plymouth and District

The city of Plymouth has one of the finest natural sites in Britain, and ranks with Edinburgh, Bath, Cambridge and Bristol for position and historic interest. Although tucked away in one corner of Devon, its influence has been felt far and wide. This is exemplified by its having given its name to forty other Plymouths throughout the world. The deep, wide and fast-flowing waters of the River Tamar effectively prevented much westwards expansion of Plymouth into Cornwall, so that it is only in the last hundred years or so since the railway bridges were built across the Tamar and Tavy that Saltash, and to a lesser extent, Bere Alston, Calstock and Gunnislake have come under the influence of Plymouth.

The city pushed north and east, to Crownhill (where the massive fort, built in the 1860s, is the finest of Plymouth's Victorian fortifications) and Roborough, Plympton St Mary and Plympton St Maurice, Plymstock, Elburton and Wembury. More recently, the growth in car ownership has pushed Plymouth's sphere of influence out to Tavistock in the north and Ivybridge in the east, and the Tamar road bridge has made commuting possible from deep into east Cornwall.

Just across the water, at **Mount Batten**, much evidence was turned up early this century of an Iron Age and Roman settlement, perhaps lasting for a thousand years. The diversity of artifacts discovered indicates another trading settlement. The name Stonehouse for a district west of the present central city area may have first been given to a masonry structure found by the wood-building Saxons, who found

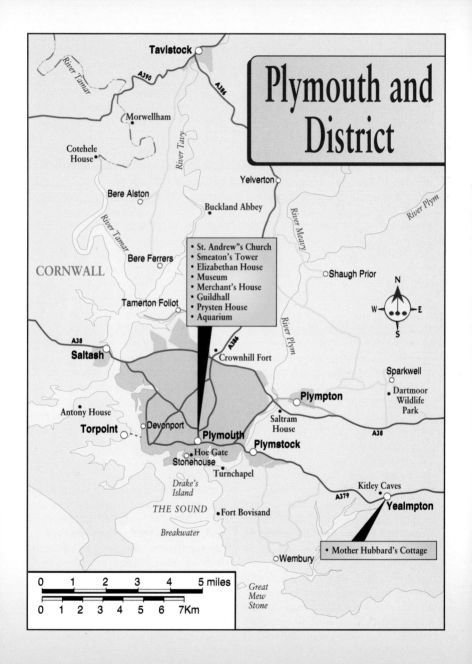

Plymouth and District

Tavistock

River Tamar

A390

A386

Morwellham

River Tavy

Cotehele House

Yelverton

Bere Alston

Buckland Abbey

River Meavy

River Plym

CORNWALL

River Tamar

Bere Ferrers

- St. Andrew"s Church
- Smeaton's Tower
- Elizabethan House
- Museum
- Merchant's House
- Guildhall
- Prysten House
- Aquarium

Shaugh Prior

N

W E

S

Tamerton Foliot

River Plym

A38

Saltash

A386

Crownhill Fort

Sparkwell

Dartmoor Wildlife Park

Plympton

Antony House

Devonport

Saltram House

A38

Torpoint

Plymouth

Plymstock

Hoe Gate

Stonehouse

Turnchapel

Kitley Caves

Drake's Island

A379

Yealmpton

THE SOUND

Fort Bovisand

- Mother Hubbard's Cottage

Breakwater

Wembury

| 0 | 1 | 2 | 3 | 4 | 5 miles |

| 0 | 1 | 2 | 3 | 4 | 5 | 6 | 7Km |

Great Mew Stone

it sufficiently unusual to accord it the permanence of a place name, and Romans are the most likely builders.

There are other equally hazy descriptions of Roman and Dark Age settlement, but what is undisputed is the development of medieval Plymouth round Sutton Harbour and the area to the north-west. St Andrew's Church on the present Royal Parade is an ancient foundation, and Old Town Street nearby has an early origin; so the Plymouth of the Middle Ages should be sought in the arc encompassed by the mouth of Sutton Harbour, behind New Street to St Andrew's Church, north to Old Town Street and back to the waterfront on the east side of Sutton Harbour.

At **Plympton**, a few miles to the east, a castle was built by the Norman Richard de Redvers, and it was a stannary town in medieval times. (Here the tin from the south-west side of Dartmoor was weighed and stamped – coigned – before being sold. *Stannum* is the Latin word for tin.) Plympton itself was two settlements – Plympton St Maurice and Plympton St Mary – and the difference is markedly discernible still. Plympton also had a priory.

One of the reasons for the growth of Sutton (Plymouth) at the expense of Plympton was the silting up of the Plym Estuary, a change brought about partly by the activities of the tin streamers on Dartmoor. So the material that contributed to Plympton's growth worked against it in another way.

Plymouth however, being nearer the open sea, was more vulnerable to raids, and in 1403 a large French force attacked the town and burnt 600 houses. The event is remembered in the name Bretonside, at the bus station site. The inhabitants asked for a wall to be built round the town, and this was eventually done; nothing of it remains to be seen today, although the names of the gates remain, Old Town Gate and Hoe Gate, for instance. One end of the wall was built against Plymouth Castle, and that too has all but disappeared. A remnant survives in Castle Street. The name Barbican, now widely applied to the area of New Street and Southside Street, is derived from a part of this castle.

The part of Plymouth known by Drake and his captains, and, later, by the Pilgrim Fathers sailing on the *Mayflower* (1620) was, therefore, Sutton. Plymouth sided with Parliament in the Civil War and suffered a three-year siege. It was King William, who had landed at Brixham in 1688 as William of Orange, who sanctioned the building of the dockyard on virgin land fronting the Tamar Estuary, where it is called the Hamoaze.

This immediately pulled development across the intervening land and Stonehouse grew, as it was situated halfway between the growing town of Dock and Plymouth itself. During the Napoleonic Wars the upstart Dock (32,000 people) outstripped its neighbour Plymouth (22,000) and Stonehouse (6,000), and in 1824 was granted the dignity of the name **Devonport**. The column in Ker Street (to be noticed later) was erected to mark the event. Nearer our own time, in 1914, the so-called 'Three Towns' were amalgamated into one municipal authority to become Plymouth. The city suffered disastrous air raids in World War II, and much of the middle was destroyed. St Andrew's Church and the Guildhall were both gutted, but have been rebuilt.

A WALK AROUND PLYMOUTH

Instead of wandering aimlessly round Plymouth (or indeed, any town!) it is a good plan to get one's bearings, perhaps by visiting a high building or some prominent landmark. In Plymouth's case the thirteenth floor of the **Civic Centre** tower block will give a comprehensive view in all directions. A small charge is made, and the facility is not available in November and December. (Should the Civic Centre be closed then stand beside it where Armada Way intersects Royal Parade, with your back to the main shopping area.)

In front, **Armada Way** rises gently up to the Hoe with the Naval War Memorial prominent in the view. About halfway up is the massive anchor, which once belonged to the *Ark Royal*, and beside where you are standing is the civic flagstaff, a shaft rising from a replica of Drake's Drum. The unveiling of this memorial in 1947 by the king marked the start of the re-building of the new Plymouth. On the left is the Guildhall, dating from 1873, but gutted in 1941 and rebuilt after the war, somewhat altered.

St Andrew's Church is the largest parish church in Devon, and, as it stands, is a post-war restoration. Only the stonework remained, and for several years it was used as a garden church before completion in 1957. It possesses some very striking modern stained glass, which may not be to everyone's taste.

Leaving the church through the south door, the **Prysten House** is opposite. The foundation of this, the oldest building remaining in Plymouth, is unknown, but a record listing a rent in 1490 is extant. The priests from Plympton Priory were probably accommodated here while ministering at the church. Stoutly built of local limestone, it contains a variety of unusual features, as well as sundry relics on show from elsewhere in the city. The carved bishop's throne and the model of Plymouth as it looked in 1620 are items of more than usual interest. Notice the Plymouth tapestry, which was executed by a team of volunteer workers, depicting the life and times of the Prysten House. Another tapestry telling the *Mayflower* story is being worked on at the present time, but will not be completed for many years.

Leaving the Prysten House, turn right and right again to see the **Merchant's House** in St Andrew's Street. This sixteenth-century four-storied town house is the best example in Plymouth of a well-to-do entrepreneur's dwelling. William Parker, an Elizabethan privateer, merchant and mayor of Plymouth, was living in the house in 1608. The house is now a museum of early Plymouth history.

Walk down St Andrew's Street, left into Notte Street and right into Southside Street, where on the right is the **Spirit of Plymouth Blackfriars Distillery** building, owned by the Coates Gin Co. This seems to have been a friary long before Coates Gin Co came on the scene in 1793, and the refectory, with a fine arch-braced timber roof, is open to the public.

Southside Street, with its neat lamps bracketed to the shop fronts, is a pleasant busy street with shops selling secondhand books, antique prints, the better type of gifts, and there are several restaurants and public houses. It once looked

PLYMOUTH

Key

1. Royal Citadel
2. Smeatons Tower/ Plymouth Dome
3. Drakes Statue/ War Memorial
4. Bowling Green
5. Theatre Royal
6. Civic Centre
7. Guildhall
8. St Andrew's Church
9. Prysten House
10. Merchant's House
11. Plymouth Gin Distillery
12. Elizabethan House
13. Island House *i*
14. Barbican Glassworks
15. Mayflower Steps & Stone
16. National Marine Aquarium
17. Bus Station
18. Museum & Art Gallery
19. Railway Station
20. Brittany Ferries Terminal
21. Saltram House

¼ ½ mile

0   250   500 metres

— Torpoint Ferry

Millbay Rd

MILLBAY DOCKS

PLYMOUTH SOUND

THE HOE

Madeira Rd

Barbican

SUTTON HARBOUR

CATTEWATER

Exeter A38 —

Citadel Rd

Notte St

Royal Parade

Armada Way

Western Approach

— Tamar Bridge A38

St Andrew's Cross

Charles Cross

Drake Circus

North Cross

St Andrew's Cross

directly out on Sutton Harbour. The north side of the street with its 'opes' (an opening onto a water-front) breaking it up into small blocks, was built later.

Now follow the quay round the western side of **Sutton Harbour**. The early nineteenth-century **Custom House** faces the old Custom House of the Tudor period, now given over to other uses. This is a lively part of Plymouth, with much fishing boat activity. Just round the corner used to be the fish market, which is now an attractive modern glass shop, **Barbican Glass.**

Mayflower Stone

Beyond the market building is the **Mayflower Stone**, one of several memorials to great events which have started from this spot. The Union flag and the Stars and Stripes fly over this shrine, marking the departure point of the Pilgrim Fathers in 1620. Other events remembered are the sailing of the *Tory* in 1839 on an early migrant trip to New Zealand, and the return of the Tolpuddle Martyrs a year earlier, who had been transported to Australia for daring to form a trade union.

Across the way from here is **Island House**, a building standing on its own, dating from about 1590, where tradition says some of the pilgrims lodged prior to their departure for North America. A board on the outside wall lists those who sailed aboard the *Mayflower*.

A short walk across the mouth of Sutton Harbour leads to the **National Marine Aquarium,** highly recommended. Here the living wonders of the ocean are revealed, with opportunities to talk to experts about the creatures on view, learn about marine conservation, watch divers feeding the fish by hand and see sharks at very close quarters.

Behind Island House is **New Street**, an attractive narrow cobbled highway, 'new' only because it came after other parts of old Plymouth. New Street is interesting as the actual stone road surface is 'listed', being of historic importance. Its builder was John Sparke, the first Englishman to describe tobacco and the potato. The original carved door frames are on Nos 34, 35, 37 and 38, and No 32 is an Elizabethan house. This original house of about 1584 was well restored from near dereliction in 1926, New Street having slipped from its former eminence as a residential area of merchants to become a street of warehouses. The house is very sympathetically furnished with pieces of the period. Notice the ship's mast round which the spiral staircase wraps itself. A rope steadies anyone using the stairs, another nautical touch. Through No 40 is a pleasant little garden behind, where plants known to have been cultivated in Tudor times are grown.

At the foot of New Street, Madeira Road has the last remaining ruin of old Plymouth Castle on the right, beneath the massive walls of the **Royal Citadel** (1666), still used as barracks for the Royal Marines. Guided tours take visitors round the walls at certain times. The baroque gateway is considered the finest in Britain.

In the opposite direction, the

Cattewater, the actual mouth of the Plym, is where Drake's fleet anchored. Beyond, the radio masts stand on **Staddon Heights** and the wall on the top is the 'safety curtain' of a rifle range. Round the corner, **Plymouth Breakwater** comes into view. This immense civil engineering project made Plymouth a much safer port, especially in the days of sail, though paradoxically, when it was completed in 1847, having been 35 years in the making, powered ships were beginning to be built. It is almost a mile long and contains 3,620,440 tons of local limestone.

Until it was destroyed in the Plymouth blitz, the 1884 promenade pier jutted out from the Hoe and provided a venue for concerts and dancing. On the Hoe itself, an elevated promenade gives views one way to the sea, and the other along the ¾ mile (1km) Armada Way. **The Hoe** gives the finest view of Plymouth Sound, which, with the Thames at London and the Dover Strait, is the most evocative maritime landscape in Great Britain. Out of this almost landlocked natural port have begun and ended countless epic voyages, from the naval task force against the Armada to the more recent task force to the Falklands.

An even better view can be enjoyed from the top of **Smeaton's Tower**, the Eddystone Lighthouse of 1759, which was superseded in 1882 by Douglass's present lighthouse. On a clear day the tower can be seen on its rock 14 miles (22km) out at sea. The cramped quarters will perhaps surprise the visitor.

Also on the Hoe is the enormous **Naval War Memorial**, surmounted by a dented globe. The damage was caused by a barrage balloon in World War II. Around its base are the names of 22,443 men who lost their lives in both wars. There are other monuments; the **National Armada Memorial**, one to the Boer War, while the jaunty figure of Sir Francis Drake looks out to sea, a copy statue of one at Tavistock, his birthplace. Not far away, probably where the Royal Citadel was later built, he is supposed to have been playing bowls when the Armada was spotted. 'Time enough to finish our game, and beat the Spaniards' he is

Drake's Island

Drake's Island, a kind of English Alcatraz, narrows the navigable channel up to the Dockyard. From being St Nicholas' Island in medieval times, it became known as Drake's Island when he was appointed island governor and began to fortify it. The island remained in military occupation until 1956, and was used as a prison for a few years after 1669. Some truly enormous muzzle loading guns of late nineteenth-century vintage were recently discovered, buried under rubble at the top. Tucked in a sea-facing site on the slopes of the Hoe is **Plymouth Dome**, a high-tech, award-winning interpretation centre for all the family. Here the whole story of Plymouth is told under one roof, with the panorama of Plymouth Sound just outside the windows.

*Above left: **The Merchant's House, Plymouth** Above right: **The Drake and Navy Memorial, The Hoe, Plymouth** Below: **Sutton Harbour and glass centre in the old fish market, Plymouth***

Plymouth Guildhall

The Plymouth Coastline

The best way to get to know Plymouth's dissected coastline is to take a boat trip as far as possible up the Tamar. The point where the boat turns back will depend on the tide, but if it reaches as far as Weir Head or Morwellham, the trip will take 5 or 6 hours. Other cruises go outside Plymouth Sound past the Breakwater and the Great Mew Stone to the Yealm Estuary. (Boats leave from the Phoenix Wharf just outside Sutton Harbour.)

supposed to have replied, knowing that wind and tide didn't allow his fleet to leave port in any case!

To return to the starting point on Royal Parade, walk north to Citadel Road. Turn left here, and follow Citadel Road to Millbay Road. On the corner is a Victorian Gothic extravaganza, the **Duke of Cornwall Hotel,** dating from 1865. Though hardly beautiful, it is enormously impressive and has managed to survive German bombs and developers' bulldozers: its roof is crowned by a château turret.

Opposite is the site of the old Millbay Station (opened 1849, closed 1941). In the great days of transatlantic sea travel, ships from the USA would put in to Plymouth Sound, to land those passengers in a hurry to reach London, before resuming their journey up Channel. A few years ago the area was given a new lease of life when Britanny Ferries developed their roll on roll off car ferry terminal on the western side of Millbay Dock by the enormous disused grain silo. Ships leave for Roscoff (France) and Santander (Spain). Millbay Road leads one back to Royal Parade.

Nearby is the distinctive architecture of **Plymouth Pavilions,** an all-purpose recreational complex for all the family. An ice rink, pool, several restaurants and a huge auditorium make it a versatile resource in bad weather.

The **Plymouth Museum and Art Gallery,** by Drake Circus, occupies one of the few buildings in the city to survive the bombing. Its collections are strong on Plymouth porcelain, Plymouth silver, paintings by local artists including Sir Joshua Reynolds, and local archaeological finds are well represented.

TOURING PLYMOUTH BY CAR

There are other parts of the city visitors should see, with a car or better still by using the Discovery bus service. This circular service links the heart of the City with most of the main attractions. A good street map of the area, including Plympton to the east, will help.

The first of the mini-tours should be to Western King Point through Stonehouse. At the end of Union Street (built in 1815 to unite the Three Towns, and the destination for thirsty sailors when they come ashore, though its disjointed and disfigured building line betrays the damage inflicted during the war), at a roundabout, turn left into Durnford Street, a road of elegant early nineteenth-century houses whose rear elevations are in many cases as attractive as the fronts. Some of these houses were occupied by retired sea captains who had balconies and large windows built at the back to give views over the Hamoaze.

On the left are the **Royal Marine Barracks** and the 1830 church of St George and St Paul, designed by John Foulston. Follow the road to its termination at a car park overlooking Firestone Bay. To the right, on a disused gun emplacement is **Western King Point,** with superb views across to Mount Edgcumbe Country Park (in Cornwall), and left to the Hoe and right towards the Dockyard. At the back of Firestone Bay is an artillery tower dating from Henry VIII's reign and now a restaurant. At low tide the shallow stretch of water between Drake's Island and the slopes of Mount Edgcumbe can be seen. This is known as the Bridge, and was made even shallower during World War II to prevent enemy penetration to the Dockyard by that route.

The channel is narrowest opposite Devil's Point, and the largest ships have to choose the right moment – high slack tide and quiet airs – before passing through the Narrows. This is complicated by tight turns before and after negotiating the constricting passage.

The **Royal William Victualling Yard** (named after King William IV, whose $13^1/2$ ft (5m) statue surmounts the main entrance) is a complex of 14 acres (5.5 hectares), designed by Sir John Rennie, who was also responsible for Plymouth Breakwater. Along Cremyll Street the rear of Durnford Street is visible, passing the **Cremyll foot ferry** on the way. A day roaming the slopes of Mount Edgcumbe (Cornwall) is well spent.

Back at the roundabout, one should turn left, heading for Devonport, and left again by the Old Chapel licensed premises into **Ker Street**. The bottom end is ordinary enough, with post-war flats on either side, but at the top is an odd collection of buildings. The classical **Doric Guildhall** of 1825, even more massive than most Doric buildings, faces down the street with the strange **Egyptian Oddfellows Hall** (1823) to one side. Behind is the 125ft (44m) column marking the change of name from Plymouth Dock to Devonport (1824). These eclectic buildings were all designed by John Foulston, the architect who had such an influence on early nineteenth-century Plymouth. A Calvinist chapel employing eastern motifs formerly stood between the Column and the Egyptian building, but has disappeared. They look forlorn now,

surrounded by late twentieth-century run-of-the-mill local authority housing, but at least we have a hint of the civic pride responsible for their construction 180 years ago.

These forays into selected parts of Plymouth do not by any means exhaust the interest of this fine city. Because so much is owned by HM Government, such places as the Dockyard, Stonehouse Hospital, the King William Yard and the Citadel are not usually open to the public, but the Dockyard, for instance, may be open one day a year for what used to be called Plymouth Navy Day: some ships may be visited.

AROUND PLYMOUTH

Further afield, about 4 miles (6km) east of the heart of Plymouth, is the delightful small town of **Plympton St Maurice**, older than the city, but now a sleepy backwater. A castle was built here not long after the Norman Conquest, and a settlement grew up nearby. Plympton Grammar School, built in 1664 and restored in 1870, is remarkable for the painters it has produced. England's finest portrait painter, Sir Joshua Reynolds, was educated here, as well as James Northcote, Benjamin Haydon and Charles Eastlake.

The town, particularly Fore Street, is unspoilt. The Guildhall juts out over the pavement, not unlike the Guildhall at Exeter, and there is a covered Butterwalk, like those at Totnes and Dartmouth. None of the buildings is in the top bracket, but together they make a very pleasing harmonious group.

Not far away is **Saltram House** (National Trust), the largest house in Devon: other superlatives apply equally. Because of Sir Joshua

Above: **Saltram House (National Trust) the largest house in Devon**
Below: **Buckland Abbey (National Trust) founded in 1278**

Reynolds' lifelong association with the owners, the Parkers, it contains many paintings by him and is the only complete example in south-west England of Robert Adam's interior design.

What's in a Name?

The origin of the name Saltram is obscure, but it must have a connection with the making of salt, for which purpose its situation beside the Plym Estuary was admirably convenient.

The house was begun in the late sixteenth century, but has been considerably changed over the years, the last alteration being in 1820, when John Foulston – whose name we have come across already – added the Doric porch and other exterior refinements.

Inside, the rooms that startle and sparkle with eighteenth-century freshness are the saloon and the dining room. The former is a double cube, the latter occupies a corner position. Neither is lit by electricity; both have Axminster carpets reflecting, but not imitating, the delicate design of the ceilings. To stand in these rooms is an unusual experience, for one is literally surrounded by beauty; beneath the feet, above your head, and of course on the walls. All so delicately done as not to be overpowering. Reached from outside is the Great Kitchen, with a variety of old utensils on show.

The gardens are of the informal kind, with trees and shrubs predominating. Near the house is the restored orangery (1775), the chapel (1776) (now an art gallery), and, scattered round the grounds, the castle (1772) and the folly-type structures of Fanny's Bower and the Amphitheatre overlooking the Plym.

Between Saltram and the sea, and occupying the broad peninsula from the Yealm to Plymouth Sound are the suburbs of **Plymstock** and **Elburton** and the sweeping pastures of **Wembury** parish. The best way to explore it is to walk the 6 or 7 miles (9-11km) of the South Devon Coast Path from Turnchapel round to the Yealm Estuary. This can be done by taking one bus to Turnchapel and returning on another from Wembury. (It is best not to rely on the ferry across the Yealm.)

The first major landmark on the circuit is **Stamford Fort**, now used recreationally, but originally built as one of a ring of forts and batteries round Plymouth in response to the threat posed by an increase in French sea power. Dover, Chatham and Portsmouth were similarly defended. They are sometimes referred to as Palmerston Follies, after Lord Palmerston, who set up the Royal Commission in 1859 'to consider the Defences of the United Kingdom'. As he died in 1865, and many of them were built after his death, he can hardly be blamed for the enormous expense of public money. The ring of forts was continued around Plymouth's northern (landward) approaches, and they represent the climax of British castellar architecture. Never again were fortifications on such a heroic scale constructed in Great Britain.

The road above **Jennycliff Bay** is a pleasant scenic drive, but where the road turns inland the coast path continues along the cliff. Soon **Fort**

Bovisand is seen below, another of the Palmerston forts and the best preserved. It is used as a training base for underwater activities, and oil rig divers come here to learn their trade. Canoeing, sailing and windsurfing are also taught. The port at Fort Bovisand, so useful for the students on their courses, was built between 1816 and 1824 to enable ships to take on fresh water without having to go right into the dockyard. A reservoir was built nearby.

The coast path descends to the back of **Bovisand Bay** and stays low for the next mile or so, where the cliffs are virtually non-existent. After Heybrook Bay, a bit of suburbia-by-the-sea, the path passes near where the guns of HMS *Cambridge* used to be. **Wembury** is soon reached.

The village is set back from the coast and largely enveloped in modern development. The church, however, stands boldly on the cliffs and should be visited, as it has some notable monuments and good woodwork. John Galsworthy's ancestors came from Wembury, and he made a pilgrimage here in 1912 – later transferring his own kinship to the fictional Forsyte family. In his *Swan Song*, Soames Forsyte visited a similarly-sited fictional church stated to be in Dorset.

Below the church is the old mill building (National Trust), used as a café in the summer. The Trust land starts here and runs for $1^1/_2$ miles (2km) to the Yealm, before leap-frogging the estuary to encompass the cliffs beyond, where the Revelstoke Drive acts as a pedestrian marine drive. (This was described towards the end of the previous chapter.) A Trust shop operates (summer only) from the stone building beside the mill café.

Inland from Wembury, at **Yealmpton** (pronounced Yampton) is the building known as **Mother Hubbard's Cottage**. This improvident lady is thought to have been the housekeeper at nearby Kitley. **Kitley Caves** are the only caves in Devon outside the Torquay area to be open to the public, and can be visited in the summer.

Before leaving the environs of Plymouth an interesting visit can be made to **Crownhill Fort,** just off the Tavistock Road to the north of the city. It is the largest and best preserved of Plymouth's Victorian fortifications. Built in the 1860s it is hidden from outside view but inside there is a complete recreation of life as it was for the soldiers of that time.

Continuing round the north-eastern outskirts of Plymouth and getting up into the foothills of Dartmoor the visitor will find the **Dartmoor Wildlife Park** at Sparkwell. Really a zoo, the illusion of animals in their natural setting is obtained by allowing them space and encouraging trees to grow, with a minimum of wire fencing and iron bars, though (obviously) the tigers and wolves are securely enclosed! Visitors are allowed to mix with the more friendly birds and animals.

Just out of Plymouth, up the Plym Valley, are **Plym Bridge Woods** (National Trust). A remarkable survival of woodland, only $3^1/_2$ miles (5.5km) from the heart of Plymouth, this strip of beautiful varied country is not quite 2 miles (3.2km) long, by half a mile wide, but it contains a truly incredible collection of industrial archaeological interest. The tracks of three old railways – all defunct – may be followed. The

Plymouth and Dartmoor Railway was the first, built in 1823 to link the two places by taking lime, sand, timber and coal up to the moor and bringing stone and peat down; horse-drawn trucks were employed. Another horse-drawn tramway passed through the woods as far as Cann quarry, where slate was quarried for the roofs of Plymouth. The railway to Tavistock was the last to be built, and the last to go out of use: it lasted from 1859 to 1962 and crossed the valley by Cann viaduct.

One further relic deserves a mention: **Cann quarry canal**, which carried the stone from the quarry before the tramway was built later on its towpath. Deer are often seen in the woods, and adders enjoy the habitat provided by the discarded slabs of slate in the enormous spoil heaps. Devon County Council has negotiated a continuous recreational footpath up the Plym Valley beyond Plym Bridge Woods to link up with the Dartmoor National Park at Shaugh Bridge.

Not far from the village of **Shaugh Prior** and overlapping the National Park boundary are the white heaps belonging to the china clay workings of Lee Moor and Shaugh Moor. This open-cast industry has expanded enormously from small beginnings early last century to the present mammoth undertaking covering several square miles. The tips of waste are the most obvious manifestations of the industry and can be seen from well out at sea on a clear day.

Granite and China Clay

Granite consists of three main components: feldspar, quartz and mica, and china clay is the product of rotted (kaolinised) feldspar. First the overburden of peat, soil and rock is removed, then high pressure water jets, called monitors, disintegrate the matrix, and the slurry finds its way to the pit bottom where the sand settles out. The china clay is then carried in suspension to a series of refining and drying plants. Apart from its obvious use in the ceramic industry – china, porcelain, tiles, sanitary ware – china clay is also used in the manufacture of paper; the paper of this book contains a proportion of china clay. Cosmetics, paint, rubber, crayons and many other commodities requiring a filler free from impurities and possessing chemical inertness all use this rare mineral, and Devon and Cornwall have the total United Kingdom reserves. Much is exported. Unfortunately the unsightly waste cannot be backfilled into the gaping pits as none of them have yet been 'bottomed', and this would inhibit future operations.

Morwellham Quay, near Tavistock – facilities include trails, museums, shop and restaurant

THE TAMAR AND THE TAVY

Once across the north-striking A386, an ancient ridgeway, the land dips to the valleys of the Tavy and Tamar, the former a private and wooded river, the latter more open, larger, and carrying on its tidal waters considerable recreational traffic. A hundred years ago much commercial transport used the Tamar also. Both rivers meander sinuously.

The undulating peninsula between the two rivers is occupied by the small town of **Bere Alston** on the top and the ancient parish of **Bere Ferrers** by the estuary edge of the Tavy. The area is still served by a branch railway line from Plymouth, which crosses both rivers by large viaducts and stops at Bere Ferrers and Bere Alston, before terminating in Cornwall at Gunnislake. The line is a delight to use. Communications were always difficult in this hilly landscape, and the rivers were used extensively until the railways arrived. The old quays are peaceful now and pleasant places to while away an hour or two. On the south and west facing slopes, quantities of strawberries are grown. Bere Ferrers church is one of the most interesting in Devon, with much fourteenth-century work, and a canopied tomb to Sir William de Ferrers and his wife.

BUCKLAND ABBEY

Overlooking the Tavy Valley near Yelverton is Sir Francis Drake's old home, **Buckland Abbey** (National Trust), like the rest of this corner of Devon, a peaceful retreat. Amicia, Countess of Devon, founded the abbey in 1278, and white-robed Cistercian brothers came to Buckland from the Isle of Wight to establish their estate.

At the dissolution the property was initially leased to George Pollard, but in 1541 the king sold the abbey to Sir Richard Grenville. His son, Roger, was the commander of the *Mary Rose* which sank with all hands in the Solent in 1545. The hulk of the ship has now been raised and will be put on show in Portsmouth when conservation work is complete. The next two tenants of Buckland Abbey were also to die at sea, notably Sir Richard Grenville (the son of Roger) of the *Revenge*. The buildings in the meantime had been converted into a country house, though their monastic ancestry is obvious.

At this point Francis Drake comes on the scene. Born not far away, outside Tavistock, he was looking for a property to match his new-found fame, not far from Plymouth. Grenville was living more at Stowe, just over the North Devon border in Cornwall. There is little doubt that the aristocrat Grenville regarded Drake as an upstart, and would not have sold the abbey to him direct. Drake knew this and persuaded two intermediaries to purchase the estate and, as Sir Francis, he moved in, aged thirty-six, in 1581; he had already achieved the circumnavigation of the world, but his victory over the Spanish Armada was still seven years away. He died of dysentery on the Spanish Main in 1596, childless. Fortunately his brother Thomas was with him when he died and must have brought home Francis' drum, Drake's Drum, such a treasure from those stirring days, and it is still on view at Buckland Abbey.

Life went on, with the Drake heirs, through Thomas, occupying the abbey. A skirmish occurred there during the Civil War in 1643, and a serious fire, which broke out in 1938, was put out before it did irreparable damage. In 1942 Captain Meyrick put the property on the market. He was the last Drake to live there, his great-grandfather's mother's mother's great-great-great-grandfather being Thomas Drake, brother of the original Sir Francis Drake. The property was bought by Captain Rodd, who gave the estate to the National Trust; after repairs it was opened to the public by Lord Mountbatten in 1951. In 1987/8 it was given a facelift to mark the 400th anniversary of Drake's defeat of the Armada in 1588. At **Buckland Monachorum**, a little way north of the Abbey, the Garden House has a magnificent 8-acre garden, one of the best in the county.

TAVISTOCK

Keeping to the valley of the Tavy, the next place of substance is **Tavistock**, the most attractive, after Totnes, of Devon's inland towns, its character wrought by the mixture of a good natural site, the presence of certain minerals in commercial quantities, a good building stone, and enterprising landowners.

Tavistock made little impression on history until a Benedictine abbey was established on the banks of the fast-flowing River Tavy near a Saxon *stoc* (a stockade or enclosure) about 974, and this part of the present-day name is the lasting memorial to the early settlement. The abbey became enormously wealthy, and a nearby borough developed, with its own market and fair, and with the discovery of workable quantities of tin on Dartmoor in the twelfth century, Tavistock became one of the three stannary towns on the edge of Dartmoor. (The other two were Ashburton and Chagford; Plympton, a fourth, is off the moor.)

To these towns the tinners brought the metal to be 'coigned' by the assay master. A small piece was struck off the corner of each ingot to test its quality, and the metal was then sold. Tin, however, made but a small impact compared with what was to come later.

When the monasteries were dissolved in 1539, the town and much land nearby was bought by the Russell family, from whom sprang the dukes of Bedford.

The Dartmoor tin was worked out in the early years of the seventeenth century, and Tavistock turned briefly to producing cloth; but this in turn failed. However, copper was fortunately discovered nearby at Mary Tavy in large quantities in the 1790s, and this caused a kind of West Devon copper 'rush'. More advanced mining techniques now enabled mining to be carried on at a greater depth, where the copper lodes were found.

The Russells, curiously, were no more anxious to exploit this underground wealth than the abbots had been to develop tin; but eventually they submitted to local pressure, and the appearance of Tavistock today is largely derived from the rebuilding they carried out. Tavistock is virtually a nineteenth-century new town.

At first sight, the abbey ruins are disappointingly incomplete, built over and around by later construction. But there are several significant parts visible within 150 yards

(136.5m) of Bedford Square. (The name 'Bedford' appears, too, in the name of the hotel, and Woburn Terrace is also a reminder of the Russell era.) **Betsy Grimball's Tower** beside the Bedford Hotel, and the Still Tower and abbey wall on the river bank, are the most substantial and unaltered remains. Who Betsy Grimball was, nobody knows. Next to the Post Office is a dining hall, preserved intact though with one end altered, and now a nonconformist place of worship, and the large Gothic gate across the way was the main entrance to the abbey. In the churchyard is a section of late thirteenth-century cloister wall.

Tavistock Parish Church

The parish church stood on its present site when the abbey was a going concern and served the common people of the neighbourhood. There is an especially good monument to Sir John Glanvill in the Lady Chapel, and the modern William Morris glass in the north-east window is worth a detailed study. Morris' father had made enormous sums of money from investments in copper mines.

Bedford Square is a product of the Victorian age, an expression of civic pride shared by the Duke of Bedford and the citizens. This duke, Francis, now looks straight down his boulevard, Plymouth Road, from his plinthed statue at another more famous Francis, Drake, who stands at the western entrance to the town. Francis Drake is believed to have

been born at Crowndale, just outside Tavistock, but while there are no other claimants, proof is lacking.

Beside the Drake statue is the rebuilt gatehouse of the Fitzford estate. Hard by the gatehouse is the Tavistock canal, on either side of which are many mid-nineteenth-century industrial cottages erected by the Duke of Bedford for the miners who flocked into the area with the copper boom. There are others at the north end of Tavistock, and they are a good example of a socially enlightened housing policy.

Dominating the south end of the town is the massive church, given to the town by the duke in 1865, and designed by Henry Clutton, using the pleasantly distinctive green Hurdwick stone in the neo-transitional Romanesque style. Built for Anglican worship, since 1951 it has been the church of the local Roman Catholic congregation. The internal height is loftier than Exeter Cathedral.

MORWELLHAM

Mention has been made of the Tavistock canal and the nineteenth-century copper boom. This brings the West Devon story neatly to **Morwellham** (the accent is on the last syllable), a place with a story. There had been a port of sorts at Morwellham for hundreds of years prior to the copper boom of the 1790s. This was the nearest point on the river to Tavistock which sea-going ships could reach, but trade was desultory. Although, as the proverbial crow flies, Morwellham is only 3 miles (5km) from Tavistock, by road the distance is nearer 5 miles (8km), and the 600ft (210m) obstacle of Morwell Down lies between, as well as the valley of the River Lumburn, no small impediments in the days of horse transport and poor roads. So, when copper was discovered at Wheal Friendship, a mine at Mary Tavy north of Tavistock, in the 1790s, an efficient way of exporting it to the South Wales smelting works had to be devised.

For twenty-seven years Morwellham was moderately prosperous, and then in 1844 much larger quantities of copper were found 5 miles (8km) north at Blanchdown. This became the Devon Great Consols mine, and it was the richest copper mine in Europe for more than ten years. The canal passed nowhere near it, and the roads were still unsuitable for the carriage of quantities of ore, so a standard gauge railway was constructed in 1858 to the top of the hill above the port and a second, larger, inclined plane built alongside the one servicing the canal.

After twenty years of continuous working, the copper lodes began to be exhausted, but a secondary product from the mines came into its own. Arsenic is found in association with copper ores, and had hitherto been little regarded. Now it was

suddenly in demand for various commercial and agricultural uses, especially as an insecticide against a cotton pest, the boll weevil. So, arsenic roasting furnaces and flues were built, and thousands of tons exported, in barrels made at Morwellham. By 1901 the mines were abandoned. 236,000 tons of copper had been produced, valued at £3 million. The canal was closed in 1872, never having been able to compete with the railway, which had reached Tavistock in 1859.

Morwellham quietly mouldered away. The docks silted up and became choked with weeds. The tiled quays were stolen, and the inn closed. However, the canal was revived in 1933 to bring water to the Morwellham hydro-electric station.

Then in 1970 Morwellham had life breathed into it again, when work began to restore its buildings, equipment and docks. It became an open-air museum with trails, museums, a shop, restaurant and most exciting of all, a trip underground after a riverside train ride to see what conditions were really like. Morwellham is now bustling with activity again.

Tavistock-Morwellham Canal

The moving spirit behind the idea of a canal to link Tavistock with Morwellham was John Taylor, a mining engineer in his early twenties and the manager of Wheal Friendship, the mine that so sorely needed relief. He calculated that by taking water off the River Tavy just below the Abbey Bridge at Tavistock, the canal could follow the contours round as far as Morwell Down, through which a tunnel, well over a mile long, could be driven. Then, from a basin at the far end, an inclined plane would take the copper ore down to the busy quays beside the Tamar.

The canal was started in 1803, and simultaneously work began at each end of the tunnel and, to achieve quicker progress, a series of shafts was sunk so that several faces could be worked at once. Even so, the tunnel took 14 years to complete. In the meantime, the canal had been finished from Tavistock to Creber, where the tunnel began, and was in use to that point by 1809.

Places to Visit

Around Plymouth

Plympton Castle

Small well preserved castle, but not open to the public.

Saltram House

Plymton (National Trust)
Devon's stateliest home, containing splendid treasures and beautiful rooms.
☎ (01752) 336546
Open: House – 12-5pm Sunday to Thursday, late March to end of October. Gardens – as house but 10.30am-5.30pm plus Saturday and Sunday during March, 11am-4pm.

Wembury Mill (National Trust)

Small mill building above Wembury beach now a summer-only café. National Trust shop nearby.

Kitley Caves

Yealmpton
Devon's only caves outside the Torbay area.
☎ (01752) 880885
Open: Monday to Sunday, Good Friday to end of October.

Dartmoor Wildlife Park

Sparkwell
Animals are allowed to roam free in large open paddocks.
☎ (01752) 837209
Open: 10am-6pm daily, all year.

Bere Ferrers Church

On the tidal stretch of the River Tavy, one of the most interesting churches in Devon.

Around Plymouth

Buckland Abbey

Yelverton (National Trust)
A monastic building, converted to domestic use and once the home of Sir Francis Drake.
☎ (01822) 853607
Open: 10.30am-4.45pm, Friday to Wednesday, April to October.

Tavistock Canal

A narrow watercourse built to carry copper to Morwellham.

Morwellham Quay

Tavistock
Nineteenth-century port on the Tamar revived as a recreational and educational attraction. Quays, museum, nature trail with bird hides, shops, and a real mine railway which takes one into a mine.
☎ (01822) 832766
Open: 10am-5.30pm daily, all year.

Plymouth

Plymouth Museum and Art Gallery

Porcelain, silver, paintings by Reynolds, archaeological finds.
☎ (01752) 304774
Open: 10am-5.30pm Tuesday to Friday, 10am-5pm Saturday and bank holiday Mondays.

The Barbican

Plymouth
Once part of the vanished Plymouth Castle, the name is now applied to the old part of Plymouth around Southside Street.

Civic Centre

Plymouth
Viewing platform on the thirteenth floor increases one's understanding of Plymouth's geography.

Plymouth Dome

A high-tech interpretation facility on the slopes of Plymouth Hoe.
☎ (01752) 600608
Open: from 9am daily, all year.

Plymouth Pavilions

An all-the-family recreation complex, with ice rink, pool and huge auditorium.
☎ (01752) 222200

Elizabethan House

Barbican
A well preserved 1584 house in New Street, suitably furnished.
☎ (01752) 253871
Open: 10am-5pm Wednesday to Sunday, April to October

Fort Bovisand

Plymouth
A nineteenth-century fort at the water's edge, now used as a training base for water activities, especially diving.

National Marine Aquarium

Opened in 1998, state-of-the-art display of life in the marine environments of the world.
☎ (01752) 600301
Open: daily all year

Mayflower Stone

Plymouth
Departure point of the *Mayflower* and many other famous voyages.

Merchant's House

Palace Street
Well restored house now a museum of old Plymouth.
☎ (01752) 304774
Open: 10am-5.30pm Tuesday to Friday, 10am-5pm on Saturday, from Easter to end of September. Closes 1-2pm.

The Spirit of Plymouth Blackfriars Distillery

Southside Street
The remains of a friary incorporated into the premises.
☎ (01752) 665292
Open: 10.30am-3.45pm Monday to Saturday, Easter to the end of October

Plymouth Guildhall

Interestingly restored hub of Plymouth's public life.

Plymouth Hoe

Breezy promenade, evocative of Drake. A passing parade of ships means a constant free show of 'something to see'.

Smeaton's Tower

The Hoe
An earlier Eddystone Lighthouse re-erected on Plymouth Hoe. Good views from the top.
☎ (01752) 600608
Open: 10am-4.30pm daily, Easter to end of October.

Prysten House

Finewell Street
Plymouth's oldest building, containing many interesting relics.
☎ (01752) 661414
Open: 9am-4pm Monday to Saturday, April to October

Barbican Glassworks

The Old Fishmarket
Demonstrations of glassblowing. Local history exhibition, gift shops.
☎ (01752) 224777

Royal Citadel

Madeira Road
Still garrisoned, but guided tours round battlements at certain times.
☎ (01752) 775841
Open: for guided tours only. 2.30pm daily, May to September. Tickets from the Dome on the Hoe.

St Andrew's Church

Devon's largest parish church, gutted in the war, now restored.

Theatre Royal

Opened in 1982, it provides splendid entertainment in comfortable surroundings.
☎ (01752) 267222 (Box Office)

Drake's Island

A fortress for hundreds of years.

Ker Street

Devonport
Interesting buildings relating to Devonport's past.

Crownhill Fort

Off Tavistock Road
Nineteenth-century cannons, barrack rooms, parade ground. Regular events depicting Victorian military life.
☎ (01752) 793754
Open: 10am-5pm daily, April to October.

4 Dartmoor

D artmoor is not only the last great wilderness in southern England. For some it is the place for an afternoon car ride or coach trip. The more energetic walk many miles across its open solitudes. Criminals have a special understanding of 'the moor'. Soldiers train on it, foresters plant it with trees, and water engineers regard its high rainfall as a valuable natural resource waiting to be impounded. Farmers try to increase its productivity.

These different objectives reflect the variety of interest within Dartmoor. From vast tracts of moorland where one is further from a road than anywhere else in Great Britain south of Northumbria, to deep-cut tree-clothed valleys, here is a mysterious, often mist-shrouded upland which at first sight may seem forbidding, empty and bleak, but which has a treasury of natural features and prehistoric and historic

remains, bewildering in their diversity. Here, too, is the highest land in England south of the Peak District.

The Dartmoor tors (the word is derived from the same root which gives us 'tower') probably stick most in the mind, although they tend to occur only locally, in clusters as it were – there are about 200 on the moor. They are mostly of granite, though a few of metamorphic or altered rock can be found on the moorland fringe. They represent the obstinately harder cores of solidified igneous material that pushed up beneath an overlay of other rock, all of which has eroded away in the 300 million years since the molten matter hardened into granite. The erosion of ages has produced rock piles of curious appearance. **Bowerman's Nose**, near Manaton, is a totally natural feature, which looks rather like an Easter Island figure. As other tors have weathered, their constituent boulders rock or 'log', thus acquiring the names of logan or nutcracker stones. Sometimes the hill slope below a tor is littered with shattered and broken rocks – the ruin of a tor – called on Dartmoor a 'clitter'.

FLORA AND FAUNA

Many rivers have their sources on the two elevated plateaux north and south of Princetown. Tiny trickles ooze from the peat bogs that blanket the area. The streams gather strength and amalgamate, leaving the moor through beautiful valleys, often densely wooded. Some of these woods give a home to deer; fallow, roe and sika. Red deer were killed off on Dartmoor by 1780, and have not been re-introduced. There seems no reason, apart from a lack of acceptance, why they should not thrive on Dartmoor as they do on Exmoor. The occasional stray comes in from the Forestry Commission plantations to the north-west of Dartmoor, but a herd has not become established.

Many square miles of moorland, and some farmland, were planted with conifers between the wars, smothering the open country and altering the landscape. The archaeological remains suffered too, until the forestry interests recently undertook to safeguard this heritage from damage by forest machinery.

Dartmoor is not particularly well endowed with heather, the best areas being on the eastern moor around the Warren House Inn/Grimspound area. When it is in bloom here, the subtle smell and delicate hues entrance the senses.

Bracken, an unloved plant, seems to be encroaching. Farmers say it shelters ticks, and its deep roots grow on the best land ('plough bracken and find gold'), sucking out the goodness from the soil which the grass should be passing on to the grazing animals.

Flora

On the higher hills are deep areas of peat, once cut for commercial and domestic purposes. Acidic and mineral-deficient, the peat supports a limited range of plants. One of the most interesting is the sundew, an insect-eating plant which seeks to extract from flies alighting on its sticky tendrils the nutrients necessary to sustain itself. A similarly carnivorous, but less common, plant is the butterwort, whose tacky leaves perform the same deadly function. Another plant of the wet areas is the cotton grass, each stalk bearing a white tuft of silken fluff. This has been used for stuffing cushions and mattresses.

Perhaps the commonest bird of the open moor is the skylark, and in the early summer the air seems to be full of its song. The raven and crow flap across the sky, stopping to feed on dead lambs or frogs. On the edge of the moor, the buzzard circles and soars, sharp eyes scanning the ground for small rodents, birds and adders. Snakes are not uncommon, but need not deter the visitor. They are sensitive to the walker's approach long before he sees them, and they slide away to hide under a rock, and so an actual encounter is infrequent.

ANCIENT TRACKS

Stone walls switchback over the hills, many of them hundreds of years old, assisting the farmers in stock control, for this is a hill-farming region. The whole of Dartmoor is grazed with sturdy sheep, cattle and ponies. The Dartmoor ponies, as well as the sheep and cattle, all belong to someone, but they stay on the moor the year through until rounded up at the end of the summer. Much of central Dartmoor is owned by the Duke of Cornwall, Prince Charles, and he takes an active role in the management of his Devon estate.

Crossing the wilder parts of the moor are ancient tracks and disused railways, which the visitor can follow on foot. Perhaps the oldest of these, the **Lich Way** (named after the Saxon word for corpse) linked the Bellever/Postbridge area with Lydford in whose vast parish they are. (In 1260, the inhabitants were granted a dispensation to use the nearer church of Widecombe for funerals to save them the harrowing journey across miles of open moor carrying a deceased relative.) Other tracks, which may enter the realm of folklore in some cases, are the **King Way**, the **Abbots' Way**, the Mariners' Way, the **Jobbers' Path** and **the Blackwood Path**. They are well described in a splendid book, William Crossing's *Guide to Dartmoor*, which was originally published in 1909 and reprinted in 1965.

ARCHAEOLOGY

The Dartmoor tin worker is less remembered than his Cornish counterpart, though in places the disturbance caused by his tin streaming activities is on a major scale. Scenes very reminiscent of the Klondike occurred, but happily the healing quality of time has returned the landscape to something approaching the natural scene. Tin streaming, which pre-dated tin mining, was very similar to panning for gold, and involved working over the valley gravels. To crush and smelt the ore, the tinner built small water-powered smelting houses – often called blowing houses on the map – which are interesting relics of this medieval industry.

Dartmoor's old buildings make it

Merrivale, Dartmoor

a fruitful locality for the study of vernacular architecture. Because the buildings were constructed of the long-lasting local stone many of the farmhouses still lived in today date back to the fifteenth and sixteenth centuries, and remains exist of houses in a similar form – 'longhouses' they are termed – going back to the twelfth century.

The Longhouse

The word 'longhouse' aptly describes their shape. Built on a slope to the approximate proportions of a shoe box, with a door in the middle of each of the longer sides, the shippon for the animals was in the lower half, while the family occupied the higher end. A screened passage with doors to the living quarters and shippon, linked the two outside doors which were shared by people and animals. In an area where it is tiresome to have to go out on a cold night to tend stock, this arrangement had much to commend it. The family end was divided into two sections with a hearth on the floor. Only later were chimneys built, roofs raised and first floors inserted, and there are still houses with smoke-blackened roof timbers and thatch, indicating an open hearth when they were first built. Few longhouses with unaltered shippons exist today; most have been altered to increase the living accommodation, but the Dartmoor National Park Authority owns one, which is shown by arrangement with the tenant.

The observant visitor will notice subtle changes in the appearance of buildings between east and west Dartmoor. On western Dartmoor the older farmhouses and cottages owe more to Cornish traditions and influence than Devon's. There is more slate, and less thatch.

FOLKLORE

It is hardly surprising that a region so overlaid with hundreds of years of history should have a rich folklore. Stories of spectral hounds and black dogs, and people turned into stones, are commonplace, though modern children with access to television are less likely to believe them than the youngsters of a hundred years ago. Of course it was to Dartmoor that Sir Arthur Conan Doyle came to gather material and atmosphere for a book about the moor that he called *The Hound of the Baskervilles*. A young coachman, Harry Baskerville, drove him round the moor, and Conan Doyle asked him if he could use his name in the book. The Dartmoor ethos is truthfully, if melodramatically, portrayed, but the places are topographically inexact. **Grimpen Mire** is probably Fox Tor Mire, one of the few valley bogs whose unpleasantness matches its reputation.

The twentieth-century story of the hairy hand defies logical explanation. In the early 1920s there were several accidents on the road west of Postbridge, and surviving drivers spoke of muscular hairy hands closing over theirs and forcing the car or motorcycle off the road.

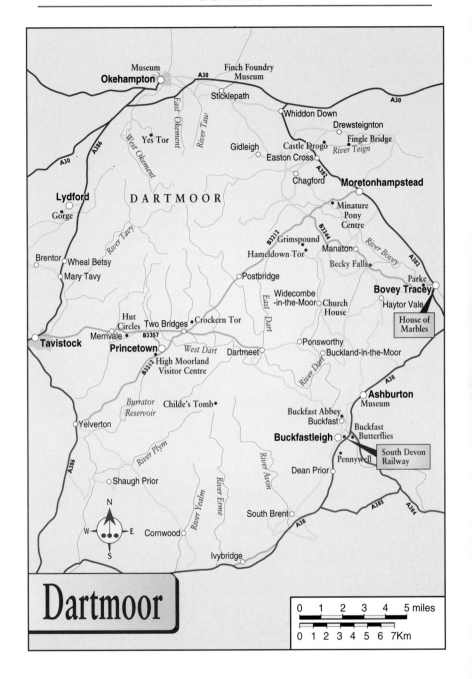

Dartmoor

Childe's Tomb

One of the best known Dartmoor stories concerns a spot beside the Mire known as **Childe's Tomb**. A fairly modern cross surmounts a circle of stones, but what one sees today is a nineteenth-century reconstruction of an older monument, possibly a prehistoric burial chamber. The tale relates that Childe, while out hunting, became detached from his friends, was benighted and beset by a blizzard. To save himself he killed his horse, disembowelled the animal and crawled into its skin, dying nevertheless. Before he expired he wrote his will on some convenient parchment (!) in the horse's blood:

They fyrste that fyndes and bringes mee to my grave The priorie of Plimstoke they shall have.

Professor Finberg has analysed this folk memory using contemporary records in a fascinating historical detective story (*Devonshire Studies*, 1951) and concludes that the tale had its origin in Saxon times.

NATIONAL PARK STATUS

In 1951, Dartmoor was declared a national park. This designation did not alter the status of the land: the moor remains in private ownership. It means that all developments are looked at very carefully by the planning authority, the Dartmoor National Park Committee. This committee also has a duty to help the public enjoy the park. This is achieved through information and interpretative services, guided walks, the erection of signposts, stiles and foot bridges, subsidised bus services and a team of rangers out on the moor making contact with residents and visitors.

ANCIENT HISTORY

Much has been written in the introductory chapter of this book about the chronology of early man and something about the stone remains that one can see on Dartmoor in great abundance. Dartmoor is probably the best place in Britain to study the homes and graves of prehistoric man. There are several reasons for this. Firstly, his settlements, burials and ritual sites were numerous to start with; secondly, they were built of the enduring local stone, granite, and lastly, they have suffered relatively little disturbance since man abandoned them.

The question is often asked, why did men live on what we regard as a fairly inhospitable, infertile upland? The answer is probably (and many of our statements about prehistoric man are qualified by the word 'probably') that the climate was less rigorous; the soil was less acid, meaning the grazing was better; man's economy demanded open pastures; the lowlands were still largely covered with trees; and if people did live in these lower areas their houses have been obliterated by later activities.

The **Bronze Age** on Dartmoor – say from 2,500BC to 750BC –has left an exceptional number of sites. The term Bronze Age indicates that man had learned to make and use metal (bronze is an alloy of 90 per cent copper and 10 per cent tin): it does not mean that the use of stone and flint implements was entirely discontinued.

The settlements are of the greatest interest; it is highly evocative to stand in the ruins of a prehistoric house and imagine life going on in this very spot 3,000 or more years ago. There are about 2,000 such sites on the moor, but some were destroyed by wall and road builders; as many were probably occupied simultaneously, only a guess at population figures is possible.

The circular stone footings we now see – called 'hut circles' by the Ordnance Survey – represent what is left of the walls which supported a conical roof of thatch propped up on a central pole or poles. A complete prehistoric Dartmoor house must have looked very like a native hut in the wilder parts of Africa. The door was usually on the south side to catch the sun and keep out the cold north wind. Some have recently been excavated which had internal plank walls. The houses were usually found in groups, and may be inside a stone wall. Such a village settlement is **Grimspound**, 300yd (274m) east of the minor road 1½ miles (2km) south of the B3212 at **Challacombe Cross**. Although some of the ruined huts at Grimspound have been 'restored' or built up, and as most of the huts on the moor are not so recognisable, it is a good introduction to similar antiquities.

At Grimspound a ruined stone wall encloses an area of nearly 4 acres (1.5 hectares) in which archaeologists found the remains of twenty-four huts, as well as what may have been cattle pens built against the wall. A stream, the Grims Lake, passes through the side of the enclosure, and was an obvious source of water, though unreliable, as it dries up in drought conditions. The paved entrance is on the higher side and gave access to the pastures on Hameldon, the high ground to the south. Its position, overlooked as it is on both sides, indicates that the inhabitants must have lived peaceably with nearby people, for the village was not defensible in an age of slingstones, arrows and spears. The wall was probably not less than 5ft 6in (2m) high and was built to keep domestic animals in and wild animals out.

The inhabitants were certainly not ignorant savages, although their skills were used for different occupations from ours. They could weave and spin, and make pottery, but their pots could not withstand direct heat. Water was heated by placing hot stones in a pot. Meat was cooked by packing it round with hot cooking stones.

In the past few years, much attention has been given to extensive systems of fairly straight, parallel land boundaries or field banks, called 'reaves' on Dartmoor. These are made of stone or soil, and extend for many miles, leap-frogging considerable natural obstacles like the Dart Valley near Dartmeet. Here and there, the ruins of circular houses are found among the strips. Their vastness and complexity are only beginning to be understood, and the theories on Dartmoor prehistory are being revised from year to year.

To these wide-ranging remains of domestic activity, we must add the barrows, cairns and cists where prehistoric man buried his dead, the enigmatic stone rows, and the stone circles where he probably worshipped.

When one puts together all that is known about Dartmoor's prehistory it is interesting how little is really understood. The moor dwellers of 3,000 years ago lived and died without written record, and their culture is so different from ours that it requires an enormous mental effort to subvert our own values and perceptions in order to contemplate their lifestyle.

If the main holiday area in Devon is based on Torquay, and visitors tend to come to Dartmoor while on holiday, then the approach through Newton Abbot and **Bovey Tracey** (pronounced 'Buvvy') is a natural one, and will be the starting point for a figure-of-eight journey across and around the moor. It helps to have a basic understanding of Dartmoor's shape; two upland plateaux, separated by two roads bisecting each other like a pair of scissors at Two Bridges. Within the eastern angle of these roads, and especially on the eastern side of the moor, are a tangle of minor roads for which the visitor certainly needs either the 1:25,000 Ordnance Survey Outdoor Leisure map or the sheets in the 1:50,000 Land-ranger series. (The visitor should not attempt to do everything described here in one day!).

BOVEY TRACEY

The name Bovey refers to the river, which passes through the parish, and the second element connects it with the de Tracey family, one of whose members, Sir William de Tracey, was in the party which murdered Thomas à Becket in Canterbury

Deserted medieval village at Hound Tor, Dartmoor

Cathedral in 1170. The de Traceys owned land in the area, but the re-dedication of the church to include the name of St Thomas of Canterbury six years after his assassination may not prove that the church was rebuilt by Sir William in expiation of his crime, as is sometimes suggested. The church is very beautiful, with a fine rood screen and carved stone pulpit, while the **Riverside Mill** is now home to a number of craftsmen of the Devon Guild of Craftsmen. The site includes a shop and café. To the south of the town, near the **Drum Bridges** roundabout on the A38, the **House of Marbles** and **Teign Valley Glassworks** give visitors the opportunity of watching glassmaking, as well as visiting the marbles and games museum (with probably the biggest collection in the world) and potteries museum.

At the other end of the town is **Parke**, the headquarters of the Dartmoor National Park Authority. The house and estate were left to the National Trust by Major Hole, on his death in 1974. The house was built on the site of an older building by the major's grandfather in the 1820s. The Trust leases the house to the National Park Authority. A joint National Park and National Trust information centre is incorporated in the buildings. There are other **Dartmoor National Park information centres** at **New Bridge** (Ashburton), **Postbridge, Princetown, Tavistock, Okehampton** and **Widecombe** (shared with the National Trust, and using Trust premises). To the south of Bovey Tracey, and at the extreme edge of the Dartmoor National Park, at Liverton, the **Gorse Blossom Park** has a miniature railway and various other attractions for children.

HAY TOR

Beyond Parke, the road divides at a stone direction post at Five Wyches Cross, where you should fork to the left and climb steadily for $3^1/_2$ miles (5.5km) to the car park near **Hay Tor**. Hay Tor is without doubt the most noticed, most recognised and most visited tor on Dartmoor. The superlatives arise from its position on the edge of the moor. On one side the land falls away; on the other the open moor rolls into the distance – there is no better viewpoint from which to get one's Dartmoor bearings.

The two main rock piles show it to be an 'avenue' tor (for reasons not fully understood, even by geologists), and both humps can be climbed. The right-hand tor had steps cut in the nineteenth century but this did not please a local parson who wrote of the 'unsightly stair step to enable the enervated and pinguitudinous scions of humanity of this wonderful nineteenth century to gain its summit'. The other rock is slightly higher and has iron rings as climbing aids and, by a quirk of landform, looks far superior from the north.

A few hundred yards to the northeast is a large quarry boasting a pool where goldfish lurk, saved from predatory herons by the depth of the water. A cutting leads from the lower quarry, and if this is followed, a double line of grooved stone blocks will be seen bearing round to the left beside a tip of waste rock. This is the **Hay Tor granite tramway**.

Between 1825 and 1858 stone was transported from this quarry and others nearby, on flat-top horse-drawn, wooden-wheeled trucks for 8 miles (13km), down a tramway built of continuous lines of these grooved sets. The material was available for the cost of extraction and dressing, but eventually it became uneconomic, as two trans-shipments were necessary at the end of the 'line'. The stone was loaded into boats for a journey along the Stover canal and down the Teign Estuary to Teignmouth, where it was loaded into seagoing ships. Nevertheless the enterprise supplied stone for many London buildings, including parts of London Bridge and the British Museum Library.

The stone tramway is visible for much of its course on the moor, and to follow it makes an easy and fascinating walk of discovery. The 'points' in particular are of the greatest interest. Of course, the system reverses the usual railway practice of having the flange on the wheels. Here the flange was on the 'rails', and the trucks' wheels were plain wood with iron hoops.

If the walk is extended past **Great Tor** to **Hound Tor** the interesting remains of a deserted medieval village can be explored. Enclosures, houses, including what was probably a small manor house, and corn-drying kilns can be recognised. By the fourteenth century the climate had deteriorated, so that farming on these bleak moors was not practical, and the settlement was abandoned. Alternatively by parking at the Hound Tor car park and walking the short distance past the tor, the site can be clearly seen.

WIDECOMBE-IN-THE-MOOR

After looking round the area, carry on towards **Widecombe-in-the-Moor**, 4 miles (6km) or so further

on. Over the top of Widecombe Hill, an enormous panorama is spread out in front. Southern Dartmoor and northern Dartmoor are recognisable, joined by the high saddle of North Hessary Tor beyond Princetown, this summit surmounted by a 700ft (245m) BBC television mast. The long whaleback hill 'behind' Widecombe is **Hameldon**, and Grimspound, mentioned earlier, is on the far slope at the north end of Hameldon.

Although **Widecombe** appears to be low down, the village is nevertheless 800ft (280m) above sea level, and the containing hills are as high again. The altitude brings its own weather, which has given rise to the saying off the moor to the south when it is snowing that 'Widecombe folks are picking their geese'.

Widecombe's rise to fame as a result of the popularity of the famous song 'Widecombe Fair' is probably due to the shrewd commercial sense of those who would profit from it. The song was first written down and popularised in the 1880s, when Widecombe Fair was in its infancy, and of course the individuals mentioned in the chorus – Bill Brewer, Jan Stewer, Peter Gurney, Peter Davy, Dan'l Whiddon, Harry Hawk, Old Uncle Tom Cobley and all – were all going to the fair from somewhere else. Their home territory is understood to be north of Dartmoor in the general area of Sticklepath and Spreyton.

When the fair began, it was what we would now call a market, with some revelling for good measure. Now, it is more of a gymkhana, with a sheep, cattle and pony show, demonstrations, competitions, sideshows, races and refreshments. It is held on the second Tuesday in

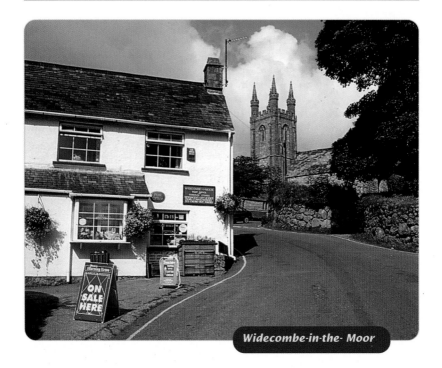

Widecombe-in-the- Moor

September, and thousands of people head in the direction of the village.

The church is the finest on the moor, with a tall tower of noble proportions. During a severe thunderstorm in 1638 one of the pinnacles was struck by lightning and fell through the roof, killing four people and injuring over sixty others. The local schoolmaster's verse about the tragedy is recorded on boards on the church wall.

Outside is the **church house**, now owned by the National Trust, and used as an information centre and shop. Church houses were originally built to serve as rest houses for the parishioners from far-flung parts of the parish – Widecombe extends to 11,000 acres (4,400hectares) – when they journeyed to the village on Sundays. This one may have been where the lord of the manor brewed ale

for the village, and later it became the poor house and, later still, the school. Part of it is used for village meetings – after 450 years it still serves the local community.

The village green was formerly called Butt Park, as this was the field ('park' means field) where the young men practised archery. Under an Act of 1466 every Englishman

...should have a bow of his own height... and that butts should be made in every township which the inhabitants are to shoot at every feast day under the penalty of a halfpenny when they should omit that exercise.'

A mile up the Natsworthy road from the village is a bucolic milestone in the hedge. The distance is carved on a natural boulder and reads '1 moil', and thus the word is still pronounced in these parts.

Driving down the valley to Dartmeet, one travels through the attractive village of **Ponsworthy**, with its watersplash and thatched cottages.

THE CENTRAL AREA

Dartmeet is a famous beauty spot where the East and West Dart Rivers come together among magnificent scenery. Just upstream from the road bridge are the flood-damaged remains of an ancient clapper bridge. ('Clapper' is an old name for a heap of stones.) The age of these primitive bridges is impossible to determine, but they are probably 700 or 800 years old.

Coffin Stone

On the hillside to the east, and rather hard to find among the gorse and bracken, is the **Coffin Stone**, a natural earthfast boulder on which it was the custom to rest the body in the days of 'carrying funerals' when the deceased was being borne to the parish church at Widecombe. A cross and the deceased's initials were incised on the stone while the bearers paused to take liquid refreshment and to get their breath. Samuel Caunter and Aaron Cleave are represented by SC and AC.

Towards Two Bridges, and 2 miles (3km) beyond Dartmeet is **Dunnabridge Pound** on the right, near some farm buildings. This is a medieval enclosure recorded as long ago as 1342, and probably built on a prehistoric site. Until recent times,

it was used as a corral for strays. Just inside the gate is a massive stone seat with uprights supporting a coverstone, perhaps the pound-keeper's shelter.

For many people, **Two Bridges** is the hub of Dartmoor, though a glance at a map of the National Park will show that Bellever Forest has more precise claims to that distinction. The Rivers Cowsic and West Dart come together here, and a five-span clapper bridge on the Cowsic may be one of the original 'Two Bridges', the one over the West Dart having disappeared.

This is a good place to begin a walk up the **West Dart Valley** to Wistman's Wood: at its shortest the return journey is 3 miles (5km). Leave your car in the quarry, noting the embryo tor in the quarry face – geologists find this a fascinating site. Walk up the track towards Crockern Farm, then follow the yellow waymarked track beyond. Do not attempt to stay close to the river; stone walls and boggy patches will impede your progress. By following the yellow blobs on boulders and gateposts an easier and drier route will make the walk more enjoyable.

Soon **Wistman's Wood** comes into sight, a long grove of gnarled and twisted trees, mostly oaks, growing out of a hillside clitter. These same rocks have safeguarded the trees from browsing animals. The wood is of interest to naturalists, as it is growing on the tree line and may represent a relic of more general tree cover in the distant past. Along its higher side are what appear to be long barrows up and down the slope, but they were thrown up by the warrener to encourage rabbits to breed. For hundreds of years, rabbits were 'farmed' on Dartmoor for their flesh and fur. The last warren survived in the Plym Valley until the 1950s. The warrener's hut at Wistman's Warren was near the north end of the wood on a small flat platform, and was only a wooden shed.

On the opposite side of the valley is an early nineteenth-century leat (artificial water course), which takes West Dart water many miles round the contours and through a tunnel, to help top up Plymouth's water supply.

Perhaps before returning to the road you may like to walk up to the pyramid of earth and stone on the ridge above the wood, **Longaford Tor**. It is an easy but rewarding climb to the top. One of Dartmoor's greatest assets is its sense of freedom – the feeling that you can go where you like. This is only partly true, however, as much of the moor is farmed in a conventional way, and this imposes restrictions on the walker as much in the National Park as elsewhere. However, since the passing of the Dartmoor Commons' Act in 1985, the public has a right of access to most common land in the national park. The Act also imposes certain standards of conduct on those using the moor, whether as walkers, riders or graziers, and regulates the number of animals which may be pastured. Dartmoor's bogs are not dangerous to healthy humans taking reasonable care; they are usually obvious for what they are, and the walker can circumvent them.

So if you want to go further up the valley you are free to do so, but do take proper precautions before setting off on a walk, however short, over the moor. Boots are the best footwear, and a waterproof advisable. A map and compass should go into a small rucksack with a spare jumper and some food and drink. Those who are heading into the high land of northern Dartmoor should first ascertain whether the Services are using any of their live firing ranges. The firing programme is distributed widely to Dartmoor National Park information centres, post offices, police stations and hotels in the area.

Back at the road, continue towards Tavistock, taking the right fork after crossing the West Dart. The road climbs, soon crossing the leat, which has been contouring the slope opposite **Wistman's Wood**. **Dartmoor Prison** comes into view (left) and the road passes through prison farmland. The prison is virtually self-supporting so far as meat and vegetables are concerned. On **North Hessary Tor** is a BBC television mast, erected in 1954-5.

Over the rise at **Rundlestone Cross** an extensive view into Cornwall opens up. About $1^1/_2$ miles (2km) from this spot, just after a left-hand bend, cars may be parked in a quarry on the left, for a 1-mile (1.5km) walk over the moor to see the best and most accessible collection of Bronze Age antiquities on Dartmoor. Within a small area every type of relic is represented. Near **Merrivale** a large stone quarry may be seen on the opposite hillside. It ceased working a few years ago.

Walk up the hill on a line with the television mast. After about 250yd (229m) will be seen a large worked stone propped on small stones. This was meant to be an edge-runner or crushing stone, but for some reason it was abandoned in the working about 150 years ago. It stands within a prehistoric stone enclosure – the walls are broken and scattered, and 15yd (14m) beyond are the ruined circular walls of a Bronze Age house. Turn right towards King Tor and you will see others ahead. In fact there must have been a considerable settlement here, as there are more above the road.

Walk towards a line of upright stones. As you reach them, you will find there are two double rows, each with a large stone at the uphill end. If you walk along the more southerly line, a burial chamber (a cist), with a partly destroyed coverstone, will be noticed, offset a few yards, and at the halfway point another burial chest within a cairn of stones. A little distance to the south is a large standing stone (a menhir) and a low circle of stones. Return to the car, and down the hill from the quarry you will see what appears to be a gatepost standing by itself. This bears a T on one side and an A on the other, and was one of a line of guidestones hereabouts marking the route from Tavistock to Ashburton. These mute memorials give an idea of what cross-moor travel was like 200 years ago. A journey we can now accomplish in half an hour would not have taken an ordinary person less than a day.

THE WESTERN SIDE, LYDFORD

Back in the car, pass through Merrivale, look on the left for a very large lump of rock, **Vixen Tor**, and carry on down into Tavistock (described in the previous chapter). Turn right and follow the A386 north to Mary Tavy where you should take the turning left, signposted **Brent Tor**. Drive to the car park below the church-crowned

tor, which gives its name to the village, and walk up the path to the summit. A direct assault is not recommended; take the longer, but less steep, way.

Brent Tor

The view from the top is one of the finest in England. A clear day will enable you to see right into the inner recesses of northern Dartmoor, where Fur Tor and Cut Hill stand out. Even Exmoor appears as a blue blur to the north. The dark rounded slopes of **Gibbet Hill** a mile or so away once carried a hanging tree, as the name suggests.

The tiny church was built in 1130 and stands 1,130ft above sea level, a useful conjunction of numerals. Burials have taken place up to the present time, and one marvels that a sufficient depth of soil exists for the purpose. Now take the road signposted to Lydford, a small village, but a vast parish, about 4 miles north-east. **Lydford** is superficially a very unprepossessing village, cast in a Cornish mould, with none of the thatched-roof cosiness of eastern Dartmoor. The small castle dominates one end of the single street, it is true, but the fascinating story of Lydford has to be sought out, and the casual, uninformed, visitor could miss a great deal.

The village's situation was its *raison d'être*. **The deep gorge** of the River Lyd blocks the approach on one side, with a secondary valley forming the other. King Alfred adapted these natural advantages by raising an earth bank across the third

Above: *The ancient clapper bridge at Dartmeet* **Opposite top:** *Lydford Gorge* **Bottom:** *Lydford Castle*

side, to create Lydford, one of his four strategically-placed *burghs* or fortified positions in Devon against the Danes. (A possibility that Lydford was built on an earlier Celtic site cannot be ruled out.) A mint was established, and it became an important local meeting place, and, as a by-product, the administrative headquarters for Dartmoor. But it never developed to any extent, and was overtaken by Okehampton and Launceston, which lay on the main route through the south-west peninsula, and by Tavistock, with its abbey. For this reason, Lydford's ancient road pattern has not been overlaid by later building. Some of the original Saxon plots and lanes laid out on a grid model can be seen, as well as Alfred's earthbank.

Soon after the Norman Conquest, the invaders refortified the site by building a fort on a corner overlooking one of the steep slopes, but this had a short life, as **Lydford Castle** dates from about 1195. Although it has the appearance of a keep, the

The Gubbins Tribe

Charles Kingsley, in his *Westward Ho!*, mentions the Gubbins tribe, a kind of Dartmoor Doone family, as lawless and predatory as the Exmoor clan. He based his description on an account written down by Thomas Fuller in about 1650. They seem to have been long-lived, fleet of foot, above the law, revengeful and totally pagan, although he wrote that '... they begin to be civilised, and tender their children to baptism .. .'. Lydford Gorge is sometimes thought to have been their home, but as the river occasionally rises to fill the defile, it affords no permanent security.

have been a noxious dungeon.

Early in the last century the castle fell into disuse, and has only given up many of its secrets as the result of excavations in the past few years. Beside the castle is Lydford church, dedicated to a Celtic saint, St Petrock, which gives credence to the suggestion that there may have been a Celtic community here before Alfred established it as one of his *burghs*. The font is the oldest feature in the church, and the screen is a splendid example of modern (1904) craftsmanship.

At the bottom of the hill below the church is **Lydford Gorge** (National Trust), down which rushes the River Lyd. In places 200ft (70m) deep with 60ft (21m) vertical walls at the bottom, the gorge has been formed by the urgent passage of the river carrying rocks which have scoured out potholes along its course. The best is called the **Devil's Cauldron**, and it can be reached by an exciting path cut along the side

castle was constructed for the custody of those who broke the strict forest (hunting) and stannary (tin working) laws. The castle is not built on the mound, as it would appear, for the earth was drawn up round the base of the walls at a later date, for an unknown purpose. The courts were held in the second floor room, and the prisoners confined in the two lower levels. The cellar must

of the gorge. Much of its course is truly awe inspiring and a little frightening, and other parts are very beautiful. At the far end of the gorge, which is over a mile (2km) long, a 100ft (35m) waterfall, called the **White Lady** the highest on Dartmoor, adds her veil of spray to the Lyd. If you visit Lydford in the winter, when for safety's sake the Gorge is closed, the flavour of the place can be felt by looking over Lydford Bridge into the deepest section.

Pass through Lydford and rejoin the A386 at the Dartmoor Inn, turning left, and heading for Okehampton. The high moor is very near the road along here, and by glancing right you will see the prominent stone cross on Brat Tor erected in 1887 to mark Queen Victoria's silver jubilee. A few miles on, turn right towards **Okehampton**, getting a glimpse of Dartmoor's highest tor, Yes Tor 2,030ft (710.5m), if it is not obscured by cloud.

OKEHAMPTON

The dramatic ruin of Baron Baldwin's **Norman castle** on the right down a winding tree-lined road into the town is the great attraction of Okehampton. It is reached by a side road beside the post office. The castle was built along a narrow ridge, with ancillary buildings leading up the slope from the barbican to the keep, past the great hall, guard room, chapel, kitchen and other quarters. Garderobes – medieval lavatories – are built into the outside walls to take advantage of the slope. On a fine spring day when the bluebells are blooming in bud-bursting time, with the chorale of

the nearby West Okement River as background music – fairyland seems to have come to mid-Devon.

The town suffered from the lack of a bypass but one was opened in 1988. On a quiet day, the distinguished town hall in Fore Street can be appreciated. This three-storied building was built in 1685, as a private house for John Northmore, and converted to its present use in 1821.

The **Museum of Dartmoor Life**, on the opposite side of the road, reveals how people lived and worked in the area for hundreds of years.

Above the town looms the high ground of Dartmoor; from the cowering town it has an oppressive presence, a feeling which evaporates when you drive up on to the moor. Here the military are active, for soldiers have trained on Dartmoor for about a hundred years. The public are excluded from the range during advertised firing times, but on other days they may walk the high open moor without concern, except that metal objects should not be touched.

THE NORTH-EAST

About 4 miles (6km) east of Okehampton is **Sticklepath**, a village frequently visited by John Wesley during the eighteenth-century preacher's journeys to and from one of his most frequented evangelistic areas, Cornwall. Here Wesley found kindred Christian spirits in a community of Quakers, and he preached from the White Rock on the Mount at the Okehampton end of the village. This is whitewashed regularly, and is marked by a flagstaff. The Quaker Burying (sic) Ground by the River Taw is a beautifully peaceful spot.

In the centre of Sticklepath is the

Finch Foundry Museum of Waterpower. From 1814 to 1960 agricultural equipment was made here by Heath Robinson-type machinery, powered by water from the Taw. After closure, a band of interested people preserved the machinery which is now shown to the public. The giant trip hammer and shears seem unbelievably primitive to have been operating commercially as recently as 1960. It was given to the National Trust in 1993.

Head eastwards from Sticklepath, and fork right at Whiddon Down, along the A382 as far as Easton Cross. Take the right turn here to **Chagford**. The name means gorse ford, although the town stands well above the beautiful River Teign, here crossed by a lengthy line of stepping stones known as Rushford Steps, over which sacks of grain were carried to **Rushford Mill**.

The church of St Michael is stoutly built of granite, and contains some fine monuments to local gentry. Facing it is the sixteenth-century Three Crowns Inn, with jutting porch, where a young cavalier, Sidney Godolphin, was killed in a Civil War skirmish. The middle of the town is remarkable for its sense of focus. All roads lead to the Square, with its 1862 market house and comprehensive range of shops. Chagford exudes self confidence.

Chagford was one of Devon's four stannary towns, but nothing survives of that era, except the remains of mining activity for those who search diligently in the surrounding countryside. If the tortuous network of lanes can be unravelled, the open moor at **Kes Tor** is worth discovering for the tor, the view, and the wealth of prehistoric antiquities – stone rows, burial chambers, huts, field systems and standing stones – which are scattered over Chagford Common.

Chagford is a good spot for exploring this corner of Dartmoor. To the north of Kes Tor is the elusive village of **Gidleigh**; elusive, as there are those who say that Gidleigh doesn't exist. Although signs point in its direction from Chagford, the serpentine lanes defeat many who set out. There is no village in the usual sense, merely a church, a tiny late Norman castle and one or two houses tucked away in the folds of the Dartmoor foothills, between Chagford and Okehampton.

On the open moor nearby is **Scorhill Circle**, a Bronze Age ritual monument, and, where the North Teign River and Walla Brook come together, a strange naturally-holed stone called the Tolmen sits in the bed of the stream above normal river levels. It is said that to crawl through will cure rheumatism, but sufferers would probably find the effort too difficult to accomplish. A single-span clapper bridge, made of one piece of granite, crosses the Walla Brook just upstream.

To reach these monuments, park your car in the small pull-in outside the gate of Scorhill House, which is on the moor edge above Gidleigh and walk up to the moor between a funnel of stone walls. A path goes over the top of Scorhill and presently Scorhill Circle, perhaps the finest on the moor, is visible on the right. The Tolmen and the clapper bridge are as described. This is a gentle walk of 2 miles (3km), but should not be attempted in mist, as nothing is visible and it is easy to become lost.

CASTLE DROGO

Another expedition from Chagford must be to **Castle Drogo** at **Drewsteignton**, which is often described as the last great country house that will ever be built in England. Drogo can be seen from some parts of Chagford, its granite glistening in the sun, or, chameleon-like, glowering in the gloom, depending on the weather. A coalition of the genius of architect Sir Edwin Lutyens and the money of Julius Drewe in the Dartmoor landscape was bound to produce a building of exceptional impact. Castle Drogo was built just in time. The taxing away of family fortunes and the repressive effect of planning laws would nowadays prevent the building of such an expensive showpiece.

Opposite: Castle Drogo owned by the National Trust

Above: Chagford square with its Market House

Left: Bullers Arms Chagford

Julius Drewe

Julius Drewe made his money from the Home and Colonial Stores. Believing there to be a link between his family and the Norman Drogo (or Dru) de Teigne who gave his name to Drewsteignton, he bought land in the parish, and set his heart on a castle. Mr (later Sir) Edwin Lutyens was recommended to him and, to a budget of £50,000 for the house and £10,000 for the grounds, he began work on Drewe's romantic dream of reproducing on an exciting site, overlooking the Teign Gorge and the eastern slopes of Dartmoor, a twentieth-century version of an all-granite medieval castle.

The foundation stone was laid in 1911 and the early plans included a great hall standing on walls 6ft (2m) thick. However, possibly on the grounds of expense, or maybe because Drewe had second thoughts about living in a building so monolithic, the plans were reduced in size, and the undercroft of the hall, which was never built, became a highly atmospheric family chapel.

Perhaps feeling that the paring away of a principal feature had emasculated his grand design, Lutyens tried in 1916 to persuade Drewe to build a gatehouse at the northern approach to the forecourt, and had a full-scale timber mock-up built to impress his client. This was never built, and one may conjecture that it was the death of Drewe's eldest son Adrian in 1917 in France that sapped his enthusiasm. Work continued exceedingly slowly, and the two original masons of 1911 eventually finished the castle in 1930. Sadly, Julius Drewe died a year later. The origin of Drewe's fortune was not forgotten and local people disrespectfully christened his house 'Margarine Castle'. Even in its reduced size, Castle Drogo is massive in scale, and inconvenient for modern living. In 1973 it was given to the National Trust with 600 acres (240hectares) of land, and it has been open to the public since 1975.

The approach is along a wide drive which Drewe and Lutyens deliberately kept free of the usual lodge, and cars are sensibly kept a little way from the house. The award-winning National Trust reception area and shop is itself an interesting design.

As the visitor enters the house (beneath a Lutyens joke: a working portcullis designed to air the hall while keeping the dog in) the first things that are noticeable are the bare granite walls. The furniture is secondary to the structure. Lutyens' treatment of the corridors and the stairs reveals his understanding of spatial relationships and the texture of that most intractable of stones, granite. The impressive main staircase, lit by a window of cathedral proportions, leads down to a less successful feature, the dining room. The heavy ceiling and mahogany panelling have an overpowering effect, which the single broad window does nothing to mitigate.

The kitchen is 50yd (46m) from the dining room, along a stone corridor, and many visitors will find the domestic quarters the most interesting part of the castle. Both the pantry and the kitchen are equipped with cupboards, dressers and tables designed by Lutyens, and the kitchen is discreetly lit by a roof lantern. The slate slabs of the pre-refrigerator era larder contrast with the service lift in the scullery that took food to the servants hall one floor up and to the nurseries two further floors higher.

Off the bedroom corridor, the elaborate bathroom apparatus will cause amusement, but the memorial room, arranged by his mother in memory of the eldest soldier son Adrian, is a touching survival of a sad time in British history, and must have been something of a shrine for the grieving parents. In the gun room, the National Trust has arranged a comprehensive display of plans and photographs showing the construction and growth of Castle Drogo. Across the drive are the formal gardens, which rise to a circular lawn used by the Drewes for tennis and now adapted for croquet. A charming Wendy house nearby captivates younger visitors.

Fingle Bridge

It would be wrong to leave the neighbourhood without visiting **Fingle Bridge**, a well known, but unspoilt, beauty spot, 2 miles (3km) away, on the other side of Drewsteignton. Here the River Teign sparkles beneath the 400-year-old stone bridge, among beautiful wooded hills. A licensed restaurant, the Anglers' Rest, stands at the foot of Prestonbury, which has an Iron Age hillfort on its summit. Public footpaths lead up and downstream, and the most beguiling, the **Hunters' Path**, climbs up through the oak woods to come out above the tree line, with the spectacle of expansive views ahead to northern Dartmoor. As Castle Drogo can be reached by turning off the Hunters' Path, this route provides a most pleasant link between the two places.

MORETONHAMPSTEAD

Before driving across the moor to Princetown, the small town of **Moretonhampstead** should be visited. Standing where the A382 and B3212 intersect, it is an important road junction. The town is notable for the fine, arcaded stone almshouses dated 1637 in Cross Street. Above the nearby cross which gives the street its name, there was, until it was blown down in 1891, a pollarded elm – the dancing tree – which had a large platform built in its branches for musical performances. In 1801 a local diarist recorded that there was room for thirty people to sit around, for a small orchestra to play, and for six couples to dance. In the Napoleonic Wars, when French officer prisoners were billeted on parole in the town they performed in the dancing tree. Memorial stones to two French officers can be seen in the church porch.

The year after Trafalgar, 1806, the 'calculating boy', George Parker Bidder, was born in Moretonhampstead, the son of a stonemason. He possessed extraordinary mental powers and from an early age could work out complicated sums in his head. Before he was sixteen he could calculate the cube root of 304,821,217 instantly, and the cube root of an eighteen digit number in $2\frac{1}{2}$ minutes. He became an engineer and built the Victoria Docks in London.

The B3212 in the Princetown direction soon passes the **Miniature Pony Centre,** which has a wildfowl lake, adventure play area and pets' corner as well as the ponies of the name. Beyond, the road leads, after a further 2 miles (3km), to a steep climb onto the open moor at Moorgate Hill. The name is a reminder that not so long ago all roads giving access to the moor had gates across them, to prevent the grazing animals from straying. Cattle grids have now replaced these except on one or two minor roads. (The first turning left after reaching the moor leads to Grimspound, mentioned earlier this chapter.)

Postbridge

Postbridge is like an oasis in the middle of the moor, with beech trees instead of palms. The finest clapper bridge on the moor is easily seen a few yards down stream from the road bridge. This is a good place for a walk up the East Dart River, starting from the stile at the top of the car park. The walker can follow the river up the west bank, cross at some convenient place, and return on the east bank. But after heavy rain, the river may not be crossable, and at the end of Drift Lane, after a gate, following the river slavishly here will produce wet feet early in the walk. It is better to veer away from the river along a track, and pick up the line of the disused Powder Mills leat, which swings back to the river valley. A convenient crossing point may be the waterfall about 3 miles (5km) up the East Dart, making a walk of 6 miles (9.5km) there and back.

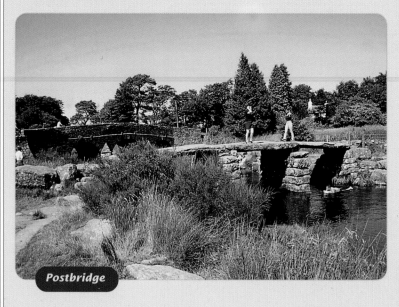

Postbridge

Crockern Tor

Gunpowder Mills near Postbridge

After the second switchback, the road levels out; beside the road on the south side is the leaning and mis-shapen **Bennett's Cross**. As a monument to medieval piety it served to mark a track over the moor before the road was formalised. WB carved on the shaft stands for Warren Bounds, for it was adapted as a boundary stone for Headland Warren, the rabbit warren in this area.

The next building to the west is the **Warren House Inn**, which once served the miners from the tin mines below the road. The deep gashes show where they followed the east-west striking tin lodes. Work went on here until earlier last century.

Carrying on towards Princetown, about 1 mile (1.5km) west of Postbridge, on the north side of the road, are the ruins of a nineteenth-century gunpowder factory, known as the **Powder Mills**. Here the three constituents of that compound were brought together – the charcoal at least was provided by locally-grown timber – and the various processes powered by water from the East Dart River. The safety factor of space was available in abundance, and batches of powder were tested by firing a proving mortar, which still stands near the cottages.

Another mile further on, a low tor, just north of the road, is **Crockern Tor**, the meeting place from 1474 to 1703 of the Stannary Court, the administrative body of the Dartmoor tinners. The moor was divided into four quarters (stannaries), which came together at Crockern Tor, and each stannary sent twenty-four representatives. Thus Two Bridges is reached by a different route. Continue on the B3212 beyond the West Dart.

PRINCETOWN

Princetown came into being through the prison, which was started in 1806 on land owned by the Prince of Wales. The prison was built by French prisoners of war, who had hitherto been incarcerated in over-crowded hulks at Plymouth, and later Americans joined the French within the walls: at one time there were 7,000 men held captive, with 500 soldiers guarding them. Initially it was referred to as the War Prison or Depot.

A weekly market was held in the yard to which farmers brought poultry, eggs, butter and vegetables, passing beneath the massive stone gateway bearing the Latin inscription *Parcere Subjectis* – 'Spare the Vanquished'. Prisoners skilled with their hands used the chicken bones to make intricate models of ships and working models of guillotines, which nowadays fetch high prices at auction. Examples may be seen at Plymouth Museum and Buckland Abbey. The prisoners sorted themselves out into a class-dominated hierarchy with 'Les Lords' at the top and 'Les Romans' at the bottom.

At the end of the wars, the prison was closed, and as a result the prosperity of its satellite, Princetown, waned. So Sir Thomas Tyrwhitt, who had initiated the prison scheme, suggested a fresh project to tap what he felt was the agricultural and mineral potential of the moor.

A horse-drawn tramway (the route was later partly converted to a standard gauge branch line) was constructed from Plymouth to bring up coal and lime, and to export stone, and he intended that the crops grown on the moorland wastes should be farmed. But there is an old saying on Dartmoor 'You scratch my back, and I'll pick your pocket', and his scheme never achieved the success he desired. The prison opened as a civil institution in 1850, after a short spell as a naphtha factory (the naphtha was extracted from peat), for transportation to the colonies was becoming increasingly unpopular in the empire. And, so it has remained to the present time.

The Plume of Feathers

The oldest building in the area is the **Plume of Feathers**, a slate-hung hostelry dating from before the prison. In 1993 Prince Charles opened the splendid **High Moorland Visitor Centre** in the one-time Duchy Hotel, and this is the best place to find out about the national park under one roof.

Modern Princetown is the home of the **High Moorland Visitor Centre**, housed in what was the Old Duchy Hotel. It provides an excellent starting point to a visit to Dartmoor with its interpretive exhibitions and wealth of information. Beyond Princetown the road once again crosses open moor, and the track of the Princetown branch railway (closed 1956) can be seen on the right. The road also passes close to several hut circles.

THE SOUTHERN FRINGE

The first turning on the left after leaving the open moor leads (by either road at a fork) to **Burrator Reservoir**, by far the most beautiful reservoir on Dartmoor. It was built in 1898 to solve Plymouth's water problems and increased in size in 1928.

From the dam the foothill lanes bring one, via Meavy and Cadover Bridge, to Shaugh Bridge, below the village of **Shaugh Prior**. From the car park beside the bridge, a delightful 2-mile (3km) walk on National Trust land to the top of the **Dewerstone** leads through woods, along a quarry tramway and up to the breezy summit. This is the Trust's Goodameavy estate; it also owns a stretch of Wigford Down, a landscape peppered with prehistoric remains. The Dewerstone is the highest inland cliff in Devon. In fact it comprises several separate crags of which the highest is the Devil's Rock.

From Shaugh Bridge, head southeastwards through Cornwood past the china clay workings (see previous chapter) to Ivybridge. Just to the north here, at Harford, the **Lukesland Gardens** are 15 acres (6 hectares) of woodland and garden, with landscaped pools and waterfalls. The rhododendron and azaleas are the highlight of this magnificent site. From Ivybridge the A38 dual carriageway can be followed as far as **South Brent**. This little town has a number of pleasant buildings, especially the Toll House with its list of charges, and the church. Originally a cruciform Norman building with a central tower, at some stage the west end was demolished. Lydia Bridge on the Avon once carried the road between Plympton and Buckfast.

On the A38, to the east is **Dean Prior**. Robert Herrick, the poet, was vicar here in the seventeenth century, and is buried in an unmarked grave in the churchyard. Sadly, the

Buckfast Abbey

A monastic community lived at **Buckfast** from before the Norman Conquest to 1539 when, with the dissolution of the monasteries, the buildings were abandoned and fell into decay. In 1882 a band of French monks acquired the site, and in 1907 the abbot decided to rebuild. The only resources available at that time were £1, a horse and cart, and much faith; none of the monks had any knowledge of building techniques. The decision made, one of the monks left Buckfast to learn the basic skills of masonry, and on his return the

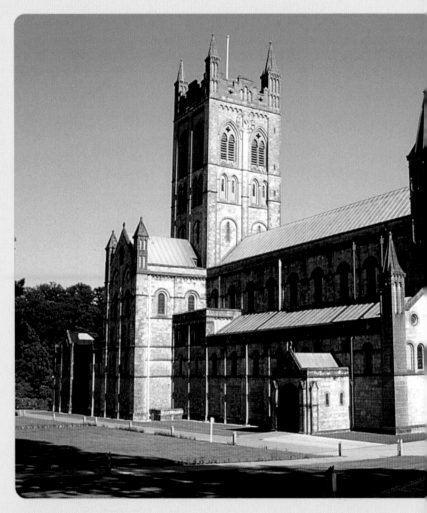

work went ahead, but with never more than six brothers working at the same time. The abbey we see today was finished exactly thirty years later.

The abbey church and monastic buildings are built throughout of West Country stone, in the transitional Norman fashion. While this style has a certain austerity not inappropriate to a monastic way of life, the fittings are lavish. The altar, centre of Catholic worship, is a sumptuous creation of the modern goldsmith's art; above hangs the richly decorated corona; the font is a magnificent conception in cast bronze. On every side is evidence that there are still craftsmen capable of producing articles as beautiful as those created by their predecessors.

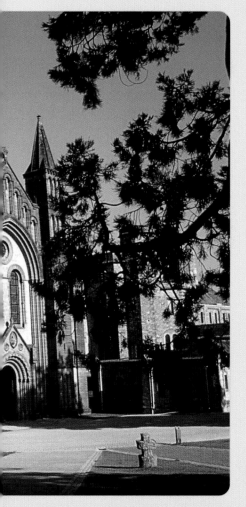

To make the monastery financially self-supporting, many activities are carried on by the monks. Dartmoor heather provides the raw material for the honey which has taken the name of Buckfast to many parts of the world. Another product that finds an overseas market is a tonic wine of secret formula. Cider is also made, cattle and poultry are kept, and the kitchen gardens are carefully cultivated. Other monks, more skilful with their hands, produce works of art in pottery, stained glass, painting, illumination and carving. All of them do what they can for the good of the community. The abbey is open to the public daily.

Buckfast Abbey

dual carriageway has isolated it from those who would worship in the church or visit it for the Herrick connection.

BUCKFASTLEIGH & ASHBURTON

Buckfastleigh was formerly a wool town that derived its power from the River Mardle. Round the edge of the built-up area are the large houses of the mill owners. Diversification has come to Buckfastleigh, however, and many different ventures now thrive in the little town where the moor meets the South Hams. The spired church, rare on Dartmoor but burnt out in the early 1990s, stands aloof from the town on a nearby hill. In the churchyard is a curious mausoleum-like structure erected over Richard Cabell's tomb following his death in 1677, to make sure his unquiet spirit could not escape to haunt the area, since he was thought to be in league with the devil. Tales of fire-breathing black dogs howling round his tomb were adapted by Conan Doyle when he was researching for *The Hound of the Baskervilles*. Newcomers to Devon will visit the area chiefly to see Buckfast Abbey and the South Devon (the old Dart Valley) Railway, and the two are conveniently sited only about half a mile apart. Just across the A38 from the town is Pennywell Farm where children can meet not only farm animals, but small mammals, falcons and owls.

The **South Devon Railway** runs along the old Ashburton line on Great Western Railway principles, from Buckfastleigh to Staverton, and on to Totnes. Here the locomotives have to change ends and pull trains back to Buckfastleigh. Many films and television serials have used the railway to achieve period atmosphere. There is much to see at Buckfastleigh Station – it has a shop, museum and model railway.

A pocket of limestone occurs in the area, and several caves are known. Scientific research continues at the William Pengelly Cave Studies Centre in Higher Kiln Quarry, which is not normally open to the public. However, the Bone Cave may be open for certain days in August. Near Buckfast Abbey is the **Buckfast Butterflies and Dartmoor Otter Sanctuary** where you can see butterflies from all over the world and watch otters being fed.

Ashburton, Buckfastleigh's twin, lies $2^1/2$ miles (4km) away up the A38, and the way passes a well-restored pigeon cote on the right. It is a pleasant little town with many attractive houses, shops and interesting corners; it repays a leisurely visit. The slate-hung front elevations are locally distinctive. In the middle of the town is a Gothic arch on the site of the Mermaid Inn, now an ironmonger's shop, where General Fairfax stayed in 1646 during the Civil War.

Ashburton had its quota of French officer prisoners during the Napoleonic Wars, and the grave of one of them, Sous-Lieutenant Francois Guidon, can be seen near the church porch. The nearby willow was grown from a cutting taken from a larger tree on St Helena, where Napoleon was exiled and died. The milestones, which marked their exercise limits, can still be seen on some of the roads leading out of the town. The church is a good example of a Devon town church, with a handsome tower. Ashburton was one of the four Devon stannary towns, but the trade died out there in about 1700.

Near the church is an award-winning new development, St Andrew's Close, and in the middle of the town, in the Bull Ring, is a well-arranged museum.

From Ashburton, 1^1/$_2$ miles (2km) up the Two Bridges road is the **River Dart Country Park**. Here is something for everyone: a privately run riverside park with walks, lakes, tennis, swimming pool and adventure playground. There is much else, too, all in beautiful grounds beside the tree-lined River Dart. Children, especially, love the sylvan spaciousness.

NORTH OF ASHBURTON

Buckland-in-the-Moor is a tiny village high up above the Dart, and reached by a signposted turning right, beyond the country park. The moorstone church of St Peter is beautifully situated on a hillside, overlooking the deep and wooded valley. The rood screen has some interesting panel paintings, but the church is chiefly visited to see the tower clock, which has letters reading MY DEAR MOTHER instead of numerals.

The memorial was provided by a local landowner who was also responsible for the famous tablets on **Buckland Beacon**, a nearby hilltop. To mark the rejection of a proposed new prayer book in the late 1920s, Mr William Whitley engaged an Exeter monumental mason, Mr W. Clement, to dress certain rocks on the summit, and to carve the Ten Commandments on them. The work was done in the summer of 1928, adding a twentieth-century folly to the Dartmoor landscape. Buckland Beacon is one of the best viewpoints on Dartmoor. Between the church and the Beacon is a well-kept group of thatched stone cottages, which seem to have come to life from a chocolate box. This is probably the single most photographed scene on the moor.

Drive on to a T-junction, turn right and 1^1/$_2$ miles (2km) further on, at the bleak crossroads known as Cold East Cross, turn left. Carry straight on at Hemsworthy Gate and make for Manaton, past **Hound Tor** (right), one of Dartmoor's finest tors.

Manaton is two places; the part round the church is delightful, with a tree-shaded green, and not a jarring note in the symphony of the senses. But half a mile down the road, a rash of modern buildings has disturbed the serenity of the scene. Another half a mile towards Bovey Tracey are **Becky Falls**, well worth a visit after heavy rain as the falls then have something to show. In dry weather the boulders, which form the cataract conceal the stream. There is a café at Becky Falls, and the oak woodland is particularly beautiful in spring and autumn.

The road towards Bovey Tracey winds vertiginously over **Trendlebere Down**, a moor-edge eminence giving expansive views eastwards. Leaving the moor, and just after the cattle grid, a turning right leads into **Yarner Wood**, where the Nature Conservancy Council has laid out two nature trails, one short, one longer. Excellent descriptive booklets guide the visitor round this varied woodland. From Yarner, a drive of 1^1/$_2$ miles (2km) brings the visitor back to Bovey Tracey, and the start of this wide-ranging tour.

During this tour, which would need about 5 days to achieve completely, a number of walks have been suggested to take the visitor away from the roads. There are two main wilderness areas which are so inviting to lovers of solitude, where one can wander at will (the Services' live firing programme permitting) all day, and maybe not see another person. The strong walker will not take too kindly to detailed advice as to where to go, preferring to look at an Ordnance Survey map and work out his own route, but a few words of advice may not be amiss. By starting high up you will save yourself a good deal of climbing, so leave your transport well up the contours. Have some goal to reach; a remote tor, antiquity or river head, and work out a circular route there and back. Do not attempt more than you can reasonably accomplish in the time available. Above all, when the days are short, start early in the day.

The custom has developed on Dartmoor of 'signing in' at visitors' books placed in waterproof tins at various remote (and not so remote) places. You can also leave a self-addressed card there for the next arrival to post, and in this way you will discover how soon after your departure someone else visited the spot. The most famous of these letterboxes is at **Cranmere Pool** on northern Dartmoor; there are others at Fur Tor and Duck's Pool (southern Dartmoor). The custom has proliferated in the past few years, with individuals establishing their own letter-boxes all over the moor, often with elaborate rubber stamps of imaginative design. Dartmoor does not need these artificial foci. It has plenty of tors to find and antiquities to discover. There are few more difficult objects to locate than a Bronze Age cist, sunk in the heather; and there is a particular satisfaction

in navigating across a bleak bit of moor in a thick mist and hitting your destination right on the nose.

Weather

A tor can be a life saver in bad weather. The wet and weary walker can nearly always find shelter in a rocky crevice or beneath an overhang. But if the only protection is in the mud under a dripping peat hag, spirits drop and the risk of exposure is very real. Inclement weather is sometimes said to be the norm on Dartmoor. The assertion that the moor attracts 'nine months winter and three months bad weather' has a grain of truth. Dartmoor is not to be trifled with; it is to be enjoyed, and this means being prepared.

Both high plateaux are flat and relatively featureless. When visibility is poor, there are few reassuring 'signposts' like rock piles or trig points. On northern Dartmoor, the red and white range boundary poles and a number of lookout huts and splinterproof shelters help as navigational beacons, though Services' paraphernalia is something most walkers can do without. Southern Dartmoor's high ground may be rather smaller in extent and of a lesser altitude, but it is more menacing when the mist is down. And it has two of the more troublesome mires, **Aune Head Mire** and **Fox Tor Mire**, though the latter is off-centre.

Threading their way through and over the watersheds of the northern blanket bog are some useful '**peat passes**', cut at the turn of the twentieth century by Frank Phillpotts and his friends, to enable them to follow hounds on horseback over this difficult terrain. They are as useful today to walkers and riders, and now appear on Ordnance Survey maps as broken lines. The one on the southern slopes of Cut Hill has acquired the name North-West Passage and winds up this broken slope, taking the easiest line through a succession of open clearings in the peat. By linking up a series of natural erosion areas continuous routes were made. After Phillpotts' death the peat passes were marked by small dressed stones, each bearing a memorial plaque.

P l a c e s   t o   V i s i t

On and around Dartmoor

Ashburton Museum

A well laid out small town museum overlooking the Bull Ring.
☎ (01364) 53278
Open: 2.30-5pm Tuesday, Thursday, Friday and Saturday, May to September.

Becky Falls

Manaton
A heap of enormous boulders down which the Becky Brook tumbles. Spectacular after heavy rain. Lovely woods.
☎ (01647) 221259
Open: 10am-6pm (dusk if earlier) daily, mid-March to end of October. February half-term and winter weekends if weather suitable.

Buckfast Abbey

A modern building constructed by the monks in the early part of the twentieth century. Physic Garden and Pleasure Garden. Monastic Produce shop.
☎ (01364) 642519
Open: 5.30am-7pm daily, all year. Services are held daily and all are open to the public. Visitor facilities open daily from 9am-5.30pm April to October; 10am-4pm November to March. Shops open at 12 noon on Sunday.

Buckfast Butterflies and Otter Sanctuary

Wander among the exotic insects from many parts of the world and view otters at close quarters.
☎ (01364) 642916
Open: 10am-5.30pm (dusk if earlier) daily, April to October.

Buckland Beacon

Buckland-in-the Moor
A splendid viewpoint overlooking the Dart. The Ten Commandments are carved on the summit rocks.

Burrator Reservoir

Sheepstor
Dartmoor's most attractive reservoir. A road passes round the lake.

Castle Drogo

near Drewsteignton (National Trust)
A granite *tour de force* by Lutyens, completed only 70 years ago.
☎ (01647) 433306
Open: Castle – 11am-5.30pm Saturday to Thursday, April to October. Gardens – 10.30am-dusk daily, all year.

Cranmere Pool

northern Dartmoor
Remote mecca for walkers

Finch Foundry Museum of Waterpower

Sticklepath
(National Trust)
Primitive industrial machinery
powered by water.
☎ (01837) 840046
Open: 11am-5.30pm Wednesday to
Monday, April to October.

Gorseblossom

Off A38 at Drumbridges roundabout

Miniature railway and adventure park

☎(01626) 821361
Open: 10.30am-5pm Monday to
Saturday, 1-5pm Sunday. Good
Friday to Easter Monday; Friday,
Saturday and Sunday plus both
bank holidays in May: daily from
late May to early September;
October half term.

Grimspound

Challacombe
Bronze Age enclosed village
settlement on the side of
Hameldon.

Hay Tor Granite Tramway

Nineteenth-century quarry
tramway which used stone 'rails'.

High Moorland Visitor Centre

Princetown
Comprehensive high-tech interpretive exhibition with national park
shop.
☎ (01822) 890414
Open: 10am-5pm daily in peak
season, 10am-4pm daily the rest of
the year.

House of Marbles and Teign Valley Glass

Bovey Tracey
Museum of Bovey Pottery, board
games and glass marbles. Glass
blowing.
☎ (01626) 835358
Open: 9am-5pm daily, all year. Free
entrance.

Lydford Castle

Built as a prison for those who
offended against the forest laws.
Open: all reasonable times, free
entry.

Lydford Gorge

(National Trust)
Awesomely deep natural defile closed
for safety's sake in winter. NB
arduous walk, needs stout footwear.
Unsuitable for those with walking
difficulties or heart complaints.
☎ (01822) 820320
Open: 10am-5.30pm April to
September; 10am-4pm October;
10.30am-3pm November to March
(limited access only).

Merrivale Antiquities

Near Princetown
The finest collection of Bronze Age remains on Dartmoor.

Miniature Pony and Animal Farm

2 miles west of Moretonhampstead
Hands on animal sanctuary. Nature trails, adventure play areas.
☎ (01647) 432400
Open: from 10.30am daily, Easter to end of October.

Museum of Dartmoor Life

West Street, Okehampton
A comprehensive and constantly growing range of local artifacts.
☎ (01837) 52295
Open: 10am-5pm Monday to Saturday, Easter to October plus Sunday June to September. Telephone for winter opening.

Okehampton Castle

Norman fortification guarding the road to Cornwall.
☎ (01837) 52844
Open: 10am-6pm (dusk if earlier) daily, mid-March to end of October.

Parke Estate

Bovey Tracey (National Trust)
Country estate with lovely riverside walks.

Pennywell

Off A38 at Buckfastleigh
Range of country activities for all the family. Adventure play, crafts, animals.
☎ (01364) 642023
Open: 10am-5pm daily, early April to October. Telephone for weekend openings in winter and February half-term.

River Dart Country Park

Ashburton
Fun for all the family beside the Dart.
☎ (01364) 652511
Open: 10am-5pm daily, April to mid-September.

South Devon Railway

Buckfastleigh
Independent steam railway run on GWR principles.
☎ (01364) 642338
Services operate daily from mid-May to early October. Reduced services at other times, telephone for details.

Widecombe Church House

(National Trust)
The ancient parish hall, partly used as a shop by the National Trust.
☎ (01364) 621321
Open: when not in use as the village hall, telephone for details.

Widecombe Church

Its lofty tower stands high above the village.

Wistman's Wood

Two Bridges
Gnarled and twisted trees growing at the highest limit of trees on the open moor.

Yarner Wood Nature Trails

Bovey Tracey
Interesting mixed woodlands with well laid out walking routes.

However the Devon guide book writer chooses to divide the county into area chapters, the result will not be totally satisfactory. Those which have gone before have a certain logic about them. Dartmoor has an identity of its own, and the South Devon holiday region hangs together reasonably well. Exeter and Plymouth, as large commercial cities, exert a powerful influence over East Devon and West Devon respectively.

The vast tract of land north of the A30 lacks a focus until Great Torrington, Bideford and Barnstaple are reached. In fact, there is a wide east-to-west swathe of thinly populated land across Devon which is no respecter of county boundaries and runs from the coast, north of Bodmin Moor in Cornwall, to the Vale of Taunton Deane in Somerset. Launceston, Okehampton, Crediton, Tiverton and Wellington form the approximate southern limits of this corridor, and Bude, Great Torrington and South Molton the northern boundary. Within the whole of this

Tourism

Tourism in this area is necessarily thinly spread, and visitors tend to pass through without stopping for long. However, more and more people are enjoying farm holidays, and in the peak weeks of the summer, accommodation is often available inland when the North Devon coastal resorts are full to overflowing. Of course, this area, being less visited than anywhere else in the county, presents a picture of unspoilt, unsophisticated charm, which has long departed from the tourist flesh-pots of the coasts and National Parks. This is a place of quiet pastoral enjoyment, of forest walks, and of drinks in real country pubs with the locals. The atmosphere is calm and unhurried, there are no dual carriage-ways, and resident and visitor alike make their own entertainment.

15 mile (24km)-wide and 70 mile (112km)-long band, there are no towns larger than Holsworthy, Bampton and Wiveliscombe, and the scene is one of scattered farms and villages in a rural landscape.

Agriculture and, to a lesser extent, forestry are the main employers, and other industries like the cheese factory at North Tawton and farm-related ventures on the old airfield at Winkleigh feed off the basic land-based economy. The reasons for this lack of population are complex, and need not be discussed here in detail, but they include geology, soil quality, communications, and quirks of history like the wars against Spain and France which made the south coast important, and North Devon less so.

The effect of this wide strip of small settlements has been to make two counties out of one, North Devon and South Devon, though the actual boundary is somewhat blurred. Those who live within this belt can go south or north for furniture and fridges, school uniforms and entertainment, and all the other once-in-a-while purchases.

The interest of the area lies in village churches, old farmhouses and manors, bridges over slow-flowing rivers and distant views of Exmoor and Dartmoor. This is undramatic Devon, where the fun is discovery and finding out for oneself.

North Devon may be split into two roughly equal halves by a line along the watershed – the Taw to the east and the Torridge/Okement river basin to the west. It is an arbitrary boundary.

NORTH-WEST OF BARNSTAPLE

When visiting North Devon, especially for the first time, many make for the ever-popular coastal resorts between Croyde Bay to the west and the twin villages of Lynton and Lynmouth to the east, often leaving the delights of places like Braunton, Barnstaple and rural villages to occasional rainy days.

The B3281 from Braunton (passing Saunton Court, a 1932 farm rebuilt by Sir Edwin Lutyens) heads straight for the sea and forms the basis of the coastal route from Croyde to Ilfracombe, one of the most popular stretches of North Devon 'seaside'.

At the sea, just beyond Saunton Sands Hotel – a 1937 modernistic building – it is worth pulling into the convenient layby to take in the view. To the left are **Saunton Sands**, with the Atlantic breakers rolling in endlessly, providing the sort of conditions surfers drive hundreds of miles to enjoy. About 3 miles (5km) along the beach, and sometimes rather difficult to see, is the estuary channel with Northam Burrows and Westward Ho! beach beyond. This is Devon's Golden Coast, and these are two of its four great beaches. Out to sea on a clear day the island of Lundy is visible. The saying goes 'If you can see Lundy it's going to rain; if you can't see it, it's raining already'! Hartland Point is the farthest mainland promontory, but, like Lundy, it may be invisible.

Round Down End, Croyde, the smallest of the four beaches, comes into view. **Baggy Point**, a National Trust headland, is the next feature to the north, and highly recommended as a destination for a $2^{1}/_{2}$ mile (4km) coastal walk, if one drives round **Croyde Bay** to the Trust car park on the Baggy Point approach, and walks out to the end.

Beside the road near the Baggy Point Hotel are some of the bones of a large whale washed up in 1915, and tucked in under the low cliff but only visible from the rocks is the **Baggy erratic**, a 50-ton boulder of granulite gneiss which found its way here in the Ice Age, perhaps from Northern Scotland. On the cliffs is the plant known as the Hottentot fig whose bright flowers bloom between May and August. (The cultivated species of the plant is the mesembrianthemum.)

Beyond a small stream, the path divides, but the two routes come together at the point. At the point, vertical cliffs fall way, a prime site for nesting birds and rock climbers. Climbers are asked not to climb between the small white posts from 15 March to 15 June. Round the cliff top, and along the north side of Baggy Point, **Woolacombe Sands**

Baggy Point

Baggy Point is made of Devonian rock, a rock named for the county in which it was first identified. The headland is composed of Old Red Sandstone, the rock below Exmoor, and is popular with nesting seabirds and rock climbers. From the headland Baggy Leap runs north-westwards, a rocky ridge on which HMS *Weazle* foundered in 1799 with the loss of her entire crew of 106 during one of Devon's most violent storms.

To the north of Baggy Point is Willer's Stone (sometimes, but wrongly, written as Wheeler's Stone), not one but two rocks which are still a hazard to shipping. The name is from William Luscombe, a sailor on the fishing boat *Bessie Gould* . One very calm day, as the *Bessie Gould* neared the rocks, Willer jumped overboard and swam to one of the rocks. He climbed on to it and claimed the pair for Queen Victoria. Sadly, history does not record Her Majesty's response to Willer's increase in the size of her realm. Equally sadly, history makes no further mention of Willer.

come into view with Morte Point the next headland to the north. A signposted path directs the walker across the neck of the point via Middleborough Hill back to Croyde Bay – the stiled path may be followed across farmland back to the car park.

From the car park there is a way through **Croyde**, passing Georgeham (the long-time home of the late Henry Williamson, the author), to **Woolacombe**. This exposed resort grew up early this century, and is now the focus of a busy camping and caravanning holiday area.

There is a road out to **Mortehoe**, an isolated village with a special church; very dark, with much old work, some of it Norman. Parking can be difficult here, but **Morte Point** (National Trust) is worth exploring. Unlike Baggy Point, as it is all gorse and rough grazing land, the walker can wander where he likes with no pressure to keep to a path: or he can head north along the Bull Point lighthouse road (open to walkers) as far as the new lighthouse (built in 1972, to replace the one which had become unsafe due to rock falls), returning to the village past Rockham Beach – about 2 miles (3km) in all. From the north coast of Devon, there are often views across the Bristol Channel to Wales.

Lee is the next place to the east, but the first turning left after Mortehoe past Higher Warcombe is not recommended; the lane is exceedingly narrow and steep at the bottom. Better to take the route the buses follow. Lee is sometimes called 'Fuchsia Valley' and the Old Maids' Cottage attracts many photographers. The beach is delightful at low tide, with a myriad of rock pools awaiting exploration, and a sandy strath giving good bathing. At high tide all this is covered, and Lee beach is then uninviting.

ILFRACOMBE

Ilfracombe is North Devon's leading holiday resort, though in the face of increasing competition from self-catering resorts, its hotel trade has fallen away. Old photographs of the quayside show several paddle steamers moored alongside each other, and until recently a summer service operated across the Bristol Channel. Pleasure trips to Bristol, Minehead, Lundy, and Clovelly used to be part of an Ilfracombe holiday. Smaller boats ply pleasure trips along the coast to Lynmouth and Combe Martin.

Hillsborough, the 447ft (156m) hill overlooking the quay from the east has an Iron Age hillfort on its summit. St Nicholas' Chapel stands on Lantern Hill, adjoining the pier, and is probably the oldest building in the town. As early as 1522 it served as a lighthouse, later suffering many vicissitudes – including being a laundry, dwelling house (two parents and fourteen children) and band practice room. It was finally restored in 1962.

At the western end of the town is the Torrs Walk (National Trust) an engineered path up the cliff, starting near the Tunnels, a similarly artificial way through a cliff to the bathing pool. Ilfracombe enjoyed its heyday in Victorian times after the railway arrived.

Ilfracombe Museum is a cherished collection of artifacts and old photographs. A mile out of Ilfracombe, up a side road, is **Chambercombe Manor**, a huddle of sixteenth- and seventeenth-century buildings round a cobbled courtyard. About eight

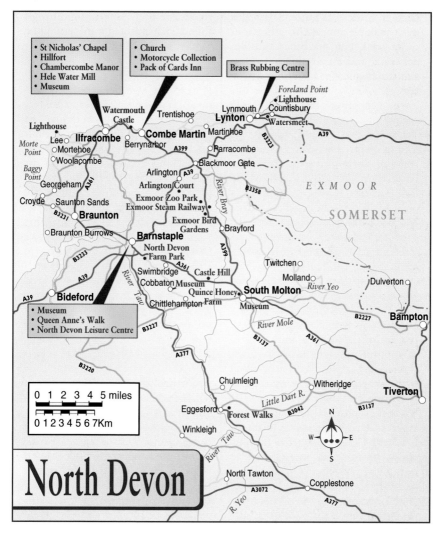

- St Nicholas' Chapel
- Hillfort
- Chambercombe Manor
- Hele Water Mill
- Museum

- Church
- Motorcycle Collection
- Pack of Cards Inn

Brass Rubbing Centre

- Museum
- Queen Anne's Walk
- North Devon Leisure Centre

0 1 2 3 4 5 miles
0 1 2 3 4 5 6 7 Km

North Devon

rooms are open to visitors and there is some good seventeenth-century furniture. At **Hele Bay**, just east of Ilfracombe, on the A399, is a completely restored **water mill**, with an 18ft (6m) overshot waterwheel.

The coast road between Ilfracombe and Combe Martin is 3 miles (5km) of winding switchback, and whether you enjoy the journey will depend on the number of other drivers on the road at the same time. Tempting,

fleeting views of the sea will occupy the passengers. After $1^1/_2$ miles (2km), **Water Mouth** is reached, a rocky boat-bobbing inlet not unlike Boscastle in Cornwall, or a small Scottish loch.

Watermouth Castle is an 1825 castellated mansion, now a full-blooded tourist attraction crammed with attractions of every kind, such as antique self-playing musical instruments, a model railway, magic lantern slides, bygone dairy and cider-making equipment, collections of bicycles, pier machines and illegal traps and a craft market. Outside are tropical gardens and a pets' corner.

To underline that Devon is a county of contrasts, after absorbing Watermouth Castle, a visit to the nearby village of **Berrynarbor** is strongly recommended. Here is a true Devonshire village, sufficiently far from the A399 to be relatively unaffected by tourism. The church has a fine eye-catching tower and a Beer stone arcade; surprising material to find so far from the quarry of origin.

COMBE MARTIN

Back on the main road **Combe Martin** is soon reached, but not so quickly passed through. It must share with Branscombe (East Devon) the distinction of being the largest village in the county, though Combe Martin is continuously built-up, whereas Branscombe is a series of hamlets. Combe Martin must certainly bow to Branscombe's superior beauty, for the North Devon village has little to commend it except the church, the Pack of Cards Inn, interesting historic associations and nearby environmental attributes. The church is one of the finest in North Devon, with a splendid tower, rood screen and parclose screen.

The **Pack of Cards Inn** is sometimes called a folly; it is more accurate to refer to it as an eccentric building (a folly implies worthless impracticality). The story is related that the inn was built in the eighteenth century to celebrate a win at cards. Fifty-two windows, four floors, each with thirteen doors,

represent the numerical multiples found in a pack of cards, and the whole heaped-up structure looks like a house of cards.

Combe Martin's silver and lead mines were worked from the thirteenth century to 1875, iron ore was mined from the beach below the Little Hangman, and manganese not far away. All these enterprises have ceased, but a few ruins remain for the diligent searcher. As a sheltered fertile valley, Combe Martin is the market gardening focus of this part of North Devon. Those who enjoy a nostalgic look at machines of the past the **Combe Martin Motorcycle Collection**, in Cross Street will prove enjoyable.

The **Exmoor National Park**'s western boundary marches with the outskirts of Combe Martin, and much of this part of North Devon is in the Park. Unlike the Dartmoor National Park, which is contained within one county, Exmoor is split between Devon (about a quarter) and Somerset (three-quarters). But Devon claims rather more than half the National Park coastline. This is one of the smallest National Parks: at 265sq miles (686km^2) it is exactly 100sq miles (259km^2) smaller than Dartmoor. Its special qualities are the coast, the red deer and the deep-wooded valleys. The Park is administered from headquarters at Dulverton in Somerset and there are seasonal National Park information centres in the Devon sector at Combe Martin and Lynmouth, and on the county boundary at County Gate.

The walk up to the summit of the Little Hangman from the beach at Combe Martin is over 700ft (245m) of climbing, about 1 mile (1.5km) each way. But the view and sense of achievement is out of all proportion

The Lynmouth Flood Disaster

Lynmouth has recovered from the devastation suffered, when, after a storm of unusual intensity, water, trees and rocks torrented down the East and West Lyn Rivers, sweeping aside bridges, riverside buildings and the harbour, in a catastrophic flood. Several inches of rain fell on an already saturated Exmoor hinterland on the night of 15 August 1952, and the steep hills did the rest. The damage was not confined to Lynmouth, the whole area suffered. Thirty-four people lost their lives, and of these, four were never found.

A wonderful job of restoration was achieved, and the harbour was re-designed. Even the Rhenish Tower, a folly building on the pier, was rebuilt. The visitor ignorant of the tragedy could be pardoned for thinking that nothing has ever happened to disturb Lynmouth's beauty. But most of the many thousands who flock to the village have heard of that terrible night and perhaps knew it before the destruction and reconstruction. On Watersmeet Road, near the car park, is the **Exmoor Brass Rubbing Centre** where visitors can make their own brass rubbings.

to the effort. Another mile further on brings you to the Great Hangman 1,043ft (365m), a mini-mountain where Exmoor meets the sea.

A day-long walk is easily devised along the **North Devon Coast Path** from Combe Martin, and takes in the Little Hangman and Great Hangman, Holdstone Down, Trentishoe Down, Heddon's Mouth, Woody Bay, the Valley of Rocks and Lynton. A bus can bring the walker back to the starting point. It is a strenuous walk, with several descents into deep valleys, and is about 11 or 12 miles (17-19km) long.

Holdstone Down 1,145ft (401m) is the highest point of a coastal outlier of Exmoor, and, regardless of weather, always seems to possess a sinister aspect, especially when seen from the A39 near Parracombe. The Aetherius Society rate it a holy mountain and hold meetings on its lofty summit. Heddon's Mouth is a deep-cut gash in the North Devon coast, with scree-scarred sides, and

a convenient pub, the Hunter's Inn, 1 mile (2km) back from the pebbly beach. High up on either side of this valley are the remote parishes of **Trentishoe** and **Martinhoe**. Both have churches with delightful exteriors, but with over-restored interiors. Woody Bay and points east are best discussed under Lynton.

The road leading east from Combe Martin meets two other main roads at **Blackmoor Gate**, a significant landmark in this part of North Devon. A country livestock market is held here, and the Lynton and Barnstaple Railway, a narrow-gauge branch line, once steamed over this high saddle of land; the station buildings can still be seen. Along the A39 eastwards, past the Parracombe bends, there is, on the left, a sign pointing down a rough lane to Parracombe church.

This is **Parracombe** old church, only occasionally used for services, as another church was built nearer the village in the 1870s. The old

Lynmouth

Watersmeet House

The Lynton-Lynmouth Cliff Railway

In the mid-nineteenth century the huge, steep cliff between Lynton and Lynmouth was affecting the tourist trade and Bob Janes, a local engineer decided to build a cliff railway to overcome the problem. After several years of raising finance from local companies and individuals, Janes started work. After the

surprisingly short time of three years the railway opened on Easter Monday 1890. The railway is very steep, rising 450 feet in 900 feet (to use Imperial measures for something so clearly Imperial) and is water-powered. At the top a 700 gallon water tank below the carriage is filled, the weight of water dragging the lower carriage (and its empty tank) up the cliff. At the bottom the water tank is emptied, the upper carriage's tank being filled to repeat the process.

The trip takes 90 seconds and on the first day cost 3d (three old pennies) for the uphill ride and 2d to go downhill. Bob Janes' design for the railway's hydraulic and emergency brakes were so good that there has been no change since 1890. In all the journeys since that first day, millions of passengers have been transported without one injury occurring, though a dog once lost part of its tail when it wandered on to the track.

church was very nearly demolished, as fears were uttered about its safety. Fortunately, the public outcry was so vocal, and was joined by no less a person than John Ruskin, that the building was saved and is now in the care of the Redundant Churches Fund. The church is a complete survivor from the late eighteenth century. Nothing has been altered since; to enter the building is to go back 200 years. The hat pegs on the wall, the rough benches and the musicians' gallery are all evocative of days when life revolved round the parish church. Now carry on along the A39 and take the B3234 to Lynton, the higher and larger of the Siamese-twin villages of North Devon, the other being Lynmouth.

These two places share the beautiful scenery of the Exmoor coast, but are very different in character. They are linked, and paradoxically separated, by one of the steepest hills in England, Lynmouth Hill. Pedestrians may use the water-operated 1890 cliff railway.

LYNTON AND LYNMOUTH

By no stretch of the imagination can **Lynton** be called a beautiful village – it is really a small town. Pleasant corners here and there and some idiosyncratic buildings like the Town Hall and the Valley of Rocks Hotel rescue it from mediocrity. The hotel is named after a craggy amphitheatre within easy walking distance – half a mile (1km) – of Lynton. Even in an area where hills dominate the scenery, one can walk to the Valley of Rocks and back along the North Walk, a well-surfaced cliffside footpath, without having to toil up steep slopes.

The **Lyn and Exmoor Museum** is in the charming St Vincent's Cottage. This is the place to discover more about old Exmoor life, the Lynton and Barnstaple Railway and the Lynmouth lifeboat. Beyond the Valley of Rocks is the aptly-named Woody Bay, once coveted for holiday development, but the plan came to nothing.

At the foot of Lynmouth Hill is the entrance to the **Glen Lyn Gorge**, a privately owned estate where the public may walk on payment of a small charge. A mile-and-a-half (2km) up the A39 valley road at **Watersmeet** the Hoar Oak Water joins the East Lyn River in valley woodland of great beauty (National Trust) beside Watersmeet House (1830). There are so many walks radiating from here, up and down the rivers, or climbing up both sides, that to suggest one in preference to another is invidious. Far better to visit the Trust's information centre and shop in Watersmeet House (it also has a small café), and buy the excellent leaflet map for the Watersmeet area, and the map of the paths around neighbouring **Countisbury**.

This is part of the same Trust property and is best reached by the A39 up Countisbury Hill. This severe ascent – 1:4 at the bottom – is more remarkable for its length, as in 2 miles (3km) it climbs to over 1,000ft (350m). **Countisbury** is a tiny huddle of stone-built buildings around the Exmoor Sandpiper Inn and the church. This inn, once the Blue Ball Inn, is a sturdy, unspoilt hostelry that used to be a stop on the Lynmouth to Minehead horse-drawn coach service which ran until 1913. Yes, horses used to draw coaches up Countisbury Hill.

Countisbury church, like others in

the district, is more interesting for its situation and exterior appearance than for its interior furnishings. From here there is a view back towards Lynmouth and a great man-made earthwork draped over the slope of Wind Hill in the middle distance like a monstrous caterpillar. This was originally built as a promontory fort in the Iron Age, say 2,000 years ago, but there is good reason to believe it was the battleground in 878 between the men of Devon and Hubba, a Danish invader.

From behind the church there is a walk a quarter of a mile up to Butter Hill 993ft (348m), crowned by a small television booster mast and a hut which gives shelter for walkers as well as protecting the instruments. This is the high open land (except for a few fields not in Trust ownership) of **Foreland Point**, and paths and a Trinity House road lead down to the lighthouse, now automatic, on the Point itself. The road zig-zags steeply down through Caddow Combe, a curious stony valley with much scree.

Eastwards from Countisbury the A39 undulates pleasantly, giving distant views of the Welsh coast and of ships using the Bristol Channel. Inland, the land falls away to the East Lyn River, then rises again to the high ground of central Exmoor. The Somerset boundary is reached at County Gate, and here an old roadside cottage has been converted into a seasonal National Park information centre.

This is a good place for starting a walk, particularly down the **Glenthorne Valley** to the beach 1,000ft (350m) below, but beware of the distance and climbing involved. The helpful staff in the information centre can tell you what to look out for, or sell an inexpensive leaflet showing the many paths giving access to the Glenthorne estate. Near the beach is the nineteenth-century house, built by the Halliday family and lived in by them until recently, which should not be approached, but there are many other goals, like the **Pinetum**, the **Sisters' Fountain** and the **Seven Thorns**, which can be found. Signposts help the searcher.

At County Gate, the visitor is near 'Doone Land', that strange *mélange* of fact and fiction, folklore and legend which has so overtaken the area that even the Ordnance Survey

Saving the Forest Hall

Before the A39 is left, it is worth pondering on the night in January 1899 when the Lynmouth lifeboat was dragged up Countisbury Hill and along this road before being launched at Porlock. A full-rigged ship, the *Forest Hall,* was in difficulties off Porlock, but the seas at Lynmouth did not allow the lifeboat to be launched there. So the whole village helped with their horses, and pulled, dragged and pushed the $3^1/_2$-ton lifeboat on its 7ft 6in (2.6m) wide carriage the 13 miles (21km) to Porlock, a party going ahead to widen the road. The effort took $10^1/_2$ hours, but the ship's crew was saved. There can never have been a more unusual lifeboat launch in the history of the service.

labels part of the Badgworthy Valley 'Doone Country' on its maps. Authorities are now agreed that the Doones existed as an Exmoor 'mafia' in the seventeenth century, and say that they lived their lawless lives near where the Hoccombe Combe meets Badgworthy Water. Overgrown remains of buildings can be seen in the Combe; grass-covered foundations going back to the moor.

Badgworthy Water is the county boundary here; other places in R.D. Blackmore's book *Lorna Doone* (1869) such as Plovers' Barrows farm, probably Oare Ford farm, and Oare itself, are in Somerset, and do not come within our purview. The Water Slide is on Lank Combe, which joins the Badgworthy Water at the southern end of Badgworthy Wood. Legends of the Doones, perhaps exiles from Scottish justice, circulated by word of mouth and in print before Blackmore wove them into his famous romance, and they continue to delight the tourist to this day.

ALONG THE COUNTY BOUNDARY

The county boundary seems carefully to exclude most of Exmoor's upland from Devon, as if to say 'you've got Dartmoor, at least let Somerset have most of Exmoor!' Even so, Chapman Barrows 1,574ft, (551m), Shoulsbarrow Common 1,564ft (547m) and Five Barrows 1,617ft (566m) are high for Exmoor and are in Devon's share. Dunkery Beacon, the highest point, near Minehead, is 1,704ft (596m). The names of these hills with the common element 'barrow' is a pointer to Exmoor's chief antiquity, the barrow. The high-level roads are a feature of the moor. Using the Ordnance Survey Tourist Map, it is possible to devise a drive of about 12 miles (19km) along the southern ridge of Exmoor, from East Anstey Common in the east to **Five Cross Way** above Brayford in the west, without dropping below 1,000ft (350m).

Occasionally one may see red deer, Britain's largest wild animal, particularly in the open, although they spend most time in the wooded combes. On Exmoor, they are hunted by hounds, a practice which is not approved of by everyone. Walkers sometimes find cast antlers. Stags grow antlers afresh each year, and Exmoor 'heads' are usually better than those from the Scottish Highlands, but less good than those from park deer.

Whoever in the past named Exmoor and Dartmoor, though obviously lacking maps, nevertheless knew which river was dominant. The Exe, with the Barle, drains nearly all central Exmoor, leaving its birthplace swollen by its tributary, the Haddeo, to run past **Bampton**, a small market town which only comes to life in late October, when the annual Exmoor Pony Sale is held. West of Bampton, and nestling in the southern foothills of Exmoor is **Molland**, a tucked away village with a lovely parish church. A three-decker pulpit, box pews and interesting monuments make it well worth a special visit.

SOUTH MOLTON

South Molton is the only place of any size in these parts, and the kind of Devon market town where one can find old-fashioned courtesy and values. Happily the North Devon link road now takes traffic past the town to the north, making South

Molton a much more pleasant place. The main street is lorded over by the Town Hall (1740), which contains the town museum. At the Barnstaple end of the town is the **Quince Honey Farm** that advertises itself as England's largest honey farm. The mysterious process of honey-making from flower to table is explained in galleries, demonstrations and observation hides.

Eggesford Forest

Before leaving this rural part of Devon – discussed in general at the beginning of the chapter – one should visit **Eggesford Forest**, which flanks the A377 halfway between Exeter and Barnstaple. It was at Eggesford that the newly-formed Forestry Commission planted its first tree on 8 December 1919, a fact commemorated by a stone unveiled by the Queen in 1956, to mark the planting of 1,000,000 acres (400,000 hectares) by the Forestry Commission. An information office, picnic site and car park are near the stone (on the east side of the road), and two walks of a mile each, the **Home Valley walk** and the **Hilltown trail**, are routed through the trees. Another walk in Heywood Wood across the valley can be either 1 mile or 2 (1-3km). Red deer live in the forest.

The rural route from here to the Barnstaple area first visits **Chittlehampton**, a large village between the A377 and the A361, with a church possessing the finest tower in Devon, 114ft (40m) tall. Inside is a medieval stone pulpit and seventeenth-century monuments. The tower may have been paid for by the offerings of pilgrims to the shrine of St Urith, the patron saint, martyred nearby in Saxon times by savage scythe-carrying villagers.

Not far from Chittlehampton, at **Cobbaton**, 2 miles (3km) northwest, is the **Cobbaton Combat Vehicles Museum**. Strange perhaps to find a collection of World War II vehicles, armoured cars and tanks in deepest Devon, but the collection began as a private one, and has just grown. A children's assault course is a bonus.

To the north the A361 leads to **Swimbridge**, where the church is splendid and should be seen. Under its fourteenth-century broach spire, the fifteenth-century church is rich and fascinating, with a stone pulpit (dating from about 1490), rood screen, bench ends and wagon roofs. The Rev Jack Russell, the original breeder of the famous terrier strain, and a notable hunting parson, was vicar here in the nineteenth century and is buried in the churchyard. Close to Swimbridge, on the road to Landkey, the **North Devon Farm Park** is a Rare Breed Centre where children can feed the animals. There is also a pets' corner and an indoor jungle world. The farm building itself dates from the fifteenth century.

Some 3 miles (5.5km) east of Swimbridge at **Filleigh**, is the very grand domed house known as Castle Hill. It stands to the north of the road and faces a triumphal arch, an eighteenth-century folly on the hill opposite at the end of a long avenue. The house is open to parties only by appointment, and individuals have to content themselves with a distant view, though there is much of interest in the house, if a visit can be arranged. It was originally built in the seventeenth century, and subsequently enlarged; the middle portion was destroyed by fire in 1934, though since rebuilt. As a stately mansion, it is probably second only to Saltram House in Devon, a county not renowned for sophisticated rural residences.

BARNSTAPLE

The A361 also leads, of course, to **Barnstaple**, the unrivalled capital of North Devon, a fact acknowledged by health and education authorities, local government, civil servants and industrialists. It is the only place in North Devon to which a railway still penetrates, though one hardly dares to ask for how long. The town, busy and well served with shops and a wonderful market, has the ethos of a county town, and it is surprising that its population falls below that of Exmouth and Newton Abbot to make it the sixth largest town in the county. But Plymouth, Torbay, Exeter, Exmouth and Newton Abbot are all in South Devon and relatively close to each other. Barnstaple is out on a limb, and is nearest to Exeter – 40 miles (64km), or at least an hour's journey away on a winding road – so it has had to be self-sufficient for goods and services.

The town's pre-eminence in North Devon goes back to Norman times; in 1086 it was one of the four Domesday boroughs in the county. Pilton, a nearby village, but now a pleasant part of Barnstaple, was the original settlement in the early tenth century, but the *burgh* was surrendered to Barnstaple a few years later, possibly because it was closer to the

ford across the Taw, later bridged about 1280. The present bridge was built about 1437, but is much altered.

The **Castle Mound** (dating from about 1100) can be seen near the Civic Centre and is now an environmental study area. Once surmounted by a wooden keep or look-out tower, it now grows a mixture of trees, shrubs and flowers, and birds are encouraged by nest boxes. Early in the twelfth century, the town was walled around, but nothing remains of that era, and all the gates have gone.

Barnstaple's early prosperity was built on wool, and much was exported. Later, it began to import Irish wool and yarn, which was carried inland to factories in East and Mid-Devon. But when the Taw began to silt up, this trade was transferred to Bideford. A sea-going trade survived, however, and, even today, coastal vessels put in with building materials and other bulk cargoes.

Pottery was an important industry for hundreds of years, and still is, and shipbuilding kept the maritime links going. Other trades were cabinet making, glove manufacture, machine-made lace and industries associated with farming, such as milling and the making of agricultural implements.

Queen Anne's Walk near the bus station is Barnstaple's most outstanding building, and a reminder of its former importance as a trading town. It was built in 1708 as the exchange for merchants but has recently been brought into use as **Barnstaple Heritage Centre**. One thousand years of history are brought to life here with interesting, interactive displays.

Barnstaple's **parish church** is more

interesting for its monuments than for its architecture, though its broach spire is worth a second glance, twisted as it is by the warp of time and temperature. Throughout the town there are quiet courts and alleys. Perhaps the best are the **Penrose Almshouses** in Litchdon Street (1627). The granite pillared arcade recalls a similar style (of 1637) at Moretonhampstead.

Barnstaple is best visited on a Tuesday or Friday when the pannier market is at full stretch. Stalls selling fruit, vegetables, dairy produce, antiques and clothing jostle each other; perhaps the dark North Devon delicacy, laver bread, may be on sale. Sold as a wet pappy heap, it is a kind of seaweed found in these parts and is highly regarded when cooked with bacon.

Standing at the south end of the bridge is the modern **North Devon Leisure Centre** which caters for most popular indoor sports, and has a bar and cafeteria. It is a good place to visit with the family on a wet day.

From Barnstaple, drive west along the A361 to Braunton, passing, some 3 miles (5km) from Barnstaple, the one-time Chivenor Air Station on the left, now a Royal Marine Base.

The hill on the right has the prominent tower of **Heanton Punchardon** church, which has a well-kept plastered interior, with many interesting monuments.

AROUND BARNSTAPLE

Braunton is sometimes spoken of as the largest village in Devon, but it has the aura of a small town. How many villages possess a good art gallery? It is one of those places which shows its least pleasant face to the casual visitor but the church and its surroundings give a very different impression. The church itself is a delight, with a lead-covered broach spire, stockier than Barnstaple's, but right for the building. Inside, the roof bosses, bench ends and Jacobean woodwork catch the eye. The small local museum nearby reflects the traditions of farming and seafaring. For Braunton was once a port; small coasting craft sailed up the Pill (the creek) to Velator on the west side of the main road. This is the way to come to see **Braunton Great Field** (shown on the 1:50,000 Ordnance Survey map), one of the few remaining open field

The Gravel Trade

A local trade of some antiquity involves the collection of gravel from tidal banks opposite Appledore, where the Rivers Taw and Torridge meet. Barges from Barnstaple arrive on the banks on an ebbing tide, allow themselves to go aground, and the crew wait for the tide to go out and expose the gravel. In former days the gravel was shovelled into the barges – a taxing task as the barge coamings were 7ft (2.5m) high! Now, the work is done mechanically, but the wet gravel has still to be shovelled on to the elevator. The barges float off on the flood tide – 'fleeting' is the term used – and set off back to Barnstaple, to be unloaded by a grab crane.

systems to be seen in England. The strips in the area are divided one from another by grass balks 1ft wide.

Beyond (south of) the Great Field is the extensive sweep of Braunton Marsh, a bit of Fenland scenery dropped into Devon, and buttressing this low-lying area from the Atlantic is the largest expanse of sand dunes in the West Country, **Braunton Burrows**, big enough to contain a nature reserve, a firing range and golf course.

The southern tip of the Burrows looks out on to the confluence of the Taw and Torridge Estuaries. North Devon differs from South Devon in not having such a dissected coastline. To travel the South Devon Coast Path from Plymouth to Lyme Regis requires the walker to negotiate nine estuaries. North Devon has only two, which come together before the sea is reached, but what a mighty obstacle they are!

One further house remains to be seen in the Barnstaple area – **Arlington Court** (National Trust), some 7 miles (11km) north-east of Barnstaple on the A39. There are usually peacocks on the approach path, and Shetland ponies in the paddock. There is much to see at Arlington, and it is worth buying a copy of the leaflet map about the estate (which incorporates a nature trail) and the catalogue of ship models in the house.

The present house was built in 1820 and succeeded two others. The Chichesters owned the estate for over 500 years, and the Trust received it on the death of the last member of the family, Miss Rosalie Chichester in 1949. She had lived there for 84 years, and the house and its contents reflect her acquisitive interests during a long life.

Exmoor Zoo

Where the road levels out on Bratton Down, on the left is the **Exmoor Zoological Park** at South Stowford. Penguins, tropical birds, waterfowl and rare poultry are on show, together with a collection of small mammals and a pets' corner.

The nature trail conducts the visitor down to the lake, with its wildlife hide and waterfowl. Jacob's sheep will be seen in the park. The handsome stables contain a collection of nineteenth-century horse-drawn vehicles. Carriage rides along the drive give an idea of what road travel was like before the internal combustion engine. The estate woodlands are extensive, and the nature trail only nibbles at the edges. A full and happy day can be spent at Arlington, and the meals in the restaurant are both delicious and sustaining.

Near the stables is the brick and timber granary which was brought here from Dunsland House – see the next chapter – after that building was destroyed by fire in 1967.

East from Barnstaple for a final flirtation with Exmoor, for the National Park boundary is only 1 mile (1.5km) from Brayford, a village on the A399 just past a succession of quarries. Also close to Brayford, at Cape of Good Hope Farm, is the **Exmoor Steam Railway**, which offers short trips on narrow gauge, steam trains.

Near the North Devon Coast

Baggy Point

Croyde (National Trust)
Mighty headland with easy circular walk.

Morte Point

Mortehoe (National Trust)
Gorse and grass-covered rocky headland with many walking possibilities.

Ilfracombe Museum

Small museum showing the rise of Ilfracombe in the nineteenth century.
☎ (01271) 863541

Torrs Walk

Ilfracombe (National Trust)
Gentle, well-engineered path up the cliffs west of Ilfracombe.

The Tunnels

Ilfracombe
Give access to Ilfracombe's tide-washed bathing pools.

Chambercombe Manor

Ilfracombe
Delightful old house containing contemporary furniture.
☎ (01271) 862624

Hele Mill

Ilfracombe
Working water mill with 18ft (6m) waterwheel.

Watermouth Castle

Combe Martin
Comprehensive tourist attraction in pleasant surroundings.
☎ (01271) 863879
Open: Easter to October, daily except Saturday. Telephone for opening times.

Combe Martin Church

One of the finest in Devon.

Combe Martin Motorcyle Collection

A museum of powered two-wheelers.
☎ (01271) 882346
Open: 10am-5pm daily, mid-May to end of October

Pack of Cards Inn

Combe Martin
Eccentric building shaped like a house of cards, with fifty-two windows etc.

Parracombe Church

An unaltered late eighteenth-century survivor.

Valley of Rocks

Lynton
Strange, rock-girt dry valley.

Exmoor Brass Rubbing Centre

Lynmouth
Make your own brass rubbings.
☎ (01598) 752529
Open: Easter to end of October, telephone for times.

Lyn and Exmoor Museum

Lynton
Fascinating ephemera collection.
☎ (01598) 752225
Open: 10am-12.30pm and 2-5pm Monday to Friday, 2-5pm Sunday, Easter to end of October.

Lynton and Lynmouth Cliff Railway

An effortless and exciting way to travel between the two places.

Glen Lyn Gorge

Lynmouth
Privately owned valley of the West Lyn River.

Watersmeet

Lynmouth (National Trust)
In valley woodlands Watersmeet House dispenses food, merchandise and information.
☎ (01598) 753348
Open: 10.30am-5.30pm daily, April to October.

Countisbury Hillfort

(National Trust)
Massive earthwork on Wind Hill.

Glenthorne Estate

Contains many walks, from County Gate (at an altitude of 1,000 ft) down to sea level.

Doone Country

Area of Exmoor made famous by Blackmore's book *Lorna Doone*.

Away from the Coast

Molland Church

Notable for its three-decker pulpit.

Quince Honey Farm

South Molton
The production of honey from plant to pot is described.
☎ (01769) 572401
Open: Shop all year, exhibition from Easter to October.

South Molton Museum

A typical small town museum in the Town Hall.
☎ (01769) 572951

Eggesford Forest Walks

Forest walks among the earliest Forestry Commission plantations.

North Devon Farm Park

Landkey, nr Barnstaple
Nature walks, animals, museum of farm life, fishing lakes.
☎ (01271) 830255
Open: 10am-5.30pm daily, April to September.

In and around Barnstaple

Chittlehampton Church

Devon's finest church tower. The pulpit and monuments are worth seeing too.

Cobbaton Combat Vehicles Museum

Chittlehampton
Collection of military vehicles.
☎ (01769) 540740
Open: 10am-6pm daily, Easter to October; most weekdays in winter.

Swimbridge Church

Splendid furnishings. The Rev Jack Russell is buried in the churchyard.

Barnstaple Market

One of Devon's premier pannier markets. Local produce.

Castle Mound

Barnstaple
Remains of Norman motte, now an environmental study area.

North Devon Leisure Centre

Barnstaple
All the popular indoor sports under one roof.

Barnstaple Heritage Centre

Queen Anne's Walk, Barnstaple
Exhibition of the history of Barnstaple.
☎ (01271 373003
Open: 10am-5pm Monday to Saturday in summer; 10am-4.30pm Monday to Friday, 10am-3.30pm Saturday, in winter.

Museum of Barnstaple and North Devon

The Square
Local antiquities from the Barnstaple area.
☎ (01271) 346747

Braunton

Pleasant spired church with many interesting features.

Braunton Great Field

Unusual medieval survivor of the open fields once common in England.

Braunton and District Museum

Small collection reflecting the town's seafaring and farming history.
☎ (01271) 816688

Arlington Court

near Blackmoor Gate
(National Trust)
Stately home containing collections of different kinds. Stands in a lovely park with a lake. Carriage collection and rides.
☎ (01271) 850296
Open: House, carriage collection and Victorian garden – 11am-5.30pm Sunday to Friday, April to early September; 11am-4pm early September to end of October (5.30pm on Sunday). Park – as house plus footpaths open from November to March during daylight hours.

Exmoor Zoological Park

South Stowford
Over 150 species, many hands-on opportunities.
☎ (01598) 763352
Open: 10am-6pm daily in summer, 10am-4pm daily in winter.

Exmoor Steam Railway

Cape of Good Hope Farm, nr Brayford
Half-size narrow-guage railway.
☎ (01598) 710711

The apologia at the beginning of the chapter on North Devon is equally appropriate here. The wide east-to-west rural corridor bulges across the whole of North-West Devon except for the lower Torridge Valley where commerce, industry and tourism have become established.

If the visitor first approaches this corner of the county from Barnstaple, as many will, along the busy bunga-low-lined B3233 through Bickington, Fremington and Yelland, this back-woods character is not obvious. The

new North Devon link road, the A39, connects Barnstaple with a high-level bridge downstream from Bideford.

INSTOW

Some 6 miles (9.5km) west of Barnstaple, **Instow** is reached, and can be swiftly bypassed if a distant destination beckons. But that would ignore a village of considerable dis-tinction. Sited in a similar position on its estuary as Starcross is on the Exe in South Devon, Instow pre-served its character by having the railway pass behind the sea front, and not in front as at Starcross. Also, it has splendid sands. Presumably a trick of the tides determines that some estuaries have muddy verges, and others have sandy beaches. Starcross is indisputably muddy, as indeed is Appledore, just across the Torridge from Instow. Mud is fine for wading birds and fishermen dig-ging for worms, but not much fun for family beach parties.

The small seventeenth-century pier hints at an early history, but major events have passed Instow by. An 1838 promotion, advertising 'newly erected baths, replete with water, hot and cold, and shower bathing', seems to have come to nothing, for no trace remains of the baths. Not the least of Instow's charms is its position facing Appledore, to which a foot ferry plies in summer.

A mile south of Instow is **Tapeley Park**, an undistinguished house with a fine garden. Originally built in the eighteenth century, it was Gothicised in the 1880s, and finally altered in 1901. The Christie family own Tapeley – John Christie founded Glyndebourne in 1931 – and his daughter still lives here. The house is open to the public in the summer, and is worth seeing for the furniture.

BIDEFORD

Bideford is, by common consent, the most attractive town in the northern half of Devon, and is reached by an ancient bridge from East-the-Water. The bridge probably dates from the end of the fifteenth century when a previous wooden bridge was used as a framework for the stone structure. Because the timbers of the old bridge were of different lengths, the stone arches inherited this uneven characteristic. Several widenings and re-buildings later, the bridge at last failed in 1968, when two arches at the west end collapsed. During the months that elapsed before restoration was complete, all traffic had to travel round narrow lanes to the south, though a footbridge was strung across the gap for pedestrians. A high-level bypass road bridge, some distance downriver, was opened in 1987.

The eighteenth-century wars and the collapse of the Devon woollen industry killed off overseas commerce, leaving a coastal trade which has survived to this day. In the nineteenth century, Bideford was a trans-shipment port for goods going further up the Torridge. Cargoes were unloaded into barges, which continued upstream to Weare Gifford or, between 1836 and 1871, up the Rolle Canal from above Bideford to upstream from Great Torrington. Bideford is now once again the port of embarkation for Lundy.

The Grenville Family

Bideford's business through out history has been the sea and ship building, and the town owes much to the Grenville family, who first acquired land there in Norman times, an interest they retained until 1744. Trade with Sir Richard Grenville's colonies of Virginia and Carolina continued until their independence, and in the meantime a wool trade had developed with Spain, Holland and France. Bideford was involved at an early stage with Newfoundland.

The town rises steeply from **the Quay**, and there are many corners worth seeking out. Bridgeland Street, at right angles to the Quay, is the street with most architectural pretensions. At the north end of the Quay is Charles Kingsley's statue. This nineteenth-century writer was born at Holne, on Dartmoor, and wrote at least some of his famous book *Westward Ho!* at the Royal Hotel in East-the-Water.

APPLEDORE AND WESTWARD HO!

Appledore must next be visited. Bideford and Appledore are inextricably linked and are only 10 minutes apart by car, though there is a pleasant 3 mile (5.5km) walk along the estuary edge footpath. The shipbuilding industry at Appledore is a present-day success story. The yard has moved with the times, is under cover and turns out ships of considerable size. Furthermore, the yard has not spoiled the town. It is therefore appropriate that the **North Devon Maritime Museum** is sited here in Odun Road above the town. Models, tools and photographs tell the story of the area's long maritime tradition.

Appledore is in two parts: the southern part behind the Quay, and Irsha Street beyond the church. This is a long narrow street, just wide enough for a car, with tempting little cobbled courtyards and slipways. Halfway along are three waterside public houses, and, at the far end, a pleasant open space with views across to Bideford Bar, the treacherous sand-shifting channel through which ships have to make their way in and out of the estuary, and only negotiable for 3 hours around high water. Imagine running for the 'safety' of the Bar in the days of sail, in failing light, and on a falling tide!

Westward Ho!, the self-catering holiday resort just 'round the corner' from Appledore is probably the only place to take its name from a book and the only place I know to include an exclamation mark. A nineteenth-century development company used the interest evoked in Kingsley's book to create a watering place at the southern end of **Northam Burrows**, a 650-acre (260 hectares) stretch of sand dunes, salt marsh and pasture. A hotel, church, a few terraces and villas were built, followed by a golf course on the Burrows – even a promenade-type pier, but the waves demolished it very quickly. Kipling was educated here in the United Services College, and later wrote up his schoolboy experiences in *Stalky & Co.* Last century, Westward Ho! expanded as a chalet, caravan and camping resort. The beach, of course, is wonderful; 2 miles (3km) of golden sand, backed by the Pebble Ridge which protects the Burrows from the Atlantic breakers, though now and again it has to be repaired. Northam Burrows is now a Country Park, administered by Devon County Council, and an excellent twenty-page guidebook describes every aspect of life on the Burrows, where the pursuits of riding and golf can be carried out, and explains where bathing is dangerous and where it is safe.

South-westwards from Westward Ho! the cliffs rise gradually and curve in a parabola towards Bucks Mills. But North-West Devon extends many miles to the south, and this vast inland district should be described before ending at the Cornish border.

GREAT TORRINGTON

Great Torrington is a hilltop town, the more attractive parts of which motorists normally miss. A long street of dull buildings ensures that the casual passer-by goes on his way oblivious of its charms. Visitors are strongly advised to penetrate to the heart of the town and explore for themselves. From one of the car parks on Castle Hill the land falls away down a steep slope of bracken and gorse. Round three sides of Great Torrington is an open common. Indeed, Great Torrington is sometimes spoken of as being the English Jerusalem by those who have visited the Holy Land. The slopes are contoured by many well kept paths, and a walk round the circuit probably takes 1 hour. The town is focused on **the Square**, where the Town Hall stands, with the **Market House** at the bottom end. The

Continued on page 164

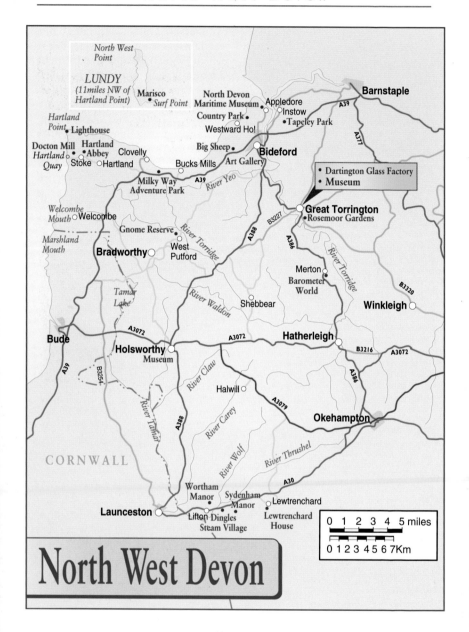

North West Devon

Instow

Bideford Bridge

museum is in the Town Hall as is Torrington 1646 heritage centre recreating an experience of life in the seventeenth century. Round the corner in Fore Street is the Plough Theatre, Cinema and Arts Centre, a lively community entertainments complex where something is going on most days.

Great Torrington has several thriving industries including the Dartington Glass factory, which opens its doors to visitors and glass is also on sale.

During the Civil War, in 1646, the church, which had been used as a powder magazine, was crowded with Royalist prisoners when the powder exploded, killing several hundred men. A mound in the churchyard may be the mass grave.

Just south of Great Torrington, beside the A3124, are the Rosemoor Gardens, well worth visiting for the variety of shrubs and plants growing in this sheltered valley.

The A386 going south towards Hatherleigh soon reaches Merton where Barometer World is a museum of the history of barometers in a workshop where barometers are still crafted. The A386 now continues through the ball clay area round Meeth and Petrockstowe. This deposit matches up geologically with the ball clay beds in the Bovey basin in South Devon.

NORTH OF DARTMOOR

Hatherleigh is a small market town with an old public house, the George, worth driving many miles to see. Market day is a wonderful gathering of rubicund farmers.

South of Hatherleigh, bestriding the A30 west of Okehampton, are three country houses of more

than usual interest. The first is Lewtrenchard House near Lewtrenchard village. This seventeenth-century house, now a hotel, was much altered by its famous nineteenth-century occupant, the Rev Sabine Baring-Gould (1834-1924), the author, folk song collector, antiquarian, and hymn writer (the author of 'Onward, Christian Soldiers').

The second house, Sydenham Manor, about 4 miles (6km) away along narrow lanes, is perhaps the finest Jacobean house in the county, but not open to the public.

About 7 or 8 miles (11-13km) north-west of Sydenham, beyond the A30 and Lifton, is Wortham Manor, an even earlier house, of the late fifteenth or early sixteenth century, somewhat reconstructed inside in the seventeenth. This splendid stone house was deteriorating when the Landmark Trust purchased it in 1969, and it has been converted into three holiday flats. The project received a Civic Trust Award in 1975. Despite being apparently at the back-of-beyond, this house has the new A30 passing nearby.

A very large reservoir to serve North Devon and Plymouth at Roadford on the River Wolf, just 4 miles (6km) to the north-east, offers fishing, sailing and picnic opportunities. Also close to Lifton, at Milford, is Dingle's Steam Village, which explores the history of steam power in the country, with various traction and other engines. There is also a village store selling souvenirs, and a childrens' play area.

The part of Devon around Halwill has a number of large Forestry Commission plantations, and several walks through the trees are laid out. As forestry operations can alter these arrangements, visitors are advised to contact the Forestry Commission office at Cookworthy Moor, near Beaworthy.

Holsworthy

Holsworthy is a market town serving a wide area of rural Devon, and is best visited on Wednesdays, when the Square swarms with traders and shoppers. Once a year, in July, the ancient St Peter's Fair is held in the town – as it has been since 1185! – and one of the charming traditions is the Pretty Maid Ceremony. This began in 1841 when a sum of money was left so that a local single woman under thirty, noted for her looks, quietness and attendance at church, should be given a small financial award. A seventeenth-century manor house contains the town museum.

At **West Putford**, not far from Bradworthy, is the **Gnome Reserve and Wildflower Garden**, where, in a woodland setting, over 1,000 gnomes may be seen living their immobile lives in a 'natural' environment. **Bradworthy** is an interesting village built round an enormous open space once used as a market. The well stocked shops are worth seeking out.

Not far away, and literally on the border with Cornwall, are the **Tamar Lakes,** two reservoirs straddling the infant River Tamar, the county boundary. In a part of Devon where there are few stretches of water, the lakes are much fre-quented by waterfowl and ornithologists. Sailing and boardsailing are possible, and there is a picnic area and water's edge footpaths. The upper lake is stocked with trout and the lower lake is a coarse fishery.

To the west of Bideford the A39 heads towards Clovelly, soon passing the **Big Sheep**, a farm experience. Children can touch the animals or try the adventure playground. Beyond, **Bucks Mills** is soon reached. The village has many similarities with Clovelly, our next stop; a steep, cottage-lined road, in a valley leading to a final drop to the beach. Bucks Mills is small and has a free car park at the top of the village. At the bottom a massive lime kiln is built above the beach.

From here the white buildings of Clovelly can be seen spilling out through the woods like a frozen coastal waterfall, and is best reached by the Hobby Drive (open from Easter to October for a small charge). This leaves the A39 a mile (1.5km) west of Bucks Cross and follows the contours of the wooded slopes for 3 miles (5km) to Clovelly. The name Hobby was given to it as its construction was the hobby of Sir James Hamlyn Williams, the landowner in the nineteenth century. Close to Bucks Mills, the **Milky Way Adventure Park** is the largest indoor children's adventure park in the south-west, with all the usual entertainments plus a few novelties – laser rifles and commando-type nets and swings.

CLOVELLY AND HARTLAND

Clovelly is the ace in the North-West Devon pack. There is nothing else like it in Great Britain. A very steep cobbled street lined with attractive flower-bedecked cottages occupies the entire width of a narrow north-facing valley. All cars are kept at the top, and supplies for properties in the valley have to be carried down or manhandled on sledges. The donkeys, which once provided transport, are retired, and there is a back road Land Rover service to the Red Lion on the Quay which takes people back up the hill. A beneficent landowner ensures that the place remains unspoilt, and despite the many thousands of visitors it receives annually, Clovelly has the strength of character to rise above the tourists. The tiny quayside has a period air about it. Fishermen are busy with their tackle and a lifeboat is stationed there.

The 8 mile (13km) walk along the **North Devon Coast Path** to **Hartland Point** is highly recommended, particularly in spring when the bluebells and primroses are in bloom. As there is no public transport at the far end, however, one must either backtrack or arrange to be met by car. The first part, as far as **Mouth Mill**, is in the Clovelly estate, and passes various small summerhouse follies, such as Angels' Wings, and Miss Woodall's Seat, an incredible clifftop viewpoint. The path descends to sea level at Mouth Mill, and there is another valley a short distance further on at Windbury but, having passed these, the path stays high all the way to Hartland Point. Just before the Point is reached, a truly beautiful beach will be seen, **Shipload Bay**, a rarity in these parts – a sandy beach, at least at low tide. The National Trust recently rebuilt the path down to the beach as the previous one had been swept away in a landslide.

The 3 mile (5km) clifftop walk from the Point to Hartland Quay is another fine walk, and is short enough for a there-and-back ramble. But most people will arrive at **Hartland Quay** by road.

In the days when England had an intensive railway network, **Hartland** boasted it was further from a railway than anywhere else in the country. Cars have made a difference, of

Continued on page 169

Hartland Point

However one returns, on foot or in a car, **Hartland Point** must be visited. This is Devon's own Land's End, a 90-degree turning point on the coast of the West Country, and here the scenery changes dramatically. Left behind are the gentle slopes and wooded combes of the Bristol Channel, for the cliffs and shoreline take on a malignant savagery not often seen even on an Atlantic-facing coast. Fretted reefs of black rock reach out like teeth on a saw.

There is a large car park (small fee), but no beach. Strongly recommended is a short stroll onto the west-facing coast, not visible from the car park. Walk along the coast path beside a wall outside the Trinity House gate as far as the first stile, from where the lighthouse can be seen. Beyond looms Lundy, 11 miles (17.5km) away, and this is the nearest point to it on the mainland.

Hartland Quay

I f Clovelly is the ace in the pack, **Hartland Quay** is the trump! On a calm day in summer everything appears benign. But a struggle to the Quay in a force nine gale in January is a very different matter. Enormous waves crash on this harsh and uncompromising coast. Yet, for over 250 years, a small harbour served this remote corner of Devon and gave a name to the spot. Skilfully sailed small boats edged in through the reefs, bringing coal, lime, slate, planks, nails and numerous domestic supplies. The record of the arrival of lead for the church roof is still in existence.

The last ship to discharge cargo was the *Rosamond Jane* in 1893, and by then the harbour had already begun to break up under the relentless battering of the Atlantic. By the 1920s it had all gone, and a major effort of the imagination is required to see where it stood. An excellent, well-illustrated 48-page book *Hartland Quay: The Story of a Vanished Port* is obtainable from the **Hartland Quay Museum**, giving the full history of this fascinating place. Two small rows of buildings at the Quay face the 'Street', where there is a hotel with a bar, a shop and lavatories. On the cliff to the north is a ruin which as it stands is probably an eighteenth-century folly, but may have been built from a earlier lookout.

North Devon Cliffs near Hartland

Tarka the Otter and the Tarka Trail

Henry Williamson settled in Georgeham, a village inland from Croyde, after his return from the 1914-18 War. There he wrote a book dealing with the life and death of an otter among the otter hunts in the Land of the Two Rivers, as the country between the Taw and the Torridge is known. The book – *Tarka the Otter* – was published in 1928 and won the Hawthornden Prize. Though Williamson lived to the north of the Torridge it was that river that he loved and he had his animal-hero born in a holt near the canal bridge on the river between Weare Gifford and Landcross, two hamlets about 3 km (2 miles) apart, Weare Gifford being about 5 km (3 miles) downriver from Great Torrington. At the end of the book the waters of Torridge close over the heads of Tarka and Deadlock, the otter-hound, as they fight their last battle close to Landcross.

Tarka the Otter is a book which arouses differing emotions: is it an indictment of the hunting of a beautiful creature by a man appalled by the casual slaughter of the trenches, or a glorification of country values, including otter-hunting?

Williamson wrote further books, several of which also document animal lives – *Salar the Salmon*, *Chakchek the Peregrine* – each of which, and most especially *The Lone Swallows*, evoke the atmosphere of North Devon in the first half of this century. He briefly moved to Norfolk, but when he died in 1977 he was buried at Georgeham.

An interesting project that takes its name from Williamson's otter hero has set up headquarters in Great Torrington – in the Eric Palmer Community Centre – with the aim of promoting conservation as well as recreation and tourism in North Devon. One aspect of the Tarka Project is of interest to walkers, as it involves the waymarking of the Tarka Trail, a 180 mile (290 km) walk. The walk is a figure-of-eight based on Barnstaple, going east and then north to Lynton and returning via Ilfracombe, and south through Bideford and Great Torrington to Okehampton, returning on a route to the east.

course, but it is still remote, and the inhabitants are more than usually self-reliant. The architecture is not outstanding, but the main street has charm, and to enter the shops or public houses is to experience old-fashioned service and courtesy. Inland from Hartland Town are extensive commercial tree plantations.

Hartland's great treasure, apart from the coastline, is its parish church at **Stoke**, 1 mile (1.5km) back from the sea, and over 2 miles (3km) from Hartland Town. The tower combines strength with grace. Inside, the main features are the late fifteenth-century rood screen, bench ends and wagon roofs. The church is worth cycling 30 miles (48km) against the wind to see, not only for the building but for its setting in a wind-torn landscape. Trees bow before the westerlies, gravestones lean, and there is a timeless aspect about everything which makes a mere mortal feel uplifted by the permanence of the place.

Hartland Abbey, a family home since 1539 with its furniture, porcelain and other family collections, is nearby. The Abbey was built in 1157 and dissolved by Henry VIII who then gifted it to the Seargeant of his Wine Cellar. Today visitors can also enjoy a beautiful woodland walk to the beach or wander the gardens, part of which was designed by Gertrude Jekyll.

A walk of about a mile (1.5km) southwards leads to **Speke's Mill Mouth** and the finest waterfall on the north-west Devon coast – a sheer 54ft (19m) drop. This walk is well worth doing, passing on the way the sliced-off hill known as St Catherine's Tor. Speke's Mill Mouth is the second valley going south. In Speke's Valley, **Docton Mill** is a working mill with Saxon origins set in delightful grounds. Its garden is open to the public, either side of the mill leat.

There is one further place on the coast that drivers can visit – **Welcombe Mouth**, though the lanes are narrow and there is little provision for parking. The church is a couple of miles inland. A sandy beach is exposed at low tide and the place is unspoilt, except for the cars. To escape one can climb out of Welcombe Mouth up the coast path to the south and as steeply descend to **Marsland Mouth**, a kind of replica valley, but devoid of vehicular intrusion, and briefly pretend that the twenty-first century doesn't exist, for Marsland Mouth is untainted by technology. What is more, it is only half Devon; beyond the stream is Cornwall, but that's another story...

LUNDY

The island of Lundy lies 11 miles (17.5km) north-north-west of Hartland Point. It is about 3 miles (5km) long and roughly half a mile wide. The *Oldenburg*, the island's own ship, sails from Bideford three times a week (twice a week in winter). Occasional pleasure trips by the paddle steamer *Waverley* are not to be relied upon, but are worth enquiring about. They usually go from Ilfracombe.

A recently completed pier has greatly improved disembarkation. There is then a steep climb up the beach road to the southern end of the 400ft (140m) plateau where most of the buildings are sited. The island was purchased in 1969 from the last of the private owners, the Harman family, by the National Trust, but the

Landmark Trust leases it from the National Trust and is responsible for its day-to-day running.

For those who want to stay on the island there are nineteen letting units of various types and a small hotel. Thirty campers can be accommodated. There is a small shop, a public house – the Marisco Tavern – and a church. There are no other artificial attractions; the beauty, wildlife and history are delights enough. The cliffs have a rugged grandeur unspoilt by any buildings.

The Old Light on the plateau dates from 1819, but as it was frequently obscured by fog it was replaced by the north and south lighthouses, which were built lower down the cliffs in 1896. A fog gun

battery on the west side is still *in situ* and is a fascinating place to observe sea birds and the interaction of waves and rocks. Both lighthouses are now automatic. (On a personal note the author's great-grandfather was the penultimate principal keeper of the Old Light. He left the island in 1893, and the author's grandfather spent his boyhood on Lundy).

Lundy should never be referred to as Lundy island. Lundy is Norse for 'puffin island'. The 'y' is the same suffix as is found in Guernsey, Alderney, Orkney, Anglesey, and so on.

Lundy is now linked to the mainland by telephone and a wind-powered electricity generator has been built to harness the winds that sweep across the island and to save fuel.

Places to Visit

In and around Bideford and Appledore

Tapeley Park
Instow
Fine gardens. Home of John Christie of Glyndebourne fame.
☎ (01271) 342371
Open: Easter to November, telephone for details.

North Devon Maritime Museum
Odum House, **Appledore**
Models, tools and photographs in an attractive display.
☎ (01237) 422064

Burton Art Gallery
Bideford
Exhibitions.
☎ (01237) 471455
Open all year.

Northam Burrows Country Park
An expansive salt marsh and sand dune area near Westward Ho!

Away from the Coast in North-West Devon

Castle Hill
Great Torrington
A beautiful open space beside the town, with miles of contouring paths.

Dartington Glass Factory

Great Torrington
The public may see quality glass being manufactured.
☎ (01805) 626242
Open: All year. Factory Tour/Visitor Centre – 9.30am-4pm Monday to Friday. Factory Shop – 9.30am-5pm Monday to Saturday, 10.30am-4.30pm Sunday.

Great Torrington Museum and Torrington 1646

Displays show how the Civil War affected the town.
☎ (01805) 624324 and 626146
Open: telephone for details

The Plough

Fore Street, Great Torrington
Theatre, cinema, arts centre and community enterprise.
☎ (01805) 624624

Rosemoor Gardens

Great Torrington
RHS gardens offering a great variety of settings and plants.
☎ (01805) 624067
Open: 10am-5pm (6pm in summer) daily, all year.

Barometer World

Merton
World's largest specialists in barometers. Museum and showroom.
☎ (01805) 603443
Open: 9am-5pm Tuesday to Saturday, all year.

Lewtrenchard House

Once the home of the Rev Sabine Baring-Gould, author and hymn writer, now a hotel.

Sydenham Manor

Lifton
Probably the finest Jacobean house in Devon. Not open to public.

Wortham Manor

Lifton
Early sixteenth-century house rescued from dereliction by the Landmark Trust.

Holsworthy Museum

A small town museum of considerable charm.
☎ (01409) 259337

Dingles Steam Village

History of steam power.
☎ (01566) 783425
Open: 10.30am-5.30pm Saturday to Thursday, Easter to the end of October.

Halwill Forest Walks

Holsworthy
Several opportunities to walk in one of Devon's largest forests.

Gnome Reserve and Wildflower Garden

West Putford
Hundreds of gnomes in a 'natural' environment.
☎ (0870) 8459012
Open: 10am-6pm daily, mid March to end of October.

Tamar Lakes

Bradworthy
Fishing possibilities on the Devon/Cornwall border.

Big Sheep

Abbotsham, Bideford
Themed farm with all-weather attractions.
☎ (01237) 472366
Open: 10am-6pm daily, April to October. 10am-5pm weekend and half-terms only, November to March.

The North-West Devon Coast

Milky Way Adventure Park

Voted one of the best 50 theme parks in the world.
☎ (01237) 431255
Open: Easter to end of October plus weekends and school holidays in winter.

Bucks Mills

A narrowly confined valley village leading down to a beach that disappears at high tide.

Clovelly

A beautifully-kept village with an extremely steep main street leading to the harbour.

Hobby Drive

Clovelly
A winding, wooded, private (small toll), unsurfaced drive from which you have glimpses of the sea.

Mouth Mill

Clovelly
Only to be reached by walking. A deep valley usually devoid of people.

Hartland Abbey

Sixteenth-century family home, gardens, dairy, museum.
☎ (01237) 441264
Open: 2-5.30pm Wednesday, Thursday, Sunday, bank holidays and Tuesdays in July and August, April to September. Gardens open Sunday to Friday April to October.

Hartland Church

Stoke
Wonderful tower, screen, bench ends and roof in bleak setting.

Hartland Point and Lighthouse

Savage turning point on coast where the Bristol Channel ends and the Atlantic begins.

Hartland Quay

The quay has gone, but the place remains. The small museum here should be visited.

Speke's Mill Mouth

Hartland
Has the finest coastal waterfall on the northern coast of Devon.

Docton Mill and Gardens

South of Hartland Point
Gardens around a working mill.
☎ (01237) 441369

Lundy

Unique and unspoilt, traffic-free island, owned by the National Trust; administered by the Landmark Trust.
☎ (01237) 431831 (island) (01237) 470422 (shore office)

HOW TO GET TO DEVON

Fact File

By Car
M4/M5 or M25/M3/A303/A30 to Exeter. A38 Devon Expressway links Exeter to Plymouth with access to all destinations in between. For north Devon leave M5 at J27 to Barnstaple.

By Rail
Direct services from London (Paddington), the Midlands, North of England, South Wales and Scotland. Contact National Rail Enquiry Office ☎ (0345) 484950 for further details or website, www.rail.co.uk/ukrail/home.htm

By Coach
National Express runs regular services to Devon from most areas of Britain. ☎ (0990) 808080 for details or website, http://www.eurolines.co.uk

By Air
Direct flights to Plymouth from Cork, Jersey, Guernsey, Paris and London Gatwick. Connecting flights from other UK destinations. Contact British Airways for further details, ☎ (0345) 222111 or website, www.british-airways.co.uk

By Sea
To Plymouth from Roscoff, Brittany and Santander, Spain. Contact Brittany Ferries, ☎ (0990) 360360 (Plymouth); ☎ (298) 292800 (Roscoff); ☎ (942) 220000 (Santander) or website, www.brittany-ferries.co.uk/home.htm

ACCOMMODATION

There is a very wide range of accommodation available throughout the area, from hotels, guest-houses, farmhouses, bed and breakfast establishments, inns and youth hostels, to caravan and camp sites, self-catering in all types of property and camping barns.

Hotels, Guest Houses, Bed and Breakfast, Inns
Details of this type of accommodation can be obtained from the appropriate local Tourist Information Centre. These are listed towards the end of the Fact File.

The Dartmoor Tourist Association issues a comprehensive guide to both serviced and self-catering accommodation in the Dartmoor area, ☎ (01822) 890567 or write to Dartmoor Tourist Association, The Duchy Building, Tavistock Road, Princetown, PL20 6QF. E-mail: enquiries@dartmoor-guide.co.uk

Farm Holidays

Cream of West Devon Farm Holiday Group
Helen Alford
☎ (01837) 861381

West Devon Friendly Farm Holiday Group,
Jane Pyle
☎ (01363) 82510

Farm and Cottage Holidays
☎ (01237) 479698 or website:
www.farmcott.co.uk

Heart of Devon Farm Holiday Group
Mrs L Olive
☎ (01884) 252321

Youth Hostels

Details of YHA hostels in the area from Youth Hostel Association, Via Gellia Mill, Bonsall, Matlock, Derbyshire. ☎ (0870) 870 8808 or website: www.yha.org.uk

Caravan and Camp Sites

Devon County Council produces a leaflet *DEVON Self-catering Holiday Parks, Caravan and Camping* which may be obtained from Devon Tourist Information Centre, Exeter Services, Sidmouth Road, Exeter, EX2 7HF, ☎ (01392) 437581 or e-mail ahopkins@mf.devon-cc.gov.uk or local Tourist Information Centres.

Self-Catering

Local Tourist Information Centres and the following agencies will be pleased to supply details of properties available or contact Devon TIC as above:

Dartmoor and South Devon Farm and Country Holidays
☎ (01364) 621391

Devon Connection
☎ (01548) 560964 or website
www.devonconnection.co.uk

Helpful Holidays
☎ (01647) 433593

North Devon Holiday Homes
☎ (01271) 376322 or website
www.northdevonholidays.co.uk

Salcombe Holiday Homes
☎ (01548) 843485 or website
www.salcombe.co.uk

South Devon Holiday Group
Linda Harvey
☎ (01626) 833266

Camping Barns

There are a number of camping barns on Dartmoor. For details ☎ (01271) 324420.

Specialist Holidays

For details of "Activity Holidays, Learning Holidays and Event Packages" contact Economy and Tourism, Exeter City Council, Civic Centre, Paris Street, Exeter, EX1 1JJ. ☎ (01392) 265900.

'Last Minute' Bookings
Contact the Devon TIC
☎ (01392) 437581 or e-mail
ahopkins@mf.devon-cc.gov.uk
Give details of the location, type and price range of the accommodation being sought and they will try to find what is wanted and make the booking.

BIRD WATCHING SITES

Berry Head Country Park, Brixham
Dawlish Warren, east of Dawlish.
Exe Estuary, reserves on east and west shores.
Fernworthy Reservoir, approx. 6 miles west of Mortenhampstead
Lundy, 10 miles off north Devon coast.
Prawle Point, south of Kingsbridge.
Slapton Ley Nature Reserve, nr Torcross.
Tamar Lakes, north-west of Holsworthy
Yarner Wood, between Bovey Tracey and Manaton.
Taw Estuary, near Barnstaple

BOAT TRIPS

Dart Pleasure Craft Ltd
Dartmouth
☎ (01803) 834488
Cruises and private hire.

Estuary Boat Trips
Salcombe
☎ (01548) 844475

Ocean Adventures
Torquay
☎ (01803) 770666.
Wildlife cruises.

Plymouth Boat Cruises Ltd
☎ (01752) 822797/822202

Rivermaid
Salcombe
☎ (01548) 853525/853607
Kingsbridge to Salcombe ferry cruises and scenic creeks and coastal excursions.

Tamar Cruising
Plymouth
☎ (01752) 822105

Tarka Cruises, Appledore
☎ (01237) 476191

CYCLING

Devon County Council publishes details of a number of cycling routes in Devon covering long and short distances and including some off-road routes. A free leaflet, *Making Tracks – cycle routes in Devon* gives the details. ☎ (0870) 60 85 531.

The Dartmoor Way is a circular route around Dartmoor of 90 miles (145km). In addition Dartmoor National Park Authority publishes a guide to cycling on Dartmoor and three leaflets (£1.00 each) showing suitable off-road routes. They are available from all National Park Information Centres or ☎ (01822) 890414.

There are three leaflets (0.75p each) available about cycling in the Exmoor National Park. These are available from Exmoor National Park Visitor Centre, Dulverton, TA22 9EX, ☎ (01398) 323841.

Remember cycling is only allowed on public roads, byways open to all traffic, public bridlepaths and Forestry Commission roads. Cycling is not permitted on public footpaths, common land or open moorland.

FACILITIES FOR THE DISABLED

The English Riviera Tourist Board publishes a free leaflet *Information for the Disabled,* which details facilities, specialist equipment hire, transport, hotels, restaurants, tourist attractions, car parking etc and also local organisations and associations which can offer help and advice. Contact the Tourist Centre, Vaughan Parade, Torquay, TQ2 5JG, ☎ (01803) 296296 or e-mail tourist.board@torbay.gov.uk or website www.torbay.gov.uk

For information on accessible areas on Dartmoor there is a leaflet *Easygoing Dartmoor* available from local information centres or ☎ (01822) 890414.

Accessible Exmoor – a Guide for Disabled People is available free of charge, from TICs or National Park Information Centres.

FERRIES

Bideford
(and Ilfracombe in summer)
to Lundy on *MS* Oldenburg.
☎ (01237) 470422
All year, fewer services in winter.

Dartmouth to Kingswear
Operates all year, approximately every 10 minutes, vehicles and passengers.

Salcombe/East
Portlemouth Ferry
☎ (01548) 842061
Runs all year to and from Salcombe and East Portlemouth.

South Sands Ferry
☎ (01548) 561035
Runs South Sands to Salcombe between Easter and the end of October half-term.

Western Lady Ferry Service
☎ (01803) 852041 (Brixham) and (01803) 297292. Runs from Torquay to Brixham and return, May to 2nd or 3rd week in October; daily in July, August and September, not Saturdays in May, June and October. Details of other ferry services that are useful when walking the coastal paths may be found in the South West Way Association guide, ☎ (01803) 873061.

FISHING

Reservoirs in Devon are available for fishing. For details of locations, species, fishing methods, permits and seasons contact South West Water Leisure Services, ☎ (01837) 871565.
    A guide to angling in and around Torbay price £1.00 is available, ☎ (01803) 297428.

Newhouse Fishery
Totnes
☎ (01548) 821426.
offers sheltered lake for fly fishing. Beginner's lake also available with free tuition for beginners.

Home Farm Fishery
Kenton, nr Exeter
☎ (01626) 866259.
offers coarse fishing.
Bait available on site.

GOLF

There are several golf courses in the area which accept non-members on payment of green fees. A selection only is given here.

Ashbury Golf Course
Okehampton
☎ (01837) 55453

Bigbury Golf Course
nr Salcombe
☎ (01548) 810207

**Dartmouth Golf
and Country Club**
☎ (01803) 712686

Dainton Park
Newton Abbot
☎ (01803) 813812

Ilfracombe Golf Club
☎ (01271) 862176

**Mortehoe and
Woolacombe Golf Club**
☎ (01271) 870225)

Royal North Devon Golf Club
☎ (01237) 473817

Saunton Golf Club
☎ (01271) 812436

Teign Valley Golf Club
☎ (01647) 253026

Teignmouth Golf Club
☎ (01626) 772894

Torquay Golf Club
☎ (01803) 327471

Torrington Golf Club
☎ (01805) 622229

Wrangaton Golf Club, nr South Brent ☎ (01364) 73229

GUIDED CITY TOURS

Exeter City Council Red Coat Guides offer free guided walks around the City, on a variety of themes, between April and October. Most walks last 1 to 2 hours and there are between 4 and 6 a day to choose from. Between November and March there is a reduced programme of 2 tours per day (1 on Sunday, afternoon only). ☎ (01392) 265212 for full details.

GUIDED WALKS

Dartmoor National Park Authority offers a programme of guided walks from June to mid-October. They vary from gentle ½ hour strolls to full days on the high moors. All walks have a theme whether it be wildlife, archaeology, sketching, navigation skills, strolls by moonlight or picnic walks. A small charge is made for participants unless they arrive by public transport (ticket to be shown to walk leader) in which case the walk is FREE. Full programme available from local Tourist Information Centres and published in *DARTMOOR visitor*, the annual free information newspaper issued by the Park Authority. ☎ (01822) 890414 for further information.

Exmoor National Park Authority offers guided walks. Contact Exmoor National Park Authority, Exmoor House, Dulverton, TA22 9HL, ☎ (01398) 323665 or any National Park information centre for details.

LOCAL EVENTS AND FESTIVALS

Ashburton
Early July, Carnival; early November, Winter Carnival

Bampton
October, Pony Fair

Barnstaple,
Late May, Jazz Festival; September, Fair and Carnival week

Bideford
September, Carnival and Regatta

Chagford
August, Agricultural and Flower Show

Exeter
mid-May, Devon County Show; late May/early June, Exeter Festival

Great Torrington
first Thursday in May, Torrington May Fair

Hatherleigh
November, Carnival

Holsworthy
May, Agricultural Show; July, St Peter's Fair; November, Carnival

Honiton
July, Fair with Hot Pennies ceremony; August, Agricultural Show; October, Carnival

Ilfracombe
June, North Devon Festival; all summer, Evening Entertainment on the seafront; July/August, Sea Fishing Festival

Kingsbridge
July, Fair Week

Modbury
May, Carnival

Moretonhampstead
August, Carnival, Horse and Flower Show

Fact File

Newton Abbot
May, Merrymakers' Day; July, Carnival; September, Cheese and Onion Fair

Okehampton
August, Show; October, Carnival

Ottery St Mary
November, Carnival and Tar Barrel Rolling

Plymouth
August Bank Holiday weekend, Plymouth Navy Days

Sidmouth
August, International Folk Festival

South Molton
last Wednesday in August, Sheep Fair

Tavistock
May, Show; June, Annual Art Exhibition; July, Carnival; October, Tavistock Goose Fair

Torbay
July/August, Torbay Carnival, August, Regattas at Paignton, Dartmouth, Torbay and Brixham; December, Torquay Christmas Carnival

Totnes
every Tuesday morning May-September, Elizabethan Market

Widecombe-in-the-Moor
September, Widecombe Fair Many more events both large and small happen throughout the region and details will always be available at TICs and in the free tourist newspapers which are readily available.

MAPS

The following Ordnance Survey maps cover the area included in this book:

Explorer Series, 1:25 000 scale (4cm to 1km or 22in to 1 mile)
108 *Lower Tamar Valley & Plymouth*
110 *Torquay & Dawlish*
112 *Launceston & Holsworthy*
113 *Okehampton*
114 *Exeter & the Exe Valley*
115 *Exmouth & Sidmouth*
126 *Clovelly & Hartland*
127 *South Molton & Chulmleigh*
139 *Bideford, Ilfracombe & Barnstaple*

Outdoor Leisure Series, 1:25 000 scale (4cm to 1km or 22in to 1 mile)
9 *Exmoor*
20 *South Devon - Brixham to Newton Ferrers*
28 *Dartmoor*

Landranger Series, 1: 50 000 scale (2cm to 1km or 13in to 1 mile)
180 *Barnstaple & Ilfracombe*
190 *Bude & Clovelly*
191 *Okehampton & North Dartmoor*
192 *Exeter & Sidmouth*
201 *Plymouth & Launceston, Tavistock & Looe*
202 *Torbay & South Dartmoor, Totnes & Salcombe*

Fact File

PUBLIC TRANSPORT

There is an increasing network of public transport throughout the area, enabling visitors to travel in comfort without the strain of driving and the problems of parking. Everyone can enjoy the view and linear walks become possible as there is no need to return to the car at the end of the day. Fewer cars on the roads will make this lovely area a pleasanter place for everyone to enjoy. Local TICs will always be delighted to supply up-to-date information.

Traveline – all public transport enquiries in the south west - ☎ (0870) 608 2608

Devon Bus Enquiry line – timetable information for all local bus services - ☎ (01392) 382800 Monday to Friday 8.30am-5pm. www.devon.gov.uk/devonbus

In addition to the main railway line serving the south coast, the Tarka Line runs between Exeter and Barnstaple. There are also a number of private railways in the area. All rail enquiries to ☎ (0845) 748 4950.

In the Torbay area Stagecoach Devon operates local services which include rover tickets for use throughout the Torbay area. Open top buses run along the routes in the sea front area and by taking the bus to Paignton Zoo visitors receive a discount on admission. Combined tickets are available for journeys using the Paignton to Kingswear Steam Railway, the Dartmouth Ferry, a cruise from Dartmouth to Totnes and return from Totnes by bus. Contact Stagecoach Devon, ☎ (01803) 613226 or enquire at the Tourist Information Centres for more details.

There are regular interlinking bus services to and across Dartmoor. Trains run along the Exeter to Plymouth line, the Tamar Valley line and on Sundays the Exeter to Okehampton line. These give access to towns on the edge of Dartmoor and, by connecting buses, to areas further afield. Anyone joining a Dartmoor National Park Guided Walk who arrives by public transport will not have to pay a fee for the walk.

The Dartmoor Public Transport Guide (published late May), available from National Park Information Centres gives all details or contact the Devon Bus Enquiry Line ☎ (01392), (01803) or (01271) 382800.

Exmoor National Park Authority produces a Public Transport leaflet for the area, available from information centres or ☎ (01398) 323665.

Plymouth Citybus operate The Discoverer, a regular circular service round the City which connects the railway station with the main tourist attractions. Day tickets enable unlimited travel round the city for the day, visiting as many attractions as possible in the time. Combined rail/Discoverer tickets available from all stations in the region. ☎ (01752) 222221 for details.

SWIMMING POOLS (INDOOR)

Brixham Pool
Higher Ranscombe Road
☎ (01803) 857151

Holsworthy Leisure Centre
☎ (01409) 254013

South Dartmoor
Leisure Centre
Leonards Road
Ivybridge
☎ (01752) 896999

Quayside Leisure Centre
Rope Walk
Kingsbridge
☎ (01548) 857100

Torbay Leisure Centre
Paignton
☎ (01803) 522240

Central Park Leisure Pools
Plymouth
☎ (01752) 560436

Seaton Pool
Plymouth
☎ (01752) 778355

Plymouth Pavilions
☎ (01752) 222200

Plympton Pool
☎ (01752) 348459

Meadowlands Leisure Pool
Tavistock
☎ (01822) 617774

Chestnut Avenue
Torquay
☎ (01803) 299992

Swim Torquay
Plainmoor
Torquay
☎ (01803) 323400

Torridge Pool
Northam, Nr Appledore
☎ (01237) 471794

Torrington Leisure Centre
☎ (01805) 623085

TOURIST INFORMATION CENTRES

Those Centres marked with asterisks are open in the summer only.

*Axminster
☎ (012970) 34386

Barnstaple
☎ (01271) 375000

Bideford
☎ (01237) 477676

Bovey Tracey
☎ (01626) 832047

Braunton
☎ (01271) 816400

Brixham
☎ (01803) 206306

Budleigh Salterton
☎ (01395) 445275

*Combe Martin
☎ (01271) 883319

*Crediton
☎ (01363) 772006

Dartmouth
☎ (01803) 834224

Dawlish
☎ (01626) 863589

Exeter
☎ (01392) 265700

Exmouth
☎ (01395) 222299

Holsworthy
☎ (01409) 254185

Honiton
☎ (01404) 43716

Ilfracombe
☎ (01271) 863001

Ivybridge (South Dartmoor Tourist Information)
☎ (01752) 897035

Kingsbridge
☎ (01548) 853195

Lynton
☎ (01598) 752225

*Modbury
☎ (01548) 830159

*Moretonhampstead
☎ (01647) 440043

Newton Abbot
☎ (01626) 367494

*Okehampton
☎ (01837) 53020

*Ottery St Mary
☎ (01404) 813964

Paignton
☎ (01803) 206306

Plymouth
☎ (01752) 304849

Salcombe
☎ (01548) 843927

Seaton
☎ (01297) 21660

Sidmouth
☎ (01395) 516441

*South Molton
☎ (01769) 574122

Tavistock
☎ (01822) 612938

Teignmouth
☎ (016260 779769

Tiverton
☎ (01884) 255827

Torquay
☎ (01803) 206306

Torrington
☎ (01805) 626140

Totnes
☎ (01803) 863168

*Woolacombe
☎ (01271) 870553

WALKING

There are a number of walking trails in the area. Contact any TIC for a free leaflet *Making Tracks – walking trails in* Devon, outlining the routes or ☎ (0870) 6085531.

The Dartmoor Way is a 90-mile (145km) walking route around the moor. For detailed information and map packs ☎ (01364) 653426. Additional information about walks on Dartmoor can be obtained from High Moorland Visitor Centre, ☎ ((01822) 890414 or www.dartmoor-npa.gov.uk

For information about walking on the 700 odd miles of footpaths and bridleways on Exmoor contact the National Park Office ☎(01398) 323665 or www.exmoor-nationalpark.gov.uk

The South West Coast Path runs for part of its 630 mile length along the South Devon coast. The South West Way Association produces a guide to the route with details of accommodation, transport, ferries and tide tables. South West Way Association ☎ (01803) 873061.

WATERSPORTS

All forms of watersports can be enjoyed around the coast of Devon. For up-to-date information on facilities, tides, weather etc. contact the nearest TIC.

WEATHER

For 1 to 10 day forecasts for Devon call Weatherline
☎ (0891) 600256
For coastal forecast for sailors use Marine Call ☎ (0891) 500458

LANDMARK VISITORS GUIDES

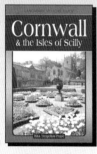

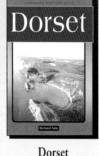

Cornwall
ISBN: 1 901522 09 1
256pp, Full colour
£9.95

Oxford
ISBN: 1 84306 022 1
224pp, Full colour
£9.95

Dorset
ISBN: 1 84306 001 9
240pp, Full colour
£9.95

Somerset
ISBN: 1 901522 40 7
224pp, Full colour
£10.95

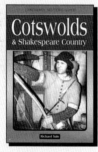

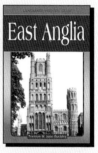

Cotswolds
ISBN: 1 84306 002 7
224pp, Full colour
£9.99

Hampshire
ISBN: 1 901522 14 8
224pp, Full colour
£9.95

East Anglia
ISBN: 1 901522 58 X
224pp, Full colour
£9.95

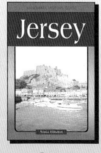
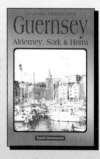

Scotland
ISBN: 1 901522 18 0
288pp, Full colour
£11.95

Jersey
ISBN: 1 901522 93 8
224pp, Full colour
£9.99

Guernsey
ISBN: 1 901522 48 2
224pp, Full colour
£9.95

Harrogate
ISBN: 1 901522 55 5
96pp, Full colour
£4.95

To order send a cheque/Visa/MasterCard/Switch details to:
Landmark Publishing, Waterloo House, 12 Compton, Ashbourne, Derbyshire
DE6 IDA England Tel: 01335 347349 Fax: 01335 347303
e-mail: landmark@clara.net web site: www.landmarkpublishing.co.uk

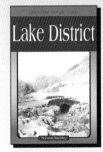

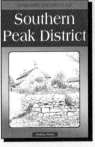

Lake District
ISBN: 1 901522 38 5
224pp, Full colour
£9.95

Peak District
ISBN: 1 901522 25 3
240pp, Full colour
£9.99

Southern Lakeland
ISBN: 1 901522 53 9
96pp, Full colour
£5.95

Southern Peak
ISBN: 1 901522 27 X
96pp, Full colour
£5.95

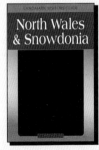

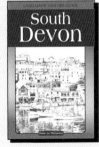

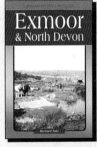

N. Wales & Snowdonia
ISBN: 1 84306 043 4
96pp, Full colour
£5.95

South Devon
ISBN: 1 901522 52 0
96pp, Full colour
£5.95

Exmoor & N. Devon
ISBN: 1 901522 95 4
96pp, Full colour
£5.95

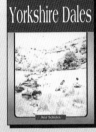

New Forest
ISBN: 1 901522 70 9
96pp, Full colour
£5.95

Isle of Wight
ISBN: 1 84306 053 1
96pp, Full colour
£5.95

Yorkshire Dales
ISBN: 1 901522 41 5
224pp, Full colour
£9.95

Pack
2 months
into
2 weeks
with your
**Landmark
Visitors
Guides**

Index

A

Abbots' Way, *Dartmoor* 105
Allhallows Museum 33
Ancient tracks 104
Anstey's Cove 53
Appledore 160
Arlington Court 154
Ashburton 132
Ashclyst Forest 36
Ashcombe Family Activities 52
Athelstan's Tower, *Exeter* 24
Aune Head Mire, *Dartmoor* 134
Axe Valley 33
Axminster 33

B

Babbacombe Model Village 54
Badgworthy Water 150
Baggy erratic 141
Baggy Point 141
Bampton 150
Barbican Glass, *Plymouth* 84
Barnstaple 152
Barnstaple Heritage Centre 152
Barometer World, *Merton* 164
Bayard's Cove 60
Becky Falls, *Dartmoor* 133
Beer 32
Beer Heights Light Railway 33
Beer Quarry Caves 32
Bennett's Cross, *Dartmoor* 128
Bere Alston 95

Bere Ferrers 95
Berry Head Country Park 58
Berry Pomeroy Castle 57
Berrynarbor 144
Betsy Grimball's Tower 97
Bickleigh 37
Bickleigh Castle 37
Bickleigh Mill Craft Centre and Farm 37
Bideford 160
Bigbury-on-Sea 70
Blackmoor Gate 145
Blackpool Sands 65
Blackwood Path, The 105
Bolt Head 69
Bolt Tail 69
Bovey Tracey 110
Bovisand Bay 92
Bowden House 64
Bowerman's Nose 103
Bradley Manor 50
Bradworthy 165
Branscombe 32
Branscombe Bakery 32
Branscombe church 32
Branscombe Mouth 32
Braunton 153
Braunton Burrows 154
Braunton Great Field 153
Brent Tor, *Dartmoor* 117
Brixham 57
Brixham Museum 58
Broadhembury 33
Bronze Age, The 8, 108
Brunel's 1846 Atmospheric Railway 39
Brutus Stone 63
Buckfast Butterflies and Dartmoor Otter Sanctuary 132
Buckland Abbey 95

Buckland Beacon 133
Buckland Monachorum 96
Buckland-in-the-Moor 133
Bucks Mills 165
Budleigh Salterton 29
Buller's Hill 38
Burgh Island 70
Burrator Reservoir 129
Butterwalk, *Bayard's Cove* 60
Butterwalk, *Totnes* 63
Bygones Museum 53

C

Cann quarry canal 93
Canonteign Falls and Farm Park 48
Castle Drogo 123
Castle Mound, *Barnstaple* 152
Cathedral Close, *Exeter* 25
Cattewater, *Plymouth* 85
Chagford 121
Challaborough 70
Challacombe Cross, *Dartmoor* 109
Chambercombe Manor, *Ilfracombe* 142
Chanter's House 35
Childe's Tomb, *Dartmoor* 108
Chittlehampton 151
Chudleigh 48
Chudleigh Rocks 48
City wall, *Exeter* 20
Clovelly 165
Cobbaton 151
Cobbaton Combat Vehicles Museum 151
Coburg Terrace 31
Cockington 53

Coffin Stone, *Dartmoor* 115
Coldharbour Mill 36
Coleton Fishacre Garden 60
Colyton 33
Combe Martin 144
Combe Martin Motorcycle
    Collection 144
Compton Castle 57
Connections Discovery
    Centre, *Exeter* 24
Cookworthy Museum,
    Kingsbridge 68
Copplestone 13
Cornhill 35
Countess Wear 28
Countisbury 148
Countisbury church 148
Cranmere Pool,
    Dartmoor 134
Crediton 37
Cremyll foot ferry,
    Plymouth 89
Crockern Tor,
    Dartmoor 128
Crownhill Fort 92
Croyde 142
Croyde Bay 141
Cullompton 36
Custom House, *Exeter* 20
Custom House,
    Plymouth 84

D
Dark Ages, The 12
Dartington Glass factory,
    Great Torrington 164
Dartington Hall 64
Dartmeet 115
Dartmoor National Park
    Information Centres 112
Dartmoor Prison 116
Dartmoor Wildlife Park 92
Dartmouth 60
Dawlish 51
Dawlish Museum 51

Dawlish Warren 39
Dean Prior 129
Devon War Memorial 24
Devonport 80
Dewerstone 129
Dingle's Steam Village 164
Docton Mill 169
Doric Guildhall,
    Plymouth 89
Drake, Sir Francis 16
Drewsteignton 123
Duke of Cornwall Hotel,
    Plymouth 88
Dunnabridge Pound 115

E
East Budleigh 29
East Prawle 66
Eggesford Forest 151
Egyptian Oddfellows Hall,
    Plymouth 89
Elburton 91
Erme Estuary 70
Exeter 19
Exeter Cathedral 24
Exeter Phoenix 25
Exeter War Memorial 24
Exmoor National Park 144
Exmoor Steam Railway 154
Exmoor Zoological
    Park 154
Exmouth 28
Exmouth Dock 28
Exmouth Museum 29

F
Fairlynch Arts Centre and
    Museum 29
Farway Countryside Park 33
Filleigh 151
Finch Foundry Museum
    of Waterpower,
    Sticklepath 121
Five Cross Way 150
Flete 70

Forde House 50
Foreland Point 149
Fort Bovisand 91
Fortfield Terrace 31
Fox Tor Mire,
    Dartmoor 134
Fursdon House 37

G
Gallants Bower 61
Gammon Head 66
Gibbet Hill 117
Gidleigh 121
Glen Lyn Gorge 148
Glenthorne Valley 149
Gnome Reserve and
    Wildflower Garden 165
Gorse Blossom Park 112
Great Exmouth 'oo' Model
    Railway 29
Great Tor, *Dartmoor* 113
Great Torrington 161
Grimpen Mire,
    Dartmoor 106
Grimspound,
    Dartmoor 109
Guildhall, *Exeter* 23

H
Haldon Hills 38
Haldon Racecourse 39
Hallsands 66
Halwill 164
Hameldon 113
Hartland 166
Hartland Abbey 169
Hartland Point 166
Hartland Quay 166
Hatherleigh 164
Hawkins, Sir John 16
Hay Tor, *Dartmoor* 112
Hay Tor granite tramway,
    Dartmoor 112
Hayes Barton 29
Heanton Punchardon 153

Hedgehog Hospital 49
Hele Bay 143
Hembury Fort 33
Hemyock 36
Hemyock Castle 36
High Moorland Visitor
  Centre, *Dartmoor* 129
Higher Ley 65
Higher Market, *Exeter* 21
Hilltown trail, *Eggesford
  Forest* 151
Hoe, The 85
Home Valley walk,
  Eggesford Forest 151
Honiton 33
Hooken Landslip 32
Hope Cove 69
Hound Tor, *Dartmoor*
  113, 133
House of Marbles, *Bovey
  Tracey* 112

I
Ilfracombe 142
Ilfracombe Museum 142
Instow 159
Iron Age, The 8
Iron Bridge, *Exeter* 21
Island House, *Plymouth* 84

J
Jennycliff Bay 91
Jobbers' Path, *Dartmoor*
  105

K
Kenton 39
Kent's Cavern 7, 53
Ker Street, *Plymouth* 89
Kes Tor, *Dartmoor* 121
Killerton 35
King Way, *Dartmoor* 105
Kingsbridge 68
Kingswear 60
Kirkham House 56

Kitley Caves 92
Knightshayes Court 36
Knowle House, *Kingsbridge*
  68

L
Lawrence Castle 38
Lee 142
Leech Wells, *Totnes* 64
Lewtrenchard House 164
Lich Way, *Dartmoor* 105
Lifton 164
Little Dartmouth 61
Longaford Tor, *Dartmoor*
  116
Longhouse 106
Lorna Doone 150
Loughwood Meeting House
  33
Lukesland Gardens 129
Lundy 169
Lydford 117
Lydford Castle 118
Lydford Gorge 119
Lympstone 28
Lyn and Exmoor Museum,
  Lynton 148

M
Manaton 133
Market Square, *Dartmouth*
  60
Marsland Mouth 169
Martinhoe 12, 145
Mayflower Stone,
  Plymouth 84
Meadfoot Beach 53
Merchant's House,
  Plymouth 81
Merrivale 116
Merton 164
Middle Ages, The 15
Milky Way Adventure
  Park 165
Minadab 51

Miniature Pony Centre
  126
Modbury 70
Molland 150
Mol's Coffee House,
  Exeter 25
Moretonhampstead 125
Morte Point 142
Mortehoe 142
Morwellham 97
Mother Hubbard's
  Cottage 92
Mount Batten 78
Mouth Mill 166
Museum of Dartmoor Life,
  Okehampton 120
Museum of Maritime and
  Local History, *Salcombe*
  69

N
National Armada
  Memorial, *Plymouth* 85
National Marine
  Aquarium, *Plymouth* 84
Naval War Memorial,
  Plymouth 85
New Street, *Plymouth* 84
Newcomen, Thomas 61
Newton Abbot 49
Newton Ferrers 70
Norman Lockyer
  Observatory, *Sidmouth*
  31
Normans, The 13
North Devon Coast Path
  145, 166
North Devon Farm Park
  151
North Devon Leisure
  Centre, *Barnstaple* 153
North Devon Maritime
  Museum, *Appledore* 161
North Gate, *Exeter* 21
North Hessary Tor 116

Northam Burrows 161
Northernhay Gardens,
   Exeter 24
Noss Mayo 70

O
Oddicombe 53
Okehampton 120
Old Blundells School,
   Tiverton 36
Old Burrow 12
Old Chancel, *Sidmouth* 31
Oldway 56
Orchid Paradise 49
Otterton 30
Otterton Mill 30
Ottery St Mary 35
Overbecks House,
   Salcombe 69
Overbecks Museum,
   Salcombe 69

P
Pack of Cards Inn,
   Combe Martin 144
Paignton 54
Paignton and Dartmouth
   Steam Railway 56
Paignton Zoo 56
Paradise Copse 36
Parliament Street,
   Exeter 24
Parracombe 145
Paternoster Row 35
Pecorama 33
Penrose Almshouses,
   Barnstaple 153
Pinetum 149
Plym Bridge Woods 92
Plymouth 81
Plymouth Breakwater 85
Plymouth Museum and Art
   Gallery 88
Plymouth Pavilions 88
Plympton 80

Plympton St Maurice 89
Plymstock 91
Ponsworthy 115
Poultry Walk, *Totnes* 63
Powder Mills, *Dartmoor*
   128
Prawle Point 66
Prayer Book Rebellion 16
Princetown 128
Prysten House, *Plymouth*
   81

Q
Quay House, Exeter 20
Quaywest 56
Queen Anne's Walk,
   Barnstaple 152
Quince Honey Farm, *South
   Molton* 151

R
Revelstoke church 70
Revelstoke Drive 70
River Dart Country Park
   133
Riverside Mill, *Bovey
   Tracey* 112
Rock End Gardens 54
Romans, The 9
Rosemoor Gardens 164
Rougemont Gardens,
   Exeter 24
Royal Albert Memorial
   Museum, , *Exeter* 21
Royal Citadel, *Plymouth*
   84
Royal Glen Hotel 31
Royal Marine Barracks,
   Plymouth 88
Royal Naval College,
   Dartmouth 60
Royal William Victualling
   Yard, *Plymouth* 89
Rundlestone Cross 116
Rushford Mill 121

S
Salcombe 68
Salcombe Regis 32
Salcombe Youth Hostel 69
Saltram House 89
Sandy Bay 29
Saunton Sands 141
Saxon, The 13
Scorhill Circle, *Dartmoor*
   121
Seaton 32
Seven Thorns 149
Shaldon 52
Shaldon Wildlife Trust 52
Shambles, *Kingsbridge* 68
Sharp Tor 69
Shaugh Prior 93, 129
Shinner's Bridge 64
Shipload Bay 166
Shobrooke Park 37
Sidmouth 30
Sidmouth Museum 31
Sisters' Fountain 149
Slapton 66
Slapton Ley Field Centre
   65
Slapton Sands 65
Smeaton's Tower,
   Plymouth 85
Sorley Tunnel Adventure
   Farm, Kingsbridge 68
South Brent 129
South Devon Coast Path
   33, 52, 58
South Devon Railway 132
South Gate, *Exeter* 20
South Hams 64
South Molton 150
Spanish barn 53
Speke's Mill Mouth 169
Spinster's Rock 8
Spirit of Plymouth
   Blackfriars Distillery 81
St Andrew's Church,
   Plymouth 81

St Mary Steps church,
Exeter 21
St Nicholas' Priory,
Exeter 21
Staddon Heights,
Plymouth 85
Stamford Fort 91
Starcross 39
Start Point Lighthouse 66
Sticklepath 120
Stoke 169
Stoke Point 70
Stover Country Park 49
Sutton Harbour 84
Swimbridge 151
Sydenham Manor 164

T
Tamar Lakes 165
Tapeley Park 159
Tarka Trail 168
Tavistock 96
Teign Valley Glassworks,
Bovey Tracey 112
Teignmouth 51
Teignmouth Museum 52
Telegraph Hill 39
The Deep, Brixham 58
The Lower Ley 65

Thurlestone 70
Tiverton 36
Tiverton Museum 36
Topsham 25
Torbryan 50
Torcross 66
Torquay 7, 52
Torquay Museum 54
Torre Abbey 53
Torre Abbey Sands 53
Totnes 61, 63
Totnes Museum 63
Trago Mills 49
Trendlebere Down 133
Trentishoe 145
Tucker's Hall, Exeter 21
Tucker's Maltings 49
Two Bridges 115

U
Uffculme 36
Ugbrooke House 48

V
Vixen Tor, Dartmoor 117

W
Warren House Inn,
Dartmoor 128

Water mill, Hele Bay 143
Water Mouth 143
Watermill, Exeter 20
Watermouth Castle 143
Watersmeet 148
Welcombe Mouth 169
Wembury 91, 92
West Dart Valley 115
West Putford 165
Western King Point,
Plymouth 88
White Lady, Dartmoor 120
Widecombe-in-the-Moor
113
Williamson, Henry 142,
168
Wistman's Wood 115, 116
Woodbury Common 30
Woodlands Leisure Park 64
Woolacombe 142
Woolacombe Sands 141
World of Country Life 29
Wortham Manor 164
Wynard's Almshouses,
Exeter 20

Y
Yarner Wood 133
Yealmpton 92

Published in the UK by:
Landmark Publishing Ltd,
Ashbourne Hall, Cokayne Avenue, Ashbourne, Derbyshire DE6 1EJ England
E-mail landmark@clara.net Web-site www.landmarkpublishing.co.uk

ISBN 1-84306-003-5

Landmark Visitors Guide - Devon

© **Brian Le Messurier 2002**

British Library Cataloguing in Publication Data:
A catalogue record for this book is available from the British Library

Print: Gutenberg Press Ltd, Malta
Cartography: Mark Titterton
Design: Mark Titterton

Front cover: Kingswear from Dartmouth
Back Cover top: St. Lawrence Lane, Ashburton
Back Cover bottom: Hallsands, near Start Point

Picture Credits
Exeter City Council: Page 19
Richard Sale: Page 23
All other slides: Lindsey Porter